DOING HUMAN SERVICE ETHNOGRAPHY

Edited by
Katarina Jacobsson and Jaber F. Gubrium

P

First published in Great Britain in 2021 by

Policy Press, an imprint of
Bristol University Press
University of Bristol
1-9 Old Park Hill
Bristol
BS2 8BB
UK
t: +44 (0)117 954 5940
e: bup-info@bristol.ac.uk

Details of international sales and distribution partners are available at
policy.bristoluniversitypress.co.uk

British Library Cataloguing in Publication Data
A catalogue record for this book is available from the British Library

ISBN 978-1-4473-5579-3 paperback
ISBN 978-1-4473-5581-6 OA ePub
ISBN 978-1-4473-5580-9 OA ePdf

Cover design: Robin Hawes
Cover image credit: iStock-490247468

Contents

About the editors   v
Notes on contributors   vi

Introduction: What is human service ethnography?   1
    Jaber F. Gubrium and Katarina Jacobsson

PART I Capturing professional relevance
1   Shadowing care workers when they're 'doing nothing'   19
    Doris Lydahl
2   Two worlds of professional relevance in a small village   35
    Christel Avendal
3   Capturing the organization of emotions in child welfare   49
   decision-making
    Tea Torbenfeldt Bengtsson

PART II Grasping empirical complexity
4   Sensitizing concepts in studies of homelessness and disability   67
    Nanna Mik-Meyer
5   Grasping the social life of documents in human service   83
   practice
    Emilie Morwenna Whitaker
6   Debating dementia care logics   101
    Cíntia Engel, Janaína Aredes and Annette Leibing

PART III Challenges of multi-sitedness
7   Social worlds of person-centred, multi-sited ethnography   119
    Aleksandra Bartoszko
8   'Facting' in a case of concealed pregnancy   133
    Lucy Sheehan
9   Ethnographic challenges of fragmented human services   153
    Tarja Pösö

PART IV Noticings from ethnographic distance
10 Ethnographic discovery *after* fieldwork on troubled youth   171
    Malin Åkerström and David Wästerfors
11 Looking beyond the police-as-control narrative   191
    David Sausdal

12   Embracing lessons from ethnography in non-Western   209
        prisons
        Andrew M. Jefferson

Index   227

About the editors

Jaber F. Gubrium is Professor Emeritus and former chair of sociology at the University of Missouri–Columbia, USA. He is an ethnographer and conducts research on the narrative organization of service and care in human service institutions. His interest in discursive practice, organizational embeddedness and intertextuality has been applied to the everyday contours of professional work in nursing homes, physical rehabilitation, mental health, dementia and residential treatment for emotionally disturbed children. Gubrium is co-editor of *Turning Troubles into Problems* (2014) and *Reimagining the Human Service Relationship* (2016).

Katarina Jacobsson is a sociologist and Professor of Social Work at Lund University, Sweden. With a general interest in qualitative methodology and sociology of knowledge, her current projects deal with documenting practices among human service workers, particularly within social work. Her writings on methodology deal with the analyses of documents from an ethnographic approach (for example, in D. Silverman (ed) *Qualitative Research*, 2021) and interviewing ('Interviewees with an agenda', with M. Åkerström in *Qualitative Research, QRJ*). Together with colleagues, Jacobsson published *Hidden Attractions of Administration* (2021).

Notes on contributors

Malin Åkerström is Professor of Sociology at Lund University in Sweden. Her earlier ethnographic studies have concerned social control and deviance, for example, *Suspicious Gifts: Bribery, Morality, and Professional Ethics* (2014). She has published articles in, among other journals: *Sociological Focus, Social Problems, Symbolic Interaction* and *Sociological Perspective*. Her current research focuses on involvement and embracement in bureaucratic concerns among human service staff, and together with co-authors published *Hidden Attractions of Administration* (2021).

Janaína Aredes is Professor at José do Rosário Vellano University, Brazil. She holds a PhD in public health with an emphasis in medical anthropology from the Oswaldo Cruz Foundation and a master's in social anthropology from the Federal University of Minas Gerais, Brazil. She is a member of the research team of the Centre for Studies in Public Health and Aging/ FIOCRUZ; in the Group of Studies in Collective Health/ CNPq and the Observatory of Cultural Diversity, Brazil. As a researcher, she has experience in anthropology of the body and health, with an emphasis on the following areas: qualitative methods, life cycles, functional capacity, health education, palliative care, bioethics and medical professionalism.

Christel Avendal is a PhD student in social work at Lund University in Sweden. Her dissertation project is the ethnographic study *Heightened everydayness: Young people in rural Sweden doing everyday life*. Her previous ethnographic study was carried out in urban Ghana, looking at indigenization of social work in an African context and the integration of professional practices and the traditional extended family system. She has done ethnographic observations in various organizational settings, for example prisons, probation offices, schools, urban planning departments, youth clubs and university departments.

Aleksandra Bartoszko is a social anthropologist and associate professor at VID Specialized University in Oslo, Norway. She has researched and published on addiction, legality, risk, disability, activism and social policy, with ethnographic fieldworks in Nicaragua and Norway. Among others, she co-edited the volume *The Patient: Probing the Inter-Disciplinary Boundaries* and published an ethnographic graphic novel, *The Virus*, on injecting drug use and hepatitis C. She is deputy editor of the *Journal of Extreme Anthropology*. Her first monograph, *Treating Heroin Addiction in Norway: The Pharmaceutical Other*, is forthcoming in Routledge Studies in Health and Medical Anthropology.

Tea Torbenfeldt Bengtsson is a senior researcher at VIVE, the Danish National Centre for Social Science Research. She is a qualitative sociologist in the fields of sociology of youth, criminology and social work. Her research includes qualitative studies of social work practice and young people in locked secure care facilities, focusing on processes of marginalization and the experience of social interventions. Her current ethnographic research explores violence in young people's everyday lives and their encounters with criminal court.

Cíntia Engel is Professor at the Federal University of Bahia and a Brazilian researcher with a PhD in social anthropology from the University of Brasília, Brazil, and an MA in sociology from the same institution. She is one of the editors of the book *Antropologias, saúde e contextos de crise* (2018), which discusses ethnography, health and care problems in face of Brazilian crises. She is currently working on the subjects of dementia, geriatric and home care, and drug complexity.

Andrew M. Jefferson is a senior researcher at DIGNITY, the Danish Institute against Torture. His research focuses on prisons and prison reform in the Global South, with a particular interest in countries undergoing transition and the relationship between confinement and subjectivity. Jefferson uses the prison as an entry point for exploring the intersection between societal and personal processes. His current research includes a project on legacies of detention in Myanmar (https://legacies-of-detention.org/) and a study of quality of life in Tunisian prisons. He co-convenes the Global Prisons Research Network.

Annette Leibing is Professor of Medical Anthropology in the Faculty of Nursing at the University of Montreal, Canada. As Professor at the Institute of Psychiatry at the Federal University of Rio de Janeiro, Brazil, she founded and directed the Centro de Doenças de Alzheimer e outras Desordens Mentais na Velhice—a multidisciplinary centre for older people with mental health issues. Since then she has studied—as an anthropologist—topics related to aging: dementia, Parkinson's disease, heart disease, stem cells as technologies of hope and medications. She is currently doing research on the prevention of dementia, together with colleagues from Brazil, Germany, Canada and Switzerland. She is the editor of *Preventing Dementia? Critical Perspectives on a New Paradigm of Preparing for Old Age* (with Silke Schicktanz, 2020).

Doris Lydahl is a researcher in sociology at the University of Gothenburg, Sweden. She is interested in qualitative methods in general, and ethnography in particular. In her research she draws upon perspectives from science and technology studies. Her research is focused on issues relating to healthcare, care and medicine. She published an article on ethnography and the production of data, 'Doing data together—affective relations and mobile ethnography' in *Qualitative Research* (with S. Holmberg, K. Günther and J. Ranta, 2020). Lydahl is currently leading an ethnographic project on 'the values of welfare technologies'.

Nanna Mik-Meyer is Professor at Copenhagen Business School, Denmark. She is trained as an anthropologist and her areas of research are identity work in organizations, micro-sociology, qualitative methodology and processes of marginalization (the sociology of the body, disability, homelessness). She has published books with Routledge and Manchester University Press, and co-edited *Qualitative Analysis* (with M. Järvinen, 2020). Her works appear in journals such as *Human Relations, Work, Employment and Society, Sociology of Health and Illness, Gender, Work and Organization, British Journal of Sociology* and *Journal of Classical Sociology*, among others.

Tarja Pösö is Professor in Social Work at Tampere University, Finland. She also works as a part-time professor in the Centre for Research on Discretion and Paternalism at the University of Bergen, Norway. She has studied child protection for a number of years with a keen interest in social work practice, ethics and methodologies as well as comparative child protection research. She is one of the co-editors of *Errors and Mistakes in Child Protection* published by Policy Press (2020) and *Adoption from Care—International Perspectives on Children's Rights, Family Preservation and State Intervention* (Policy Press, 2021).

David Sausdal is a criminological ethnographer and tenure-track assistant professor of sociology at Lund University, Sweden. He is also associated with University of Copenhagen's Centre for Global Criminology, Denmark. Sausdal's research focuses on issues of transnational crime and policing—issues on which he has published in top tier criminological, sociological and anthropological outlets. Currently, one of his central interests revolves around matters of nostalgia and, more particularly, why many police officers nowadays express a longing for the 'good old days'.

Lucy Sheehan is a PhD student at Cardiff University, Wales. She is an ethnographer engaged in a humane exploration of child protection social work, with a particular interest in the methodical, collaborative practices of change talk in the context of institutional and societal requirements for self-transformation. She has a professional background in social care, including work in the voluntary and statutory sector, most recently as a social worker in child protection and substance misuse services. Alongside her PhD, Lucy teaches and works as a research associate for Cascade, and is a member of the Cardiff Ethnography, Ethnomethodology, Interaction and Talk research group.

David Wästerfors is Professor in Sociology at the Department of Sociology, Lund University, Sweden, and teaches in sociology and criminology. His research is often focused on interactions, institutions, emotions and social control. He has completed three research projects with ethnographic data from Swedish detention homes (on conflicts, schooling and violence). A related interest is qualitative methodology, shown in the book *Analyze! Crafting Your Data in Qualitative Research* (with Jens Rennstam, 2018). Other interests include narrative analysis, social psychology, disability studies and ethnomethodology. At the moment he is working on two projects, one on accessibility for people with disabilities in urban and digital settings, and another one on people's digital discussions and crowdsourcing activities around criminal events.

Emilie Morwenna Whitaker is a sociologist and lecturer in social policy at the University of Salford, England, and an honorary lecturer at Cardiff University, Wales. Her work is ethnographic and explores relationships between people, emotion, place and time. She has published in *Qualitative Inquiry*, *Qualitative Research*, *Journal of Organizational Ethnography* and the *Journal of Integrated Care*.

Introduction: What is human service ethnography?

Jaber F. Gubrium and Katarina Jacobsson

Once the exclusive method of sociologists and anthropologists, the use of ethnography in social research—broadly *in situ* participant observation—has expanded across disciplines and settings. Ethnography now appears prominently in social work, public health, management, nursing and criminology, among other disciplines, with settings of interest across the board. Ethnography now tends to be less about societies as a whole and more about specific characteristics *of* the whole, such as language variation, narrative structures, migration, gender, race, class, age organization, power differentials and diverse human needs. From the start, its findings have proven to be enormously important in challenging prejudicial beliefs, unjust social arrangements and biased public policies. *Doing Human Service Ethnography* takes some of its significance from this research context.

Additional significance stems from the specific purpose of the book, which is to recognize that ethnography, despite having general features that apply in all disciplines, has substantive and procedural characteristics specific to particular fields of application. The field of human service provision is no exception. Being field specific, we refer to it as 'human service ethnography'. The goal of human service ethnography is to make visible forms of service-related personal experience and social organization that are either unrecognized, misunderstood or otherwise hidden from view. This relates in particular to areas of service provider and recipient experiences and complexities otherwise taken for granted or trivialized in the simplifying practices of accountability. This is especially pertinent in the current public policy environment where trends for evaluating human service work are decidedly non-ethnographic, favouring rampant quantification.

Preliminary matters

Three preliminary matters should be noted that apply to the following chapters. One is disciplinary and relates to the difference between general ethnography and field-specific ethnography. General ethnography is a prominent and time-honoured method of procedure for researching fields of social interaction (Atkinson, 2017; Hammersley and Atkinson, 2007). Field-specific ethnography focuses on particular interactional fields such as hospitalization, schooling and policing. Emblematic across the board is theory-based participant observation. The perspective of this book is that in an increasingly complex organizational environment and with the multi-sitedness of so many services, it is fruitful to consider how the general is shaped substantively and procedurally by the living and working conditions of specific fields.

The second matter is conceptual and pertains to different uses of the term 'practice'. One usage draws from the distinction commonly made between social policy and policy application, which is well worn in human service intervention. This hinges on the tension between what social policy formally designates as opposed to what transpires on the ground in practice. A different usage refers to the focus of the form of social theorizing that informs the perspective of this book. It conceptualizes and studies what are termed 'everyday' constructive practices regardless of the field (Goffman, 1959; Douglas et al, 1980; Smith, 1987; Shotter, 1993). In the human service area, this would include both social policy and policy application. This is sometimes referred to as 'praxis', the everyday sense of practice. Both usages are evident in the book.

The third preliminary matter relates to empirical scope. The chapters present ethnographic research sited either within or in connection with *formal* human service provision. While it can be convincingly argued that informal acts of service and care occur in all places where people helpfully relate to each other, all sites in view here are in some fashion officially designated. In that regard, as organizational operations and professional accountabilities are inevitably in place, service provision is continually subject to administrative hurdles and documentary red tape. Often raised in frustration, the existential question 'What is this all about, really?' doggedly lurks in the background of decision-making and intervention.

The general and the specific

Following decades of studies of providers and recipients within and outside of human service organizations, *Doing Human Service Ethnography* joins a growing literature packaged as the ethnography of specific fields of practice. Long the subject of education and publication, the idea and method of ethnography in and of itself as a general undertaking short-changes the associated procedural diversity of today's applicable environments. There is a realization that ethnography can no longer be understood and properly applied as a method of procedure without due consideration for what the ethnography is about. Conditions on the ground are sufficiently varied in their operational logics to warrant separate research statuses, and are referenced accordingly in field-specific terms such as 'street ethnography', 'school ethnography', 'business ethnography' and now 'human service ethnography'.

What makes field-specific ethnography such as the human service variety different from others? Much of the difference, of course, stems from what is being substantively observed. Substance matters, grossly at times. It differentially affects ethnographers' thoughts, sentiments and research questions about the subject matter. Some of it relates to the personal stakes and risks, the worries and the cautions of being ethnographically present in particular sites as opposed to others, navigating entry, establishing rapport and managing ongoing participation, even exiting. The local operational contingencies of participant observation in prisons are not the same as those in nursing homes or on street corners. The everyday thoughts, sentiments and actions of the ethnographer regarding rapport, personal danger, secrecy, violence, succour, care, sympathy and collaboration combine in distinct ways to facilitate or threaten what it means to effectively 'be there' as a participant observer in various fieldsites. These weigh heavily on the method and, of course, on the researcher engaging in it. Still, not everything is field specific, some elements being rather general to ethnographic presence. Regardless of the field, there is still observational work undertaken (for example Atkinson, 2017), still the matter of writing ethnographic field notes (for instance Emerson et al, 1995; Atkinson, 2019) and still the business of completing ethnographic reports and publication (Van Maanen, 1988, Emerson, 1995; Goodall, 2000, for example), let alone the issue of conceptualization.

Like other field-specific ethnographies, human service ethnography has been influenced by social theorists who have dealt with the general question of what a field is in the first place, regardless of field particulars. In that regard, field-specific ethnographies have much in common. Pierre Bourdieu (1977, 1990), for one, conceives of fields as being constructively sited in both the varied substances and operational logics of everyday life. For Bourdieu, fields are not 'just there', separate from the constructive practices that bring into being what is there. While 'being' has a gigantic philosophical heritage, it is firmly settled in everyday life (Heidegger, 1962; Wittgenstein, 2009 [1953]). Michel Foucault (1995) has formulated discursive histories, among them one centred on incarceration, for example; the formulation encourages us to think of the meanings and consequences of incarceration as working discourses set in time. The 'present' relevancies and urgencies of one discourse can be radically different from another. Incarceration in this case is not 'just there' as a continuous configuration of being, but is brought to life in discursive formations in practice (compare Mol, 2008).

The continuing significance of the general also relates to groundbreaking conceptual changes, leading the units of analysis away from broad nebulous forms towards smaller units closer to the scale of everyday life. Here, ironically, the significance of the general relates existentially—and in practice, rhetorically—to the specific. The concept of culture has been rethought as being too experientially grand, if not too globally parochial, not adequately attuned to local categorical understandings and practices (see Geertz, 1973; Said, 1978; Bauman, 1986; Clifford and Marcus, 1986; Fox, 1991). Anthropologist Lila Abu-Lughod (1991) has suggested that it is important to 'write against culture' as much as about it, locating culture as much in myriad configurations of references to it as in general patterns of conduct. The sociological concept of society has been similarly reconditioned on many fronts, fuelled by the idea that society is a diverse set of social constructions and associated material conditions. It is as much a fluid body of representational opportunities and performative occasions as it is a coherent structure of social relationships (see Berger and Luckmann, 1966; Garfinkel, 1967; Goffman, 1959, 1974; Smith, 1987, 2005). New terms of reference for what society is and what social structures are in practice converge on a reimagined understanding of human service provision (Gubrium et al, 2016).

The shift in emphasis away from broad wholes and more towards everyday particulars affects ethnographic focus. The outcome is a flourishing critical consciousness that takes account of the range of what it means existentially to be, say, a patient and an aide in a nursing home as opposed to what it means to be an inmate and a guard in a prison (see Fox, 1991; Wortham, 2001; Puddephatt et al, 2009). This has vivid narrative resonances, turning ethnographers away from purely geographic senses of fields and fieldwork towards the everyday narrative spaces of articulation (see Schuman, 1986; Czarniawska, 1997; Gabriel, 2000; Langellier and Peterson, 2004; Riessman, 2008; Gubrium and Holstein, 2009; Plummer, 2019).

Problematizing everyday life

The chapters of this book focus on everyday life in relation to the formal content and quality of providers' or recipients' activities. Neither the nature of professional services provided as such nor the extent and quality of provider/recipient relations is the primary subject matter. The latter, especially, has received enormous attention in an era of service accountability saturated by quality indicators, the priority of enumeration and statistical representation, best-practice manuals and the like, which, of course, diverts attention from the complex lived experiences and social relations of service provision, away from what Dorothy E. Smith (1990) calls 'the relations of ruling'. The aim is to make visible, within areas of service provider and recipient experiences, complexities otherwise taken for granted, rendered invisible or trivialized in the simplifying practices of accountability, as noted earlier (see Gregor and Campbell 2002).

One procedural step of problematizing everyday life consists in tentatively suspending belief in the presumed or official realities in place, shifting the angle of vision to how those realities are constructed, managed and sustained in everyday practice. For example, ethnographic research can be conducted on the practice of what is called 'documentation' in human service (for instance, Gubrium et al, 1989; Jacobsson and Martinell Barfoed, 2019; Jacobsson, 2021), which is a key concern of Chapters 5 and 8. This requires some form of belief suspension, not taking documents at face value in order to discover their social construction, how they come into being as applicable facts of human service for all practical purposes.

The procedural step is sometimes called 'bracketing', and has phenomenological sources (see Berger and Luckmann 1966; Gubrium and Holstein 1997). The authors of all chapters have engaged in a form of this in fieldwork. Fieldwork is not just a process of detailing the everyday *whats* or substance of human service provision, such as contending discourses and fragmented services, but is undertaken in tandem with a view to uncovering the constructed *hows* entailed (Gubrium and Holstein, 1997). This serves to reveal the way in which what is presumed to be real or taken for granted exists or is accomplished in place and time, which may be strikingly varied. Some researchers simply incorporate a healthy scepticism into their field observations. Others come at it more deliberately, with the decided aim of making 'facting' visible in unfolding detail, such as in Lucy Sheehan's case of a concealed pregnancy discussed in Chapter 8. In Chapter 11, David Sausdal takes the perspective of 'looking beyond' the dominant police-as-control narrative as a way of reimagining policing as a service profession.

A second procedural step of problematizing everyday life is what anthropologists refer to as being 'experience-near' in fieldwork. This means being bodily present in the field of interest, not applying 'experience-distant' tools such as office interviews as a substitute for what could be directly observed and recorded. Ironically, even in the time of the COVID-19 pandemic, it remains utterly clear that 'one profound truth about ethnography…is that intimacy, and not distancing, is crucial' (Fine and Abramson, 2020). The timing of the first step and this second procedural step need not be sequential. The reverse might be the case, as when one already is close up to service provision of some kind and then, even inadvertently, temporarily suspends belief in what is ostensibly in view in order to, say, study the 'social life of documents', as Emilie Morwenna Whitaker does in Chapter 5. There also is the option of proceeding with the first and second steps shuffle-like, moving back and forth reflexively throughout fieldwork, alternately attending to the *whats* and *hows* of the matter in view.

A third procedural step of problematizing everyday life is to critically present the value of ethnographic research results. Ethnography always has had a critical consciousness. Even early and mid-20th-century ethnographers who carefully documented the substance and moral contours of distant cultures as well as unknown nearby communities were critical in a fashion. If not explicitly, they were informing us that there is value in recognizing diverse ways of constructing experience—of being—and presenting empirical proof of that. There is no universally correct way of living, they were telling us. Ways of being human need to be understood in and on their own terms. The significance of Christel Avendal's portrayal of the daily lives and sentiments of small village youth in Chapter 2 emerges in this context, in which the youths' allegedly trouble-ridden world appears on its own to be completely bereft of this understanding.

Some ethnographers have been rather blunt about this, as the following extended extract shows. It is taken from the introduction to American sociologist William Foote Whyte's (1943) classic ethnography *Street Corner Society*. Whyte casts clear judgment on depictions to the contrary, forcefully stating that 'no human beings are in [them].'

> In the heart of 'Eastern City' there is a slum district known as Cornerville, which is inhabited almost exclusively by Italian immigrants and their children. To the rest of the city it is a mysterious, dangerous, and depressing area.

Cornerville is only a few minutes' walk from fashionable High Street, but the High Street inhabitant who takes that walk passes from the familiar to the unknown.

For years Cornerville has been known as a problem area, and, while we were at war with Italy, outsiders became increasingly concerned with that problem. ...They have long felt that Cornerville was at odds with the rest of the community. They think of it as the home of racketeers and corrupt politicians, of poverty and crime, of subversive beliefs and activities.

Respectable people have access to a limited body of information upon Cornerville. ...In [their] view, Cornerville people appear as social work clients, as defendants in criminal cases, or as undifferentiated members of 'the masses.' There is one thing wrong with such a picture: no human beings are in it. Those who are concerned with Cornerville seek through a general survey to answer questions that require the most intimate knowledge of local life. The only way to gain such knowledge is to live in Cornerville and participate in the activities of its people. (Whyte, 1943, p xv)

Human service ethnography

The importance of field specificity warrants further contrast. While ethnographic fieldwork in general has had a very broad and useful empirical remit, the breadth overlooks significant differences. Doing human service ethnography is not the same, say, as doing ethnographic fieldwork on city street corners (for example, Anderson, 1999; Sandberg and Pedersen, 2011; Goffman, 2014). Monographic subtitles can be quite telling in this regard. As the subtitle of Elijah Anderson's (1999) urban ethnography *Code of the Street* indicates, the field-specific language of ethnography in that field was ridden with the conduct and concerns of *decency, violence,* and the *moral life of the inner city.* Doing human service ethnography is not the same, for instance, as doing fieldwork within what David Grazian (2008) calls *the hustle of urban nightlife,* the subtitle of his book *On the Make.* Both ethnographies contrast with the conduct and concerns of the organizational ethnography reported in Robert M. Emerson's (1969) book *Judging Delinquents,* for example, the subtitle of which is *Context and process in juvenile court.* Or the conduct and concerns of the ethnographic account by Robert Dingwall, John Eekelaar and Topsy Murray (1983) titled *The Protection of Children* and subtitled

State intervention and family life. As important ethnographically as street corner and nightlife sites are, they are largely bereft of the organizational bearings, the officially designated professional rules and responsibilities, and the documentary responsibilities of concern in the following chapters of this book.

The four-part division of *Doing Human Service Ethnography* reflects a spectrum of field-specific conditions and issues centred in a distinct social world that range from the everyday professional relevance of human service practices to the mundane logics of need and care, and to the everyday relational challenges of fragmented and multi-sited human service intervention. What is general to ethnography is shaped substantively and procedurally by these specific conditions of the field, converging here on need, suffering, care, help, healing and recovery in professional application. Part I of the book, 'Capturing professional relevance', brackets the assumption that applications of service provision ideally coincide with professional understanding. Chapters rather seek to capture the everyday *wheres* and *whens* of professional intervention. The resulting ethnographic lesson is that what is officially assigned can have different working borders than what is organizationally designated or professionally articulated in practice.

Chapter 1, by Doris Lydahl, is titled 'Shadowing care workers when they're "doing nothing"'. Lydahl seeks to observe the *wheres* and *whens* of caregiving in practice, both in and around formally designated work times. In the process, she opens up to view a world of care that falls outside the bounds of what is organizationally recognized as caregiving. From two empirical cases she concludes that some essential everyday practices of care were rendered invisible as they were not easily captured in quality assessment forms or accounted for by evidence-based methods. Chapter 2, 'Two worlds of professional relevance in a small village', presents the findings of Christel Avendal's field observations. She reports initially being surprised by the degree to which village adults, both professional service providers and nonprofessionals, are on the proverbial same page regarding troubled youth. Avendal is amazed by how far the language of social problems and service intervention for ostensibly troubled youngsters has penetrated one of the smallest corners of society. It is only when Avendal starts to observe and listen to youngsters themselves on their own turf that she captures something else, retrospectively, *then* seen as the separate and seemingly self-generating and problematized world of youth service provision she began with. In Chapter 3, titled 'Capturing the organization of emotions in child welfare decision-making', Tea Torbenfeldt Bengtsson asks herself, during fieldwork, why it is that the service providers she is observing become so emotional at times in making welfare decisions. Is it because the matters they are required to make decisions about are so heartbreaking? In which case, they might be continually emotional, as service intervention is often conducted for heartbreaking reasons. Conducting field observation with this question in mind, she captures a world of emotion related to organizational accountability. The emotions appear to be integral components of social organization, in other words, rooted in the frustrations that accompany wanting to do the right thing when thwarted by organizational hurdles or red tape. Service providers can literally scream with rage over demands that divert them from what they consider to be more desirable actions. The 'organizational embeddedness' of everyday life has rhythms of its own that mediate individual attitudes and sensibilities (compare Gubrium, 1992; Gubrium and Holstein, 1993).

Part II of the book is titled 'Grasping empirical complexity'. Its chapters seek to grasp an understanding of the complex practices in place that generate inconsistencies and contradictions in the meaning of service provision. Bracketed is the assumption that terms of reference such as homelessness, disability and dementia and their documentation have reliably consistent meanings across space and time. The resulting ethnographic lesson is that meaning is constructively contingent on the related working issues, the immediate relations of ruling, that arise in the circumstances of consideration.

Chapter 4, by Nanna Mik-Meyer, is titled 'Sensitizing concepts in studies of homelessness and disability'. It brings to light the dynamics of unintentional problematization in two service populations. Mik-Meyer compares the differential challenges to a coherent understanding of homelessness and disability. In one case, there appears to be an attribution of contradictory agency to homeless clients, who are constructed as both helpless individuals and active agents capable of making decisions on their own. The other case is a study of 'othering', illustrating how, in practice, able-bodied workers and managers at a research site who viewed themselves as avoiding the othering of disabled colleagues wound up unintentionally marginalizing them. Chapter 5, titled 'Grasping the social life of documents in human service practice', is by Emilie Morwenna Whitaker. It opens up to analysis what is called 'the social life of documents'. The gaps in and contradictions of documented information are traced and their resolutions made visible as the paperwork undertaken traverses the shoals of demands for effective and coherent care, on the one hand, and the complex and often emotional practices of caregiving on the other. Finally, in Chapter 6, which is titled 'Debating dementia care logics', authors Cíntia Engel, Janaína Aredes and Annette Leibing compare two ethnographies of dementia care, one where care is carried out at home, and one situated in a geriatric outpatient clinic. They describe the competing everyday logics within sites of care attendant to what is otherwise understood as a single disease entity with identifiable needs unbound by care context.

Part III of the book addresses the 'Challenges of multi-sitedness'. Its chapters open to ethnographic consideration the everyday consequences of human service provision constructed across the borders of different operational and interpretive sites of service. Bracketed in this part of the book is the idea that the coherence of social policy and the consistency of service interventions can be understood in principle as independent of the contexts of application. The ethnographic lesson here is akin to the lessons of what Janet Newman (2016) calls 'border work', in which the meaning and coherence of social policy and human service provision are better understood as the border crossings of multiple sites of translation.

Chapter 7, titled 'Social worlds of person-centred, multi-sited ethnography', is authored by Aleksandra Bartoszko. She describes her decision in fieldwork to turn one of her respondents, named Siv, into a kind of ethnographic assistant she calls a 'seed patient'. The expectation is that Siv, in time, will grow into a co-ethnographer, helping Bartoszko to understand from a client's perspective the constructive work of meaning-making and coherence-building as they move along together crossing the multiple sites of service provision. Chapter 8 by Lucy Sheehan is titled '"Facting" in a case of concealed pregnancy'. Referring to the interpretive processes in question, or 'facting', the leading idea is that matters of fact are not as solid or rational as they might appear to be (see Raffel, 1979). Rather, they are artefacts, so to speak, products of the varied interpretive actions that enter into concealment in the case under consideration. Chapter 9 by Tarja Pösö is titled 'Ethnographic challenges of fragmented human services', and builds on several empirical studies of child protection that nowadays takes place in many locations such as family homes, courts, social work offices or even on social media sites. As Pösö explains, there is a need to pay ethnographic attention to 'fragments, multiple locations and moments of human services' and the ways providers combine their influences into site-adequate coherences in formulating service plans.

Part IV, titled 'Noticings from ethnographic distance', shifts gears by stepping outside of participant observation per se to feature the ways that the reconceptualization of field understandings can alter the empirical substance in view. Explored here are questions of what field notes are telling us, what looking beyond established understandings offers in terms of what is ethnographically noticed, what a comparative ethnography can provide by marking the content and borders of field specifics and even what the unschooled, ordinary ethnographic musings of members of the fields we study can teach us. The lesson is that what is noticed ethnographically, even in the most careful fieldwork, is intimately tied to views, even metaphors, of what is there in the first place.

Chapter 10, authored by Malin Åkerström and David Wästerfors, is titled 'Ethnographic discovery *after* fieldwork on troubled youth'. 'After' refers to the stepping outside of participant observation by rereading field notes well after fieldwork has been completed or by reading field notes taken by a co-researcher. In the process, the authors learn through 'key readings' how central the social world of meetings is to organizational accountability. Initially, meetings were taken to be merely the locations for focal descriptions of everyday decision-making. The later reading found that meetings in practice were places for (re)constructing, if not laundering, representations of care for a variety of administrative purposes (compare Schwartzman, 1989). In Chapter 11, titled 'Looking beyond the police-as-control narrative', David Sausdal, when doing so, finds a narrative that brings on board a conception of policing as service provision. Sausdal asks what might be noticed ethnographically if the perspective were shifted accordingly. Sausdal's findings, indicating that police officers are often caring and considerate, do not correspond well with the police-as-control image. Yet, he argues, they are important to a profession that would benefit from a more nuanced police narrative. Finally, Chapter 12, by Andrew M. Jefferson and titled 'Embracing lessons from ethnography in non-Western prisons', details what can be learned about the concept of imprisonment from conducting ethnography in a non-Western context. From the distance of non-Western ethnographic findings, he brings back home the usefulness of an approach that bridges the institutional on one side with the concrete situatedness of everyday life on the other. This can result in the noticing of striking parallels in matters of confinement and control between the lived experience of prisoners and prisoners-of-life in human service institutions such as nursing homes. It is no wonder that residents of confining institutions of all kinds use metaphors and common narratives of 'imprisonment' in their own ethnographic musings to describe, rightly or wrongly, what 'they live by' day in and day out (see Lakoff and Johnson, 1980; Gubrium, 1993; McAdams, 1993; Rosenblatt, 1994).

Taken together

Empirically focused on a specific field of interest—human service provision—the working contours and challenges of participant observation are presented in ethnographic detail in this book's individual chapters. Case material is discussed by seasoned human service ethnographers, collected from service activities in fields ranging from child welfare to nursing homes, from homelessness and home care to imprisonment and from hands-on service provision to administrative paperwork. Taken together within a human service landscape that has changed enormously from the early years of one-on-one service encounters with individual nurses, social workers, community police officers, counsellors and disability workers, the chapters offer exemplary observational studies of organizationally embedded, field-specific human service work.

References

Abu-Lughod, L. (1991) 'Writing Against Culture', in R.G. Fox (ed) *Recapturing Anthropology: Working in the Present*, Santa Fe, NM: SAR Press, pp 137–162.

Anderson, E. (1999) *Code of the Street: Decency, Violence, and the Moral Life of the Inner City*, New York: Norton.

Atkinson, P. (2017) *Thinking Ethnographically*, London: Sage.

Atkinson, P. (2019) *Writing Ethnographically*, London: Sage.

Bauman, R. (1986) *Story, Performance, and Event*, Cambridge: Cambridge University Press.

Berger, P.L. and Luckmann, T. (1966) *The Social Construction of Reality: A Treatise in the Sociology of Knowledge*, New York: Vintage.

Bourdieu, P. (1977) *Outline of a Theory of Practice*, Cambridge: Cambridge University Press.

Bourdieu, P. (1990) *The Logic of Practice*, Stanford, CA: Stanford University Press.

Clifford, J. and Marcus, G.E. (eds) (1986) *Writing Culture: The Poetics and Politics of Ethnography*, Berkeley, CA: University of California Press.

Czarniawska, B. (1997) *Narrating the Organization: Dramas of Institutional Identity*, Chicago, IL: University of Chicago Press.

Dingwall, R., Eekelaar, J. and Murray, T. (1983) *The Protection of Children: State Intervention and Family Life*, Oxford: Blackwell.

Douglas, J.D. (1980) *Introduction to the Sociologies of Everyday Life*, Boston, MA: Allyn and Bacon.

Emerson, R.M. (1969) *Judging Delinquents: Context and Process in Juvenile Court*, Chicago, IL: Aldine.

Emerson, R.M., Fretz, R.I. and Shaw, L.L. (1995) *Writing Ethnographic Fieldnotes*, Chicago, IL: University of Chicago Press.

Fine, G.A. and Abramson, C.M. (2020) 'Ethnography in the time of COVID-19: Vectors and the vulnerable', *Etnografia e Ricerca Qualitativa*, 13(2): 165–174.

Fox, R.G. (ed) (1991) *Recapturing Anthropology: Working in the Present*, Santa Fe, NM: SAR Press.

Foucault, M. (1995) *Discipline and Punish; the Birth of the Prison*, New York: Random House.

Gabriel, Y. (2000) *Storytelling in Organizations*, Oxford: Oxford University Press.

Garfinkel, H. (1967) *Studies in Ethnomethodology*, Englewood Woods Cliffs, NY: Prentice-Hall.

Geertz, C. (1973) *The Interpretation of Cultures*, New York: Basic Books.

Goffman, A. (2014) *On the Run: Fugitive Life in an American City*, Chicago, IL: University of Chicago Press.

Goffman, E. (1959) *The Presentation of Self in Everyday Life*, New York: Doubleday.

Goffman, E. (1974) *Frame Analysis*, New York: Harper and Row.

Goodall, H.L. (2000) *Writing the New Ethnography*, Lanham, MD: AltaMira.

Grazian, D. (2008) *On the Make: The Hustle of Urban Nightlife*, Chicago, IL: University of Chicago Press.

Gregor, F.M. and Campbell, M.L. (2002) *Mapping Social Relations*, Toronto: University of Toronto Press.

Gubrium, J.F. (1992) *Out of Control: Family Therapy and Domestic Disorder*, Newbury Park, CA: Sage.

Gubrium, J.F. (1993) *Speaking of Life: Horizons of Meaning for Nursing Home Residents*, New York: Aldine de Gruyter.

Gubrium, J.F. and Holstein, J.A. (1993) 'Family discourse, organizational embeddedness, and local enactment', *Journal of Family Issues*, 14(1): 66–81.

Gubrium, J.F. and Holstein, J.A. (1997) *The New Language of Qualitative Method*, New York: Oxford University Press.

Gubrium, J.F. and Holstein, J.A. (2009) *Analyzing Narrative Reality*, Los Angeles, CA: Sage.

Gubrium, J.F., Buckholdt, D.R. and Lynott, R. (1989) 'The descriptive tyranny of forms', in J. Holstein and G. Miller (eds) *Perspectives on Social Problems*, Greenwich, CT: JAI Press, pp 195–214.

Gubrium, J.F., Andreassen, T.A. and Solvang, P.K. (eds) (2016) *Reimagining the Human Service Relationship*, New York: Columbia University Press.

Hammersley, M. and Atkinson, P. (2007) *Ethnography*, London: Routledge.

Heidegger, M. (1962) *Being and Time*, New York: Harper and Row.

Jacobsson, K. (2021) 'Analyzing documents through fieldwork', in D. Silverman (ed) *Qualitative Research* (5th edn), London: Sage, pp 167–183.

Jacobsson, K. and Elizabeth, M.B. (2019) *Socialt arbete och pappersgöra. Mellan klient och digitala dokument* [Social Work and Paperwork], Malmö: Gleerups.

Lakoff, G. and Johnson, M. (1980) *Metaphors We Live By*, Chicago, IL: University of Chicago Press.

Langellier, K.M. and Peterson, E.E. (2004) *Storytelling in Daily Life: Performing Narrative*, Philadelphia, PA: Temple University Press.

McAdams, D.P. (1993) *The Stories We Live By*, New York: Guilford.

Mol, A. (2008) *The Logic of Care*, London: Routledge.

Newman, J. (2016) 'Border work: Negotiating shifting regimes of power', in J.F. Gubrium, T.A. Andreassen and P.K. Solvang (eds) *Reimagining the Human Service Relationship*, New York: Columbia University Press, pp 318–335.

Plummer, K. (2019) *Narrative Power: The Struggle for Human Value*, London: Polity.

Puddephatt, A.J., Shaffir, W. and Kleinknecht, S.W. (eds) (2009) *Ethnographies Revisited: Constructing Theory in the Field*, London: Routledge.

Raffel, S. (1979) *Matters of Fact*, London: Routledge and Kegan Paul.

Riessman, C.K. (2008) *Narrative Methods for the Human Sciences*, Los Angeles, CA: Sage.

Rosenblatt, P.C. (1994) *Metaphors of Family Systems Theory*, New York: Guilford.

Said, E. (1978) *Orientalism*, New York: Pantheon.

Sandberg, S. and Pedersen, W. (2011) *Street Capital: Black Cannabis Dealers in a White Welfare State*, Bristol: Policy Press.

Schuman, A. (1986) *Storytelling Rights*, Cambridge: Cambridge University Press.

Schwartzman, H.B. (1989) *The Meeting: Gatherings in Organizations and Communities*, New York: Plenum.

Shotter, J. (1993) *Cultural Politics of Everyday Life*, Toronto, Canada: University of Toronto Press.

Smith, D.E. (1987) *The Everyday World as Problematic*, Boston, MA: Northeastern University Press.

Smith, D.E. (1990) *Texts, Facts, and Femininity: Exploring the Relations of Ruling*, London: Routledge.

Smith, D.E. (2005) *Institutional Ethnography*, Oxford: AltaMira.

Van Maanen, J. (1988) *Tales of the Field: On Writing Ethnography*, Chicago, IL: University of Chicago Press.

Van Maanen, J. (ed) (1995) *Representation in Ethnography*, Thousand Oaks, CA: Sage.

Whyte, W.F. (1943) *Street Corner Society: The Social Structure of an Italian Slum*, Chicago, IL: University of Chicago Press.

Wittgenstein, L. (2009 [1953]) *Philosophical Investigations*, reprint, Malden, MA: Wiley-Blackwell, 2009.

Wortham, S. (2001) *Narratives in Action*, New York: Teachers College Press.

PART I

Capturing professional relevance

1

Shadowing care workers when they're 'doing nothing'

Doris Lydahl

Methods of evidence-based medicine and practice (EBM and EBP) are increasingly used to study and evaluate healthcare. In this chapter, I discuss shadowing as a technique of importance for articulating *ideals* and *practices* that are made silent, taken for granted, excluded or forgotten in methods of evidence-based medicine emphasizing accountability. As I will show, one highly pertinent thing that tends to be made invisible or forgotten through the methods of EBM/P is the actual daily activities that make up everyday care (Pols, 2008).

I focus on two empirical cases. The first case consists of observational studies of a mental healthcare unit performing home-based care for people in the margins of welfare. This case exemplifies practices not readily captured by evidence-based quality assessment forms, such as the importance of staff's bodily postures and their clarifications to patients. The second case derives from observational studies undertaken in an internal medicinal ward that introduced a specific framework of person-centred care. The work at this hospital ward was structured according to EBM and work was assessed by means of EBM but there were, as I will show, practices of care within the ward that were not easily accounted for by methods of EBM and which were therefore rendered invisible both to the hospital ward and to the professionals performing them.

Standardization and 'nothingness'

Methods of EBM and EBP are currently upheld as superior for studying human service organizations and for evaluating the quality of the work performed within these organizations. Proponents of EBM/P argue that it provides an unsurpassed way of integrating individual clinical experience with best available evidence in making decisions about the care, treatment and service for patients and clients alike. It is argued that to decrease variation in healthcare there needs to be assurance that medical decision-making is not dependent on the subjective opinions of doctors or social workers but instead relies on standardized scientific knowledge and research (Berg, 1997).

Critics, however, warn that EBM/P might result in ' "Cookbook medicine"—reducing medicine from a clinical art to following a standard "recipe"' (Knaapen, 2014, p 829), furthering a 'standard approach to healthcare problems advocated by the guidelines, in which every patient problem would be addressed generically, as one more instance of the same' (Timmermans and Berg 2003, p 19). EBM/P is also said to destabilize humanism, and in failing to consider 'the uniqueness of patients, their individual needs and preferences, and their emotional status are easily neglected as relevant factors in decision-making' (Bensing, 2000, p 17). Finally, but relatedly, some argue that an important critique of EBM/P is that it builds on a reductionist and exclusionary approach to knowledge making (Epstein, 2007). EBM/P is undeniably a movement of standardization (Lydahl, 2021), and reductionism is necessary for any universal standard to work (Knaapen, 2014). Therefore, when studying and evaluating healthcare, EBM/P tends to focus on reduced and specific aspects, as they are used to evaluate and measure specific interventions with pre-specified variables, outcome measures and target groups. In this process, some points of view are necessarily valorised while others are silenced (Bowker and Star, 1999). In this sense, one can argue that the EBM/emphasis on standardization makes some things visible and other things invisible, or even leaves them untouched, creating as much 'nothingness' as evidence.

One way of approaching the silencing consequent to standardization is by way of a metaphor borrowed from the sociologist Howard Becker. He argues that all methods by default will find some situations uninteresting or not worth looking into, because *seemingly* 'nothing's happening' (Becker, 1998, p 133). He argues that something is, however, always happening, albeit sometimes 'it just doesn't seem worth remarking on', rendering it organizationally invisible (Becker, 1998, p 135). In the case of EBM/P, some aspects of healthcare are silenced as nothing while others are accounted for and measured. Some aspects are deemed worth proving, while others are left untouched.

Importantly, Becker's argument about studying cases wherein 'nothing is happening' is prefaced by the word 'seemingly'. 'Nothing' is not an absolute, but instead only makes sense in relation to 'something'. This 'something' refers to things that are perhaps too readily organizationally quantifiable. Things that are not are 'nothing'.

But the point is, 'nothings' may be something for other viewpoints or interests. Another way of approaching this is in the language of visibility, asking what a particular method makes visible and, equally important, what it renders invisible. So invisible that they're not even discussed because, well, they are 'nothing'. Who would want to discuss nothing?

One such 'nothing' that is certainly *not* nothing but which tends to be rendered invisible or non-valorised by EBM/P (Moser, 2010) is the actual and specific daily activities, events and routines that make up the *practices of care* (Pols, 2008). Ceci et al (2012, p 11) describe care 'as attentive, meaning paying attention to the particularities of the situation of the people being cared for'. Similarly, Mol (2008, p 64) describes care as being 'knowledgeable, accurate and skillful. But, added to that, it also involves being attentive, inventive, persistent and forgiving'. Here the main question is not about who is in charge 'but whether or not the various activities involved are well attuned to one another' (Mol, 2008, p 64). Care is the 'practical care work that is aimed at stabilizing or improving the situation of those cared for' (Pols 2015, p 82).

What would happen if one tried to quantify, evaluate and count care, and what would be lost in such a process? In a study on dementia care, Moser (2010) makes an argument against the enforcement of EBM in practices of care. Tears, she argues, should not be counted but wiped away:

> The method does not fit. ...It does not make sense to require that effects and efficiency should be measured against single and individualized parameters for the health of brains and bodies, when improvements are sought for situations, activities and daily life in wards involving not just single patients and their individual conditions, but fellow patients and carers, too. (Moser, 2010, p 278)

Shadowing the everyday practices of care

I am not arguing that EBM/P should expand its horizon and include practices of care in its scope. However, I think that practices of care are worth attending to. In this chapter I therefore suggest *shadowing* as a practical approach to studying practices of care where seemingly 'nothing's happening', or differently put, when care workers officially 'do nothing'.

I study practices of care by building on data from ethnographic fieldwork carried out in two research projects and exemplifying two different empirical cases. One of the projects is concerned with the turn towards home-based care for people in the margins of welfare and the other with the relation between person-centred care and standardization. Both projects have employed mobile ethnography in the form of shadowing as ethnographic technique. According to Czarniawska, shadowing signifies 'following selected people in their everyday occupations for a time' (Czarniawska, 2007, p 17). It thus denotes fieldwork on the move whereby the researcher moves with the professionals through their daily activities and tasks. Shadowing further suggests an attitude of 'outsidedness' because, while observers do not know better than an actor does, they can see different things (Czarniawska, 2007, pp 20–1).

While all direct observations are to some extent participatory, Czarniawska notes the difference between shadowing and participant observation. She argues that shadowing is easier compared to participant observation 'because it does not require a simultaneous action and observation, and because participation in complex, professional activities would be impossible for most researchers.' (Czarniawska, 2007, pp 55–56). Moreover, while a participant observer risks 'going native', shadowing allows one to keep an attitude of 'outsidedness'.

For me, however, it has never seemed reasonable to be a detached observer, without any interaction or for that matter engagement and attachment with and to those I have studied (see Lydahl et al, 2020). While I acknowledge that I don't have the professional competence necessary to be a participant observer, I think it is important to acknowledge, make visible and document the relations and emotions developed in field. Not keeping distance allowed me to build relations and rapport with those I shadowed, which improved my observations. This is especially important when shadowing someone in intimate home spaces as the 'home in itself is always a place associated with affect. It is a private space full of culturally, materially, and bodily constructed meanings that influence people's actions during home visits' (Lydahl et al, 2020, p 13). One can, as a matter of fact, become conspicuously invisible if one tries to keep too much distance when shadowing in the home, which may in fact hinder the observation (Lydahl et al, 2020).

This acknowledgement of relations and attachments is similar to Haraway's (1988) call for acknowledging the situatedness and embodiment of knowledge. This approach of *feminist objectivity* 'is about limited location and situated knowledge, not about transcendence and splitting of subject and object. It allows us to become answerable for what we learn how to see' (Haraway, 1988, p 583). My own version of a situated shadowing thus means a form of shadowing that acknowledges and describes how one is situated, attached and related in field.

Care practices in the home

Consider the first empirical case, taken from a mental healthcare unit performing home-based care in the form of home visits as part of its outpatient work in the context of psychiatric care. The patients at the unit, who mostly suffered from schizophrenia, commonly lived in their own apartments in a supported housing facility. Each patient had two case managers who made visits to their home once a week—or if the patient preferred, they met at the clinic. Some home visits were done indoors sitting at a kitchen table while others took place outdoors at, for example, a boules court. There were no specific stipulations attached to the care provided in the unit. Once you had become a patient at the unit, you could not be kicked out. This was care for the long run, aimed at improving or at least stabilizing the lives of the patients, while also acknowledging the bad periods of living with schizophrenia.

The unit worked in accordance with a model of care called 'resource group assertive community treatment', which builds on evidence-based routines and interventions. Assertive community treatment is a multi-disciplinary support service for individuals with serious and enduring mental health problems such as schizophrenia spectrum disorders. The model was first developed in the US and was created to care for clients in their own apartments or in group homes in the community after deinstitutionalization, and it is today one of the most well-known evidence-based practices of mental healthcare (Brodwin, 2013). Still, these routines did not decide or guide the actions of the workers at the unit during home visits. Instead, 'the exception (to any rules) is the norm' at the mental healthcare unit (Lydahl and Hansen Löfstrand, 2020, p 9).

Football and singing: relations and persistence in care

Studying home-based care for people in the margins of welfare, my colleague and I identified the relationality of care as a strong ideal (Lydahl and Hansen Löfstrand 2020). How this relationality played out depended on institutional settings and relations to other ideals. In the mental healthcare unit, establishing a relationship with the patient was seen as pivotal to good care (Lydahl and Hansen Löfstrand, 2020, p 7).

The following example, taken from field notes, illustrates the importance of relationship building and the attentiveness of good care.

During this home visit, which lasted for about 45 minutes, I shadowed Nurse Elsa. She had been working in the unit for quite some time. Tommy, the client we were meeting that day, was rather new to her. She had taken over as his case manager just a month or so previously. Tommy lived in a two-room apartment in a supported housing facility. His apartment was cosy and filled with pictures and football merchandise from his favourite team. He suffered from schizophrenia and had recently returned home after being hospitalized during a longer period, due to worsened symptoms. From the field notes:

> Tommy sits on his couch and counts money when nurse Elsa knocks on his door. He lets us in and explains that he won money betting on his favourite football team. After introductions Tommy invites us to sit down at his kitchen table. Nurse Elsa asks how Tommy finds his new antidepressants and explains that there is an initial risk of hypomania when one starts with these medicines. Tommy says that he feels fine so far, and Nurse Elsa encourage him to keep track of his mood, and of potential mood swings. They talk about strategies for what Tommy can do if something would happen or if his symptoms would worsen. He can contact the mental healthcare unit, the staff at his supported living facility and his legal custodian. 'I have you', Tommy says. 'Yes, you have me and you can always call me or leave a message at the unit if I am not available', Nurse Elsa confirms.
>
> We continue talking. Tommy shows us pictures of his family and of himself when he was a young punker. We discuss music and family relations. He turns directly to me and tells me about the football team that he loves and shows me the many different memorabilia he has. He is most proud of a sweater his mom knitted for him in the colors of his team. He always wears it when it is cold, he explains. We talk about his walks of life and how he grew up, his early teens and his adulthood. He explains that a specific rock star has been a red thread throughout his life. I notice a poster of the rock star on the wall behind the kitchen table.
>
> Before leaving, Nurse Elsa and Tommy make plans. Nurse Elsa again mention strategies for what Tommy can do if his symptoms would worsen or if he has mood swings. She says that they shouldn't plan too much other than that. Tommy agrees. He says that life should be good. Then he says that he

wants to sing us a song. He starts singing a famous Swedish song made by a comedy troupe:

One should live a good life
Otherwise it's pointless
One should live a nice life
Otherwise it's pointless
One should live an easy life
Otherwise it's pointless
Don't be a dilly-dally
Or you will ruin everything
Don't get worked up
Life should be good, good, good
Good to live.[1]

'That's great. But if you, or the staff, feel that you have a significant mood elevation, you must let me know Tommy. Even if it feels good it is not good for you', Nurse Elsa says when Tommy has finished his song. 'No, I know', Tommy answers sombrely.

From the outside, this perhaps does not seem much of anything—nothing. It is mainly a conversation about music and football. But it is *also* an endeavour in relationship making, in building trust, and an example of attentive care. It is an illustration of the importance of clarification and that a song about the goodness of life is not necessarily just something good but can also be a sign of mood elevation, which is something to be careful with.

Throughout the conversation, Nurse Elsa skilfully asked questions about Tommy's life and illness history, and how he had been doing since he came home from the hospital, without disrupting our conversation about his love for the rock star and the specific football team. During this conversation we learned when Tommy had his first encounter with schizophrenia, and how it had affected his life and his relations since, all weaved into a story with lots of music references and old pictures. Observing this home visit allowed me to witness care in practice. I could see, and was involved in, Nurse Elsa's care. I saw and took part in her knowledgeable and skilful conversation with Tommy which both helped to build relationship and rapport and gave Elsa a much-needed insight in Tommy's life and illness. I saw how she took *cues* from Tommy's story, learning about how and at which point in his life his symptoms had worsened and when they had decreased.

The extract also tells us that relations are key to care in the mental healthcare unit. It provides examples of the texture and details of these relations, which could not have been documented without my shadowing of Nurse Elsa. Rather than ethnographically distancing myself from the situation playing out, I was open to being affected by the contact of others. I took part in the conversations; I was moved by Tommy's openness and I nearly felt Elsa's persistent attentiveness to Tommy's mood swings. Because, indeed, Nurse Elsa was attentive and persistent (Mol, 2008) in relation Tommy's mood elevations. What stands perfectly clear from this excerpt is that mood elevations are to be taken seriously. Therefore, rather than applauding Tommy after his song, Nurse Elsa talked about how things that feel good are not always good for you. Instead, things that feel good can sometimes be an indication of a mood swing, which in turn could mean worsened schizophrenia symptoms. My heart almost skipped a beat after Tommy's song when Elsa said, "Even if it feels good it is not good for you". While I was deeply touched and a little saddened by Tommy's song, Elsa managed to be *persistent* and expressed her attachment to finding ways of improving Tommy's situation. In addition, Nurse Elsa's actions also emphasized that Tommy should not be alone in keeping track of his mood. This is not his individual responsibility but the responsibility of a larger network in which he is one node. On several occasions during the home visit Nurse Elsa *emphasized* that Tommy could always call her or contact the staff at his supported living facility.

By not keeping distant but instead engaging in relation with Tommy and Elsa, a sense of comfort and ease was established, allowing Tommy and Elsa to talk about sensitive and difficult things such as mood elevations. My shadowing technique thus helped me see things otherwise difficult to see as an array of variables and quantities. In addition, I did not become conspicuously invisible or an awkward third wheel in the conversations. The field notes I took about my own feelings and situatedness and the way I reacted to Tommy's song later helped me in the analytical phase to discover and document the professionality and knowledge in how Elsa managed the situation.

Sitting on the floor: inventiveness and sensitivity work in care

One day I shadowed Doctor Anders, who also worked at the mental healthcare unit described in the previous section. On this day he was doing home visits to several clients with apartments in the same supported living facility, together with two nurses. One of the clients we visited was Nils. Before the visit Doctor Anders told me that Nils had been institutionalized for most of his life. He told me that Nils was practising yoga, was religious and had many specific dietary restrictions due to his religious believes. In addition, Nils had not left the supported living facility in almost a year, despite shorter periods at the hospital. He had taken a walk once, not too long ago during the early spring, but had forgotten to put his shoes on. This had frightened him about going out again. Nils had been hospitalized quite recently, when his symptoms had worsened, as elaborated upon in these field notes:

> Nils leads us to his bedroom [Figure 1.1]. His mattress lies on the floor and the bedframe stands empty on the other side of the room. There are books and loose paper everywhere. Nils sits down on the mattress. Doctor Anders brings me and one of the nurses chairs from the kitchen to sit on. The nurse asks where he will sit and Doctor Anders answers without hesitation, 'On the floor!' He takes a seat on the floor opposite Nils. Like Nils he sits with his legs crossed in front of him.
>
> Doctor Anders asks how Nils has been doing since he came back from the hospital. Nils constantly shakes and shivers, which is a common side effect from neuroleptics (anti-psychotic drugs), and it is a bit difficult to hear what he is saying. He says something about suffering. That he suffers? Doctor Anders asks if suffering is part of his religion. 'Krishna', Nils answers. 'Krishna', Doctor Anders repeats. And yes, there are writings about suffering in Bhagavad-Gita, Nils continues. 'Do you pray a lot?' Doctor Anders asks. 'Yes, I do' Nils answers. 'And are your prayers answered', Doctor Anders follows. 'Sometimes', says Nils. 'Did you receive any answers today?' asks Doctor Anders. Nils says that he did not.
>
> We have been in Nils' apartment for a minute, perhaps two. When Doctor Anders again asks how Nils is doing, Nils puts his hands before his chest in the 'Anjali Mudra' yoga pose and says that he cannot take it anymore and that it is too much. 'Just one more thing', Doctor Anders says quickly. He says that he has received the results of some blood samples and that Nils has a deficiency of a vitamin produced by the sun. 'Okay, so vitamin D?' Nils asks. 'So you know of it?' says Doctor Anders. Nils says that he does. Doctor Anders explains that he will add vitamin D to Nils' multi-dose drug dispenser. 'But mainly it is produced by the

sun. Perhaps you would be able to go outside 5 minutes each day the sun is shining?' Doctor Anders suggests. He explains that it is his recommendation. He also says that there is a patio outside, surrounded by a high fence for privacy. Perhaps Nils wouldn't be disturbed there and perhaps he could practice yoga outside? 'Okay. But you have to leave now', Nils says. We leave the apartment. (Field notes)

The quality of this encounter would be difficult to study quantitatively. A client like Nils would most likely not be willing or able to fill in a patient questionnaire. And what such a questionnaire would capture is uncertain. Similarly, counting the minutes doesn't say anything about this meeting. We were only there for five minutes. Would that count as success or failure?

This extract underscores that shadowing allows one to see the details and the context of daily practice. Indeed, shadowing and my informal chat with Doctor Anders made it possible for me to interpret his suggestion of five minutes outside on the patio in terms of care. Without this contextual knowledge about Nils being frightened after his previous walk outside it may even seem careless of a doctor not to order long walks. My knowledge of Nils' past experiences—or at least what the staff had told me about them—made Doctor Anders's sensitivity visible to me. Shadowing thus allowed me to see the nuances of care in this home visit. What struck me was the inventiveness, sensitivity and situatedness of this encounter.

The situatedness of care is something I have also highlighted in an article with Hansen-Löfstrand; no one home visit is like any other, instead home visits are characterized by constant exceptions and adaptations. In the mental healthcare unit, we noticed that good care was 'defined as being dependent on the circumstances and on the creativity of staff to provide care in these unique situations, given the specific context of the healthcare' (Lydahl and Hansen Löfstrand, 2020, p 10). Therefore, there wasn't really any specific principle or method of care guiding the actions of the healthcare professionals. The only way of studying this type of care is by observing it as it unfolds in practice.

The sensitivity and inventiveness are also seen in Doctor Anders's home visit to Nils (see Figure 1.1). First, Doctor Anders, myself and a nurse had to decide where to sit. Nils did not offer us anywhere to sit in particular. Instead, Doctor Anders arranged us: me and the nurse on two chairs and himself on the floor. This can be interpreted as a form of body work—Doctor Anders helped us all to adjust our bodily positions. By sitting on the floor *mirroring* Nils' position, rather than

Figure 1.1: Nils' bedroom

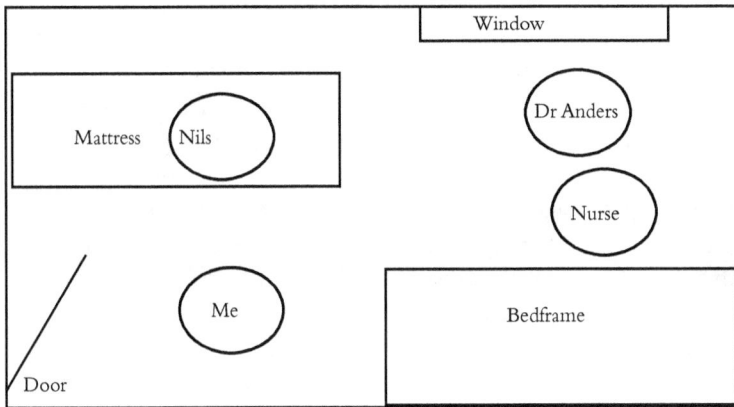

being elevated on a chair, Doctor Anders seemed to insist on some sort of equality in relation to Nils. To connect to Nils, Doctor Anders then inquired into Nils' faith when Nils talked about suffering. This can be seen as an effort to build relations around and be attentive to what is important for Nils. Indeed, it can be interpreted as sensitivity work. After answering some of Anders's questions, it was clear that the situation was a bit too much for Nils. After all, three persons were in his apartment. One of them—me—he hadn't even met before. When he put his hand before his heart and said that he couldn't take any more, Doctor Anders again had to be inventive. He had not yet had the opportunity to discuss what he wanted with Nils: the results of his blood sample and his medications. Doctor Anders explained the results in a simple way, confirmed Nils in his knowledge and again found a way of connecting to and being attentive to that which was important to Nils.

Through shadowing I could see the context of this encounter. In addition, I could see that sometimes a little is enough, and that care practices do not always consist of grand gestures or intense conversations. Sometimes it is enough to sit on the floor, suggesting that perhaps a patient could go out on the patio to do some yoga in order gain vitamin D from the sun, as this would *improve* the situation of the patient.

Care practices in the hospital

Besides studying home visits in mental healthcare I have also studied the realization of a specific version of person-centred care in practice, the focus of my second empirical example (Lydahl, 2017, 2019a, 2019b), that is, how a specific framework of person-centred care was worked with by care workers on the floors. Person-centred care has, in recent years, been heralded by healthcare researchers and politicians alike as a way of increasing patient satisfaction and furthering the efficiency of healthcare by inviting the patient in as an active participant and decision-maker in the delivery and planning of their own care.

The hospital ward where I carried out my shadowing had implemented a specific standardized framework of person-centred care, with some adaptations (Lydahl, 2021). In addition, the implementation of person-centred care at this specific ward would be evaluated according to the methods of EBM. Data would be collected about the patient experience of care, about how the staff experienced the care environment and about whether and how documentation in the patient records had changed. This would be done through questionnaires with patients and staff, and through text analysis of patient records. The work at the hospital ward was, in other words, structured according to EBM/P, but there were, as I will show, practices and situations within the ward which differed from EBM/P.

Making sandwiches: invisible work and tailored care[2]

During observations of the work of nurses and assistant nurses at the hospital ward, I found that person-centred care was presented as something primarily taking place in assessment interviews with newly admitted patients following an interview protocol, and in the setting up of a care plan with those patients (Lydahl, 2017). The hospital ward was an internal medicinal ward and new patients very regularly admitted to the ward, most commonly from the emergency ward at the hospital.

Like most implementations and their evaluation, this implementation and evaluation of person-centred care highlighted some practices, voices and points of view while silencing others. To my surprise, one practice that was silenced, or rather rendered invisible, was the work of assistant nurses in the ward. This became especially visible to me one day when I shadowed Assistant Nurse Amy, as the following extract from field notes describes:

> Peter is at the hospital for an abuse-related illness. Today, he will be discharged from ward E and moved to a rehabilitation home. It is early in the morning and Amy, an experienced assistant nurse that I am shadowing today, is talking about Peter who has fallen during the night and

injured his hand as he comes towards us. Rather than talking of his hand, Peter wants to talk about when he will be discharged. Amy is talking very animatedly and smiles and laughs when talking. She has a hand on Peter's un-injured arm. Even though Peter looks tired and worried he seems to relax somewhat when talking to Amy. Amy suggests that she can make some sandwiches he can take with him when leaving the ward as it will take an hour or two to travel to the rehabilitation home. A while later Amy prepares sandwiches for Peter. She tells me that Peter likes to eat and that he easily gets frustrated when he is hungry. However, he has not been that fond of the hospital food. But as he likes sandwiches Amy has prepared quite a few of them for him. Amy and I talk of person-centred care while preparing the sandwiches. I ask her if person-centred care in any way has changed the way she works. To my surprise she says that since she is an assistant nurse, she doesn't do person-centred care, as assistant nurses don't do assessment interviews or write care plans. Instead, their role in the implementation of person-centred care is to free up some time for the registered nurses by taking on some of the screenings usually carried out by registered nurses. (Field notes)

In line with the definition of care provided by Ceci et al (2012, p 11) as 'paying attention to the particularities of the situation of the people being cared for', Assistant Nurse Amy, like Nurse Elsa and Doctor Anders, found inventive ways of caring for her patient Peter. In this extract we can see how Assistant Nurse Amy, first through *touching*—having a hand on Peter's arm—found a way of calming him after his burdensome night. She saw that he was agitated—she noticed the particularities of the situation—and found a way of acting on it, in this case by laughing, talking and touching. Second, we can see how Assistant Nurse Amy inventively used her knowledge about Peter's eating habits and preferences to improve his situation. Assistant Nurse Amy's simple measure of making sandwiches can indeed be interpreted as way of *tailoring care* for Peter. She paid attention to the specificities of this particular troubled young man and adapted her care to suit him, to calm his mood and to make his transportation to the rehabilitation home as comfortable as possible.

Still, even when the assistant nurse saw the person behind the patient, touched him and tailored care for him, this type of care was rendered invisible in the implementation of person-centred care. Amy and other assistant nurses did not see their work as person-centred. Perhaps they did not see their work as nothing, but they clearly did not see it as person-centred. Moreover, as the care carried out by Assistant Nurse Amy and her colleagues was not classified as person-centred, it was not acknowledged in the implementation process of person-centred care, and thus also excluded from the evaluation thereof. While I am not arguing that the type of care carried out by Assistant Nurse Amy should be categorized or taken up in the routines of person-centred care, I think that shadowing can help researchers describe and illustrate practices of care taking place in settings such as hospital wards.

The extract also details that not everything in an organization, such as a hospital ward, working in accordance with EBM will be affected by EBM. There will always be practices and situations within any given discourse that are different. But this does not mean that they are valorised or given meaning. Instead there is a risk that they are seen as unimportant 'nothings'.

Conclusion

When healthcare and other forms of human service organizations are increasingly studied by methods of evidence-based medicine, the actual and specific daily activities, events and routines that make up the practice of care tend to be rendered invisible, forgotten and perhaps even made into seemingly nothing. There are a number of care practices (such as touching, laughing with someone, making food, doing sensitivity work, mirroring bodily postures, being persistent, making clarifications and emphasizing) that seem to be important for professionals to carry out even if they themselves sometimes think of them as 'nothing', and even if assessment forms and methods of EBM do not or would not include these particular practices. The reason for this abundance of 'nothings' is related to the EBM/P enterprise, which through its focus on reduction makes some things visible, and many other things invisible and untouched. However, through ethnographic methods such as shadowing, one can describe what is happening when 'nothing's happening'. This form of 'nothingness' is not possible to capture other than with ethnography.

Shadowing is therefore a suitable method for discovering and exploring practices made silent or taken for granted by methods of EBM/P. Utilizing shadowing as an ethnographic method, one can pay attention to the attentiveness, inventiveness, activities and gestures, which can be relatively small, that make up care. Through shadowing,

I have been able to illustrate that care sometimes involves talking about a song, sometimes consists of sitting on the floor and sometimes can come in the form of a sandwich.

Importantly, the attention to practices of care through shadowing generates other forms of knowledge than the type of knowledge provided by EBM/P. Rather than providing departicularized claims or guidelines about good care, shadowing of care practices provides situated knowledge with limited location. It provides suggestions for how specific practices can be developed, and shows how quality work can be accomplished in situ. Shadowing and attention to practices of care provide a way of staying open to the 'nothings' of experience.

Notes

[1] 'Gött å leva' by Galenskaparna och After Shave, my translation.
[2] This section and the empirical example build on an article previously published in *Sociologisk Forskning*, see Lydahl (2017).

References

Becker, H.S. (1998) *Tricks of the Trade: How to Think about Your Research while You're Doing It*, Chicago, IL: University of Chicago Press.

Bensing, J. (2000) 'Bridging the gap: The separate worlds of evidence-based medicine and patient-centered medicine', *Patient Education and Counseling*, 39(1): 17–25.

Berg, M. (1997) *Rationalizing Medical Work: Decision-Support Techniques and Medical Practices, Inside Technology*, Cambridge, MA: MIT Press.

Bowker, G.C. and Star, S.L. (1999) *Sorting Things Out: Classification and Its Consequences*, Cambridge, MA: MIT Press.

Brodwin, P. (2013) *Everyday Ethics: Voices from the Frontline of Community Psychiatry*, Berkeley, CA: University of California Press.

Ceci, C., Björnsdóttir, K. and Purkis, M.E. (eds) (2012) *Perspectives on Care at Home for Older People*, London: Routledge.

Czarniawska, B. (2007) *Shadowing and Other Techniques for Doing Fieldwork in Modern Societies*, Malmö: Liber.

Epstein, S. (2007) *Inclusion: The Politics of Difference in Medical Research*, Chicago, IL: University of Chicago Press.

Haraway, D. (1988) 'Situated knowledges: The science question in feminism and the privilege of partial perspective', *Feminist Studies*, 14(3): 575–599.

Knaapen, L. (2014) 'Evidence-based medicine or cookbook medicine? Addressing concerns over the standardization of care', *Sociology Compass*, 8(6): 823–836.

Lydahl, D. (2017) 'Visible persons, invisible work?', *Sociologisk forskning*, 54(3): 163–179.

Lydahl, D. (2019a) 'Standard tools for non-standard care: The values and scripts of a person-centred assessment protocol', *Health*, available at: https://journals.sagepub.com/doi/abs/10.1177/1363459319851541

Lydahl, D. (2019b) 'It is not a pill', *Nordic Journal of Science and Technology Studies*, 7(2): 4–14.

Lydahl, D. (2021) 'Standard tools for non-standard care: The values and scripts of a person-centred assessment protocol', *Health*, 25(1): 103–120.

Lydahl, D. and Hansen Löfstrand, C. (2020) 'Doing good: Autonomy in the margins of welfare', *Sociology of Health and Illness*, 42(4): 892–906.

Lydahl, D., Holmberg, S., Günther, K. and Ranta, J. (2020) 'Doing data together: Affective relations and mobile ethnography in home visits', *Qualitative Research*, available at: https://journals.sagepub.com/doi/abs/10.1177/1468794120917913

Mol, A. (2008) *The Logic of Care: Health and the Problem of Patient Choice*, London: Routledge.

Moser, I. (2010) 'Perhaps tears should not be counted but wiped away: On quality and improvement in dementia care', in A. Mol, I. Moser and J. Pols (eds) *Care in Practice: On Tinkering in Clinics, Homes and Farms*, Bielefeld: Transcript, pp 277–300.

Pols, J. (2008) 'Which empirical research, whose ethics? Articulating ideals in long-term mental health care', in G. Widdershoven, J. McMillan, T. Hope and L. Van der Scheer (eds) *Empirical Ethics in Psychiatry*, Oxford: Oxford University Press, pp 51–68.

Pols, J. (2015) 'Towards an empirical ethics in care: Relations with technologies in health care', *Medicine, Health Care and Philosophy*, 18(1): 81–90.

Timmermans, S. and Berg, M. (2003) *The Gold Standard: The Challenge of Evidence-Based Medicine and Standardization in Health Care*, Philadelphia, PA: Temple University Press.

2

Two worlds of professional relevance in a small village

Christel Avendal

First, the short of it. This chapter is about social worlds and forms of ethnographic noticing in the context of human service providers working with rural youth. During my ethnographic fieldwork in a small Swedish village, service providers' views of and actions towards village youngsters regularly formulated the young as troubled and as potential service problems (see Gubrium and Järvinen, 2014). The kinds of service provider involved were legion; it wasn't just a matter of social work. Everyone from state-employed social workers to therapists of every stripe dealing with all manner of problems and remedial conduct were involved. Nowadays, the perceived problems of the young seem to be everyone's business, be they mental health issues (Kvist Lindholm and Wickström, 2020), family relationships (Bartholdsson, 2004) or youths' presence in public space (Valentine, 2004. The emphasis on human service problems is rarely questioned; it is a professional given, taken for granted. In relation to rural youth, the problem framework is further reinforced through spatial constructions. At the time for my fieldwork, and as is still the case, Swedish public discourse portrayed the rural young as a particular concern (see Areschoug, 2019), and the challenges facing human service provision in rural settings with low population rates were on the political agenda (see SOU 2017:1, p 156ff). This suggested that doing ethnographic research on human service work in relation to village youth would produce something special.

I soon learned that matters professional and legion reverberated throughout human service organizations even into the smallest villages. Local providers narrated young people's everyday lives in these milieus as problem ridden. However, fieldwork among young villagers themselves—outside the bounds of professional service providers—showed a different picture. They, on the contrary, narrated everyday life as joyful and fun. This made possible a critical reflection on taken-for-granted and well-established 'truths' within service organizations, and fuelled a process of sceptical self-discovery on my own part. In talking to young people themselves, a different way of constructing reality was captured, a reality of as much professional relevance as the one constructed by human service providers.

Concerned villagers and problems-talk

Now for the longer story. The Swedish village, which I hereby give the fictitious name Allboda, is located in the middle of a vast agricultural area and may be described as charming, tranquil, pretty and small. About six hundred people live there. The village consists of two main roads which are crossed by smaller streets where villa gardens are located. Many of the villas boast beautiful wooden houses from the beginning of the 20th century, even though several appear to be in need of maintenance. Allboda is the hub of human service provision for the surrounding, sparsely populated rural area. The village hosts a school, grocery store, nursing home, petrol station, hairdresser, preschool, pub, playground and a small kiosk. It has "everything you need", as a young villager put it. In the past, one could travel by train to Allboda, the village being something of a social and commercial centre in the region. But the train station closed long ago and nowadays Allboda is unknown to most people outside the vicinity. Today, the village may be described as a 'remote corner'; villagers have to rely on a winding and narrow country road when undertaking the 15 km journey to the closest small town.

I started my fieldwork in Allboda eager to know how young people spend their days in the village. Predictably, and in line with a social-problems framework, at the start I concentrated on human service agencies in the village, to discover what it offers local youth. Children and young people today spend large parts of their days in human service agencies, subjected to adults' protection and control, something which is referred to as the institutionalization of childhood (Qvortrup, 2012). Perhaps rural service provision would be 'something different' considering the small population rate and presumably few service agencies—which was a source of political concern.

I quickly learned that there were plenty of 'human service workers' thereabouts—state and civil society actors and varied service professionals, as well as concerned laypersons—with the common goal of ensuring young people's access to entertaining and meaningful activities in the local community. There was quite a bit of action in the village on this front. I encountered youth workers at the local youth club, open Mondays and Thursdays; villagers who led weekly evening study circles in cooking and knitting; librarians at the small state-run library; villagers organizing collective sports such as football, tennis or gymnastics; planning professionals responsible for strategic development related to village life and living opportunities; and volunteers at the *Byalag* (the local community organization),[1] which organized activities, village happenings and various social interventions. I also encountered teachers and other staff members in local schools concerned with young villagers' doings and well-being. At first glance, state-employed school staff, strategic development professionals and village people running small, private study circles may not seem to have much in common. Yet they shared the common objective of bringing change and improvement in the life situations and life opportunities of youngsters, among others. Most often this was accomplished by identifying problems and taking action in order to solve them. In some sense, all of those concerned can be seen as occupied with problems and problem-solving in a service-problems framework.

Not only providers but also human service *researchers* are regularly concerned with problems. Dominant as this framework is, the related problems narrative can influence the researchers' assumptions and what they notice ethnographically. This generated a procedural complication in that my ethnographic fieldwork was now usefully fuelled by forms of noticing with conflicting aims. The aim of careful *empirical noticing,* which is to document the constructions of everyday life and which I started with, was joined with the aim of *conceptual noticing,* a term inspired by Anna Tsing's (2015) term noticing, which inscribes the contextual horizons of those constructions. The two forms of noticing offered the most ethnographic insight for me when they worked together reflexively. The process of conceptual noticing extends to the ethnographer's willingness and ability to observe the empirical world beyond prevailing knowledges or narratives (compare Tsing, 2015), in this case the social-problems framework. Unfortunately, ethnographic observation is often described as detailed empirical discovery only. Through attentive observation and detailed documentation, ethnographers linger on details, stay with the mundane and note seemingly trivial matters as part of a method for representing ways of life and their complexities. This practice, which I describe as empirical noticing, is fundamental to ethnographic documentation. However, no matter how detailed and attentive empirical noticing is, it cannot reveal what conceptual noticing can.

Conceptual noticing involves setting aside familiar frames of reference in order to discover matters that are not visible even with strong lenses.

It is a process of sceptical self-discovery and reflection on that which is taken for granted. It involves setting aside what is predominant in order to make visible what we haven't readily seen (compare Tsing, 2015, p 18). In my Allboda fieldwork, conceptual noticing involved setting aside the social-problems framework. This did not come easy, although it was readily adopted when it did. The service-problems framework dominated my own research milieu in a university social work department as well as service providers' assumptions and conduct in Allboda. Conceptual noticing is particularly helpful in cases like this, when ethnographer and informants share fundamental frames of reference.

The concern with problems was palpable across the board. My conversations with local social workers on the topic of 'young villagers' triggered problems-talk regardless of what I said. My conversation with librarian Charlotte provides another example. The first time we met, I told her I was visiting Allboda to learn more about youngsters' village life. I had not seen that many young people yet, I said in a cheerful tone, adding that they seemed to spend their days at school, at home or at the local youth club. Charlotte immediately responded: "There are no other places to go here!" She added that there were no cafés or shopping malls in Allboda. Later, I came to think about what she left out: the beautiful surrounding woods, the much-appreciated local grocery store, the lovely small river and the new playground where the young often hung out. Instead, implicating a possible social problem, she pointed at what was lacking, using a variation of the well-known saying: 'Nothing to do, nowhere to go' (compare Skelton, 2000).

Anna, part of the student health team in the local school, also engaged in problems-talk. Avoiding putting words in her mouth, I was careful to ensure my questions did not indicate any particular interest in problems, as I now had started to reflect on the preoccupation of those concerned with all kinds of difficulties. I asked her what young people generally do in the village. Anna responded that the village does not offer young people very much, and that the local youth club has few visitors. The latter fact worried her. I told her that many youngsters had shown up at the club lately. I knew this, I said, since I spent quite some time there. Anna was not convinced, and instead of picking up on my happy news, she turned the conversation into one about problems of idleness ("Not much to do").

> 'Mm, okay, good. Because it's so sad. I know they think
> they have very few places to be at . . . People say there is
> not much to do [in the village], more than football /—/

And we have this new sports hall and I just read in the
newspaper that there is not as many activities as people
wished for. / — / And then I feel that there is nothing for
girls to do / — / For girls who do not want to play football
there is nothing. (Anna)

Indeed, Anna frames the situation in the small village as a whole in
terms of problems. As if to say that small villages, especially for youth,
pose service problems; it did not seem to matter that the village has
a youth club, a new sports hall and a football team. When I tried to
convince her that the youth club in fact had many visitors, Anna showed
no interest in elaborating on the positive aspects of these issues. Instead,
her talk echoed familiar notions about rural living as dull (for example
see Holloway and Valentine, 2000). My impression from fieldwork was
that human service workers narrated their experiences of the young
through familiar problem stories, regardless of what questions I asked
them or my conversational encouragement. The workers seemed to use
established problem repertoires to convey their experiences, and they
especially used the problem framework when talking about the young.

Even those who talked about matters that were perceived as 'good'
related them to what I soon took to be a widespread service-problems
genre. Sissi, a youth leader at the local youth club, often emphasized
that the young villagers were "good", meaning that they were nice
and upstanding and did not engage in problematic activity or cause
any problems. The following field note describes how Sissi tried to
convince Helen, the mother of a 12-year-old girl in the village, that
the young villagers in fact are "good", as Sissi and Helen sat in the
youth club one evening talking about this and that in my company.
Notably, after a while they started talking about young people in the
village in the context of and what they were "up to". They talked
about "bad stuff" going on in village streets, referring to then recent
vandalism (smashed windows at the local grocery store and graffiti on
village walls).

Helen says she is happy that the youth club is open. This
means that someone is keeping an eye on the young, she
says. 'How can so much bad stuff happen in the village when
you never see anyone outdoors?' Helen asks rhetorically.
She adds that it is important for adults to keep an eye on
the young, to have them in the spotlight. 'You cannot do
more than be visible in the streets, so that they know you see
them'. Helen is puzzled about the fact that no one knows

who the vandals are. They were captured on CCTV, Helen says, but they have not yet been identified. 'Could it be the greasers?' Sissi asks? Helen says no. Sissi mentions that young people at the youth club are good. They are always happy to see and talk to you, she clarifies. Helen answers that not all of them are good. She starts talking about one of the girls who regularly visits the youth club, about her bad attitude and the lack of support she gets from home. Sissi answers that she shows no bad attitude at the youth club. None of the bad stuff is visible there. 'She knows how to be smooth', Helen concludes. (Field notes)

Problems-talk and the larger narrative culture

The repetition of common themes and familiar accounts, especially the kind Robert Dingwall (1977) years ago called 'atrocity stories' and which Donileen Loseke (2001) more recently referred to as 'formula stories' points to the larger narrative culture of problems-talk. Sissi, Helen, Anna and many others are, narratively, in the near and distant company of service providers in countless service institutions, organizations and associations devoted to identifying and processing people and situations as social problems (compare Gubrium and Holstein, 2001). The problems framework may be seen as an institutional discourse (Miller, 1994), which many argue has become the representational centre of the troubles culture of social life, extending not only to professional service workers but also to concerned laypersons, some of whose related talk we've heard. Institutional discourses include assumptions, concerns and vocabularies that those concerned use as shared resources when interpreting and organizing action (Miller, 1994). As taken for granted and fundamental, the discourses are virtually invisible to those who use them, and are seldom a concern in their own right. But they are highly audible and ethnographically visible for 'noticing'.

Take formula stories in particular, which are an important ingredient in the institutional discourse among workers and concerned others in Allboda. Experiences under consideration are narrated by drawing on various well-known problem accounts. Since problems–talk was so easily triggered in Allboda, accounts became *usefully* formulaic, giving the impression of being a conventional way of speaking. This was probably also triggered by my position as a researcher with a human service background. Such stories were told to an appreciative audience and evaluated as meaningful in relation to that audience (Riessman, 2008). As a social science researcher, the larger narrative culture of social problems meant that I was likely seen as someone who had a specific interest in problems and solutions, and then taken as someone familiar with 'the issues' and, as such, as an appreciative audience. Human service researchers may in this way reinforce institutional discourses.

Problems discourses should not be viewed as mere talk. In use, they organize the setting of members' actions (Miller, 1994). In this case, problems–talk and problem-solving activities are part of the same pie. Martin, a strategic development worker in the municipality where Allboda is located, talked to me about problems concerning the young, parents and place. His worry was linked to statistics that showed low grades among pupils in the municipality. In the following field note, he elaborates not only on problems but also on potential solutions while I am sitting next to him listening.

> Martin says that parents in the municipality are not able to convey the importance of education, higher education, to their children. Parents believe that in the future their children will take over the family farming enterprise, but in order to run a farm today, Martin says to me, you have to be an agronomist or likewise. Much technical knowledge is needed. Martin thinks the girls are studying hard as a way of getting away from the village. He says that the solution is to start a secondary school with academic programs, to show other possibilities to the young locals. When you walk the streets of the municipality capital, Martin continues, you see no architect companies or design enterprises. There is nothing here to inspire higher education, he says, adding that there are many entrepreneur businesses though. Walking down the street you see tinsmiths and other craft business: 'There are 140 construction firms in the municipality', Martin exclaims. He says to me that, proportionally, that is counted as many. (Field notes)

As it is in the larger narrative culture, a vital part of problems–talk and formula stories is the creation of solutions to problems, such as Martin conveyed with his thoughts on educational programmes and other types of business in the village. The human service workers in Allboda were all highly engaged and involved in producing and conveying solutions to the problems they readily described. The local youth club arranged a number of activities. "There must be at least one organized activity every week", Sissi, the youth leader, explained to me when I asked about her plans for the youth club. During my fieldwork, she organized sports games, baking competitions, card games, graffiti painting, movie nights and candy evenings for the youth, to mention just a few examples. Also, the Byalag arranged a great number of activities. During one single Byalag meeting, I observed the participants plan for National Day celebrations, night patrol (*Nattvandring*), flea markets, family gymnastics, an autumn fair and a circus school, all significantly directed at Allboda's villagers.

Social worlds and counternarratives

As fieldwork progressed, the concept of social worlds and their distinct narratives began to take shape, the former at times superseding the latter in the analytic process. Moving out of social service environs allowed me to consider empirically the possibility that problems-talk and formula stories were part of a distinct social world constructed by service providers and concerned others around the experiences of youth. This happened as I came into contact with young people themselves on separate grounds, which reflexively made me aware of counternarratives. On their own turf, the young, by and large, did not use problems-talk or problems narratives for describing daily living. By encouraging the young people with whom I interacted to talk about their everyday lives, I noticed aspects of youthful living that I had not noticed earlier. Perhaps more to a theoretical point, noticing took on conceptual as much as empirical significance. I was not just another piece of a common service-problems pie, as it were, but a different pie with the same ingredients, if that can be imagined, spoken in the language of joy, pleasure, pride and fun.

   In the following extended extract from an interview, Casper, a 12-year-old living in Allboda, tells me about his daily routine, as he calls it. In his account, rural living is depicted as a set of experiences with different moral horizons than those represented in accounts conveying problems narratives. Service problems, solutions, and human service work are noticeably absent. The account isn't exceptional; it is, rather, typical of the many responses to the interview questions I put to youngsters about what life is like for them in the village of Allboda:

> 'I get up from the bed, then I eat two toasts and a glass of milk, sit down at the kitchen table and sit there for like 20 minutes and watch YouTube and eat'. 'What do you watch on YouTube?' I ask. 'Well, I usually look at "Jocke and Jonna",[2] they are called. And sometimes I look at birds. And then I put on my jacket and shoes and go out. Then

I open for the hens, they have a trapdoor. Or now that I am at home they may roam freely in the yard, but not the pheasants, because they can escape. They don't feel at home yet. And well, I open for them, and set things right for them, and fix their water, clean a little, or something like that, and give them some new food. And now it is more work to do with the pheasants, I have no proper day routine with them yet. So, then I go around and check things out, I have a look at what they do and pick up the brood duck so she gets to bathe a little and then I take out the ducklings in the poultry yard, and then maybe I go in and get my cell phone so I don't forget it. And I usually stay indoors a bit and so, check out stuff. I also have a lot of plants that I have planted, like potatoes and stuff. Water them a little. Then I go out again and see what the others are doing. Then, well, I usually stay outside with the hens. And then I stay there and pick some eggs, and well. And then in the evening, when it is evening, I take all the chickens in. The ducks usually sleep outside, or they are not allowed to do that, but I have to chase them in, the hens go in voluntarily. And then I lock them up, wish them goodnight. And then I bring in the ducks and ducklings. If it is windy, I can't take the ducklings out, because then they blow away. And then I go indoors, I always wash my hands after I've been at the poultry yard, before I eat and so. So I wash my hands before I go in and eat. And then we usually check out a series called "Prison Break" that we watch on Netflix, ... me, dad and his girlfriend Lena. And then we go to bed, always at 10 pm. That is when we usually go to bed'. (Interview with 'Casper')

Casper's story is an interesting contrast to the notion of village life as problematic. Two parts are prominent. First, he talks at length and with enthusiasm, joy and pride about the activities in which he is involved. He does not depict his living circumstances as a problem needing to be solved. In fact, he describes himself being involved in all kinds of problem-solving activities unrelated to service problems. And he seems capable of dealing with them on his own. Second, organized human services are virtually absent from his story. Casper does not even mention school, a place that takes up a significant portion of his time, as it does for most young people. Casper is not unique in what he reports, nor are its emotional and moral contours: joy, pleasure, pride and fun. The young villagers all had stories of joy and pride to tell about everyday living. Certainly, they occasionally spoke of 'troubles', but these were workaday difficulties, such as having "to chase the ducks in". They were rarely conveyed as service problems.

Conclusion

During my fieldwork in Allboda, I learned to appreciate the utility of both forms of ethnographic noticing—both empirical and conceptual noticing. I want to point out strongly that these are reflexively related, an important first lesson. They can and should grow, in turns, out of each other as fieldwork progresses. As important as systematic participant observation and careful note taking are, it is their combination with a willingness to consider and set aside possibly dominant narratives that leads to noticing of the more conceptual kind especially. (Regarding note taking in particular, see Emerson et al, 1995).

By setting aside the service-problems narratives and moving on to what I eventually viewed as a separate social world, for example, I learned that Alice, a 12-year-old, was deeply dedicated to horseback riding. Hardly idle, she was busy as ever with that. She participated in national competitions and worked as a riding instructor for even younger persons. This knowledge enriched my empirical noticing regarding this social world. It made me tune in more conceptually to the many times when Alice and her friend Sara, also deeply passionate about horses, spoke about how, during school breaks at their desks, quietly and by themselves, they discussed horses and riding. They sometimes wrestled with difficult questions: What should Sara do now when her horse was injured? Abandon him for another healthy horse, as her parents recommended, or continue to take care of him even if this meant that she would spend fewer hours on horseback? This was a problem, yes, but not a service problem, something it could have been seen as in the context of problematic idleness and frustration. Rather, they were once more rehearsing the narratives of different social world.

Likewise, had I not talked to 12-year-old Benjamin about things he likes doing in his free (idle) time, I would not have taken notice of his kicking a football during school breaks. Using a problems narrative, perhaps I would have observed him and even felt a little bit sad, interpreting his football interest as a sign of disinterest in schooling and of the lack of leisure activities in the village (as worker Anna did previously in this chapter). Instead, by asking about matters of fun, I learned that he had been recruited by a prestigious Swedish football club and was about to change schools in order to attend the club school, which was a veritable dream come true.

A second and related lesson learned is that the idea of there being two forms of noticing did not drop out of thin air. It was concretely supported as much by a willingness to analytically take up the possible grounded borders of narrativity as by literally moving to other places with different ways of thinking and talking about life and living. A willingness to consider that what people say about, how they feel in the process and what they do about it are localized. To some extent we know very well about this, which animates the ongoing contextuality of everyday life. But the lesson has yet to penetrate thinking conceptually about the substance and limits of human service provision. The distinction between the two forms of noticing led me to see that my informants were already "going about" their own lives with as much nuance as I was now, I hoped, "going about" human service ethnography. Another facet of this, for me, came with the realization that casting light on, and emphasizing, a particular view of reality can simultaneously obscure and diminish others, making them virtually invisible in comparison. Setting aside the problems framework through conceptual noticing enabled me to see matters that had been hardly noticeable when I was focusing on the empirical landscape of the problems narratives.

Noticing details and mundane activity outside of well-established narrative spaces such as that of service problems work is challenging. One does not just move on a whim to other fields of social interaction where 'nothing (of interest seemingly) is happening' such as troubles, problems and human service provision (see Lydahl's essay in Chapter 1 of this volume). Why study troubles and problems in places other than where they are considered and where their origins and consequences are contemplated? If not scientific derring-do, it requires patience and confidence to stay with issues that at first glance may seem trivial and of no interest (Wax and Wax, 1971), especially in places without pertinent narrative landscapes.

For human service ethnographers this poses particular challenges. The combination of ethnographic methods and human service as their object of research makes for a particularly tricky case. Ethnographic fieldwork is about immersion in a place. Immersion brings advantages in terms of detailed and emplaced empirical knowledge. However, during fieldwork in human service organizations, the ethnographer is immersed in milieus where single and strong frameworks are in use and which hence make it difficult to notice and imagine things otherwise. Furthermore, research disciplines such as social work often share related human service agencies' basic assumptions, concerns and vocabularies. Practice and research thus operate under the same umbrella. This is, in many ways, necessary in order for academics to understand and provide relevant research to human service workers. Yet, when it comes to the task of developing, redefining and reinterpreting human service work, the underlying shared assumptions of the world is a hindrance.[3]

When the young people I eventually spoke with were asked to freely talk about things that interested them, they talked at length, with precision, in detail and with dedication and often passion about daily life today, their pasts and their futures. They told me about motorcycles, cooking, YouTube, ploughing on the farm, horseback riding, reading, computer games, walks in the woods, playing with pets and seeing friends, among countless interests and activities. They presented themselves as competent and active, and they narrated their experiences with pride and enthusiasm.

If not dismissed as analytically irrelevant, young people's stories can lead problems narratives to be seen in a new light when the two are juxtaposed. This opens up the possibility of seeing social-problem assessments as interpretive practices that leave out and obscure relevant parts of clients' lives and qualities. The alternative stories that conceptual noticing reveals have the potential to open new windows on reality and provide new ways of interpreting social lives (Delgado, 1989). Engaging with narratives that challenge institutional accounts may be a way for human service workers to provide new interpretations of fundamental concerns and assumptions in their work. (For a compelling example of social work research providing new ways of understanding people who typically are categorized as 'undocumented youth', see Djampour, 2018; Söderman, 2019). The young Allboda villagers' counternarratives permitted me to pose critical questions about service provision. They made me ask whether service providers really served the interest of the young, or if they rather served the interest of other people (compare Qvortrup, 2012).

Although not new, this question tends to be forgotten when operating within a service-problems landscape. The question is not just for the Allboda service providers, but for service provision as a whole, and for service providers in all sorts of agencies working with children, the elderly, people with addiction or mental health problems or detainees, among many others. Alternative narratives may, as Delgado puts forward, enrich our imagination and construct a new and richer world (Delgado, 1989, p 2415). Engaging with the youngsters and talking about their everyday doings, was, for me, significantly a consequence of my applying the helpful tool of conceptual noticing. It led me to discover that in a geographic space as small as a Swedish village there can exist, virtually side by side, the social worlds of multiple realities (Gubrium, 1974).

Notes

[1] A Byalag may be described as a local form of organization. It organizes inhabitants in a village and its function is mainly social, but it may also be advisory in political issues.

[2] Jocke and Jonna are famous Swedish YouTubers.

[3] Setting aside the social-problems framework should not be confused with the now rather well-established research practice of shifting perspective from service provider to service user. Service user is in itself an institutional category which may not assist the social work researcher in setting aside the problems framework, as the notion of service user is defined in relation to problems. In social work, there is a tradition of exploring service users' lives and perspectives. However, studies taking a 'user perspective' also run the risk of focusing on the social problem at hand, as people's lives are understood mainly in relation to the problem they are associated with. 'The addict', for example, may be portrayed in a new (more positive) way, but the person is still part of research as 'the addict' and as a 'user' of human service. We may learn more about addiction from a user perspective (obviously important knowledge in itself), yet we risk not being aware of people's experiences and qualities beyond the problems framework.

References

Areschoug, S. (2019) 'Rural failures: Representations of (im)mobile young masulinities and place in the Swedish countryside', *Boyhood Studies*, 12(1): 76–96.

Bartholdsson, Å. (2004) 'Konsten att konstruera sanning: Om barn och föräldrars tid för samtal', *Sociologisk forskning*, 41(2): 43–67.

Delgado, R. (1989) 'Storytelling for oppositionists and others: A plea for narrative', *Michigan Law Review*, 87(8): 2411–2441.

Dingwall, R. (1977) ' "Atrocity stories" and professional relationships', *Sociology of Work and Occupations*, 4(4): 371–396.

Djampour, P. (2018) *Borders Crossing Bodies: The Stories of Eight Youth with Experience of Migrating*, Doctoral dissertation, Malmö University.

Emerson, R., Fretz, R. and Shaw, L. (1995) *Writing Ethnographic Fieldnotes*, Chicago, IL: University of Chicago Press.

Gubrium, J.F. (1974) 'On multiple realities in a nursing home' in J.F. Gubrium (ed) *Late Life: Communities and Environmental Policy*, Springfield, IL: Charles C Thomas Publisher, pp 61–98.

Gubrium, J.F. and Holstein, J.A. (eds) (2001) *Institutional Selves: Troubled Identities in a Postmodern World*, New York: Oxford University Press.

Gubrium, J.F. and Järvinen, M. (eds) (2014) *Turning Troubles into Problems: Clientization in Human Services*, London: Routledge.

Holloway, S.L. and Gill, V. (2000) 'Children's geographies and the new social studies of childhood', in Holloway, S.L. and Gill, V. (eds) *Children's Geographies. Playing, Living, Learning*, London: Routledge.

Kvist Lindholm, S. and Wickström, A. (2020) '"Looping effects" related to young people's mental health: How young people transform the meaning of psychiatric concepts', *Global Studies of Childhood*, 10(1): 26–38.

Loseke, D. (2001) 'Lived realities and formula stories of battered Women'in J.F. Gubrium and J.A. Holstein (eds) *Institutional Selves: Troubled Identities in a Postmodern World*, New York: Oxford University Press, pp 102–126.

Miller, G. (1994) 'Towards ethnographies of institutional discourse', *Journal of Contemporary Ethnography*, 23(3): 280–306.

Qvortrup, J. (2012) 'Users and interested parties: A concluding essay on children's institutionalization', in A. Kjørholt and J. Qvortrup (eds) *The Modern Child and the Flexible Labour Market: Early Childhood Education and Care. Houndmills*, Basingstoke: Palgrave Macmillan.

Riessman, C.K. (2008) *Narrative Methods of the Human Science*, London: Sage.

Skelton, T. (2000) 'Nothing to do, nowhere to go?', in S.L. Holloway and V. Gill (eds) *Children's Geographies. Playing, Living, Learning*, London: Routledge.

SOU (2017:1) *För Sveriges landsbygder—en sammanhållen politik för arbete, hållbar tillväxt och välfärd. Slutbetänkande av Parlamentariska landsbygdskommittén*, Stockholm: Wolters Kluwer.

Söderman, E. (2019) *Resistance through Acting: Ambivalent Practices of the No Border Musical*, Doctoral dissertation, Lund University.

Tsing, A.L. (2015) *The Mushroom at the End of the World. On the Possibility of Life in Capitalist Ruins*, Princeton, NJ: Princeton University Press.

Valentine, G. (2004) *Public Space and the Culture of Childhood*, Aldershot: Ashgate.

Wax, M. and Wax, R. (1971) 'Great tradition, little tradition and formal education', in M. Wax, S. Diamond and F.O. Gearing (eds) *Antropological Perspectives on Education*, New York: Basic Books.

3

Capturing the organization of emotions in child welfare decision-making

Tea Torbenfeldt Bengtsson

I feel so angry with Mum here. She should step up now and take responsibility, save her sons! Is there really nothing we can do? Are we completely powerless here?! (Observation of 'Karen')

Karen, an experienced social worker, made this exclamation during the weekly team meeting at a Danish child welfare agency. At the time, I was conducting an ethnographic study of the decision-making process in child protection. Five other social workers also were present, together with a family counsellor and the team manager. Over the course of three months of fieldwork, during which I participated in all the social workers' weekly meetings, I had encountered numerous situations involving emotional expressions of this kind—of frustration, anger, worries, guilt and blame. While expressions of joy, pride, happiness and competence also were evident, the more negative and dramatic ones dominated my field notes. If such expressions provided insider knowledge about the practices of a child welfare agency, the negative ones especially could be viewed ethnographically as playing a defensive role in the practice of regulation and control.

In this chapter, I use my own emotional experiences as a starting point for arguing that both the emotional expressions and their regulation in the field spring from an inherent paradox in human service organizations, which, to a large extent, defines the practice of social work in child welfare. The paradox is formed on one side by the expected rationality of bureaucratic structures mediated by law and their associated economic-rationalistic demands. It is formed on the other side by a (sometimes frustratingly raging) humanistic care ethos built on taking responsibility for the care of human beings and related demands for flexibility, personal engagement and constant availability (Davies, 1994; Daly and Lewis, 2000; Deery, 2008; Mol, 2008).

Organizational contours of emotion

Although numerous emotions arise from navigating the complexities of social work, they are often disregarded and viewed as being irrelevant for our understanding of decision-making in human services provision. To a large extent, emotions and emotional expressions are considered to be private (or personal); therefore, they are almost naturally excluded from the bureaucratic understanding of decision-making in child welfare (Forsberg and Vagli, 2006; Ingram, 2013; O'Connor and Leonard, 2014; Harrits, 2016). Organizational logic, in effect, is seen to be a world of structures and processes, separate from the logic of personal life. However, through an analysis of emotional expressions and regulations, I seek to demonstrate how ethnography can bring forward important knowledge about the role of emotions in organizational contexts and, in particular, how emotional expressions actively inform the everyday practices of decision-making in human service provision.

While the role of social workers' emotions and their emotional intelligence is key to ongoing discussions in social work practice, there is a tendency to mainly focus on the individual social worker (such as Davis, 2001). Emotions are located within the individual as adaptive responses to current events. They are seen as underpinning decision-making through the degree of self-knowledge that social workers possess (for a more detailed discussion see Ingram, 2013). However, I found that assigning emotional responses to an individual social worker's degree of self-knowledge, self-control or to their personality traits failed to take the formative interactional and structural aspects of emotions seriously. Denzin has also addressed this point: 'All experiences of being emotional are situational, reflective and relational…[and] radiates through the lived body of the person' (Denzin, 2007, p 3). During my fieldwork, individual social workers continually expressed emotions, but I also observed that these were balanced to fit the specific cultural guidelines of care and responsibility in the organization. These observations demonstrated to me how emotional expressions were not merely internal to an individual social worker but closely connected to their organizational contours and the related cultural context of human service work (Hochschild, 2012).

In what follows, I first consider what it meant for me to be ethnographically engaged with emotional expression in a particular field. Second, I discuss the overlap between my own emotional experiences and those of the field by showing how this led me to focus on the role of emotions in social work practice. Third, I consider the role of emotions in everyday decision-making, demonstrating how ethnographic data allow for relatedly nuanced analyses of decision-making. And finally, fourth, I address how engagement with emotions is controlled both within the agency but also in the interactions between the field and myself as an ethnographer. I then conclude the chapter with a brief discussion of how ethnography may be used in the future to further investigate the role of emotions in the field of human service provisions.

Engagement with the emotions of a particular field

Ethnographically, child welfare agencies are a type of field, one with organizational contours. Not all fields are organizations, of course, such as the field of family relations. In that respect, the organizational contours of emotional expression need to be understood in their own terms, related to a specific paradoxical signature. Child welfare agencies make critical decisions regarding the futures of families, children and youth based on clear evaluations of family functioning and child well-being (Holland, 2011). Rational argumentation, legal support and systematic knowledge are paramount in this work; this is increasingly reflected in the use of manuals and control systems to ensure that social workers make ostensibly rational decisions based on the documented 'facts' of cases (Jacobsson and Meeuwisse, 2018). These are the resonances of one side of the paradox.

However, as the observation introducing this chapter shows, decision-making processes are not neutral and detached from the emotions they entail and produce. Anger is activated as a response, feeding on concern, worries and professional integrity. Similar to what other researchers have found, this demonstrates that decision-making in child welfare agencies is not a straightforward process. Despite increased systematization of the field, decision-making continues to be defined by unsystematic processes and relationships (Helm, 2016; Skotte, 2018). Emotional expressions are not metrical; moreover, they are not necessarily articulated. Nussbaum (2001) has provided important information about how we always understand, experience and evaluate the world through emotions. Yet, despite this insight, emotions continue to be disregarded and marginalized in most research processes and, thus, in what constitutes relevant scientific knowledge (Holland, 2007). As Barbalet has stated: 'Emotions are not optional extras. They are implicated in all human action, including thought'

(Barbalet, 2006, p 51). Consequently, they inform our creation of new knowledge. For many ethnographers, this insight is part of their embodied practice when conducting fieldwork (Hastrup, 1992; Coffey, 1999; Hubbard et al, 2001; Dickson-Swift et al, 2009).

Within the tradition of auto-ethnography, there has been a focus on personal and inward experiences as being relevant for research through the ethnographer's self-conscious autobiography, allowing for introspective emotional self-awareness (Ellis, 1999). While these insights clearly permit emotional expressions to be part of the generation of knowledge, not all ethnographic research that aims to investigate emotions can or should be autobiographical. While my own embodied and emotional reaction to the field became an important conduit for ethnographic understanding, it was less person-centred than organizationally mediated. I found emotional expression's pattern of organizational linkages offered insights into social regulation that a purely autobiographical approach would not (Gubrium and Holstein, 1997).

Turning to the everyday practice of emotional expression

In my search to understand the emotions involved in the meaning-making of the field, I started to focus on the overlap between my own emotional experiences and those of individuals in that field. However, this overlap only slowly revealed itself in my multiple readings of the field notes when trying to systematize and understand them as I read them (Emerson et al, 2011). While the emotional expressions of the social workers appeared in the field notes from the first meeting, my own emotional responses were only gradually formed. At the start, I set aside the feelings I had during the fieldwork as merely personal and therefore irrelevant; thus, they were rarely included in my field notes.

When I first acknowledged their personal relevance, it was because, in many ways, they resembled the emotional expressions of the social workers. I was continually drawn into cases involving multiple stories about the social problems of children and families when the social workers presented them in great detail at the meetings. Although I had never met the children or their families, their pains and struggles, as presented at these meetings, travelled home with me, provoking restlessness and worries. Questions persistently popped up in my head: What should be done? Could I do something? What if this were my child? (see also Sparkes and Smith, 2012). I stopped myself, wondering if I could call one of the social workers between the weekly meetings, or perhaps I could call the team manager to ask for status updates. I considered if I should expand the focus of my study and try to contact the children and families in question—obtaining data about the people experiencing the real issues, tackling an everyday life of struggles and pain, those facing the consequences of the decisions being made. For weeks, I found myself drawn into the multifaceted, contradictory and ambiguous nature of the field (Hubbard et al, 2001). I experienced an ongoing internal struggle to either respond to these emotional concerns and new ideas or adhere to the original plan of focusing on decision-making within the child welfare agency. Little did I know at the time, that what I and, in turn, the social workers felt and said were not just personal but had organizational contours.

At the beginning, I only attended the weekly meetings and conducted informal and formal interviews with the professionals in the child welfare agency. I rationalized that expanding my data to include meetings with the children and families would also change the subject of my ethnography. I would no longer be focused on understanding the decision-making processes in child welfare agencies; rather, I would be studying the experiences and perspectives of children and families. But, gradually, taking increasingly seriously what might be called the often agonizingly rationalistic linkages of emotional expressions, I started to reframe the study. By actively tracing the organizational resonances of emotions, which Hubbard et al (2001, p 121) describe as 'emotionally-sensed knowledge', I gained new insights that allowed me to refocus my fieldwork on the role of emotions. This process of realization led me back to focusing on the field and away from my own strong emotions, and to a focus on the field as one that was constituted as highly emotional and emotionally imbricated. This created an awareness that the emotions I experienced were not unique to me, or to individual social workers for that matter. Although the number and intensity of the emotions that I felt surprised me, they were a reflection of the emotional expressions that I observed in the field. Concerns, worries, sadness, hope and anger were overtly present at the meetings when the social workers were trying to navigate the complexity of their many cases, and were exacerbated by the social problems of the children and families.

The complex ethical issues of representation, which are pertinent when doing an ethnography of social service provision, are related to these insights. Not knowing that emotional expressions would be central in the fieldwork, I did not have a strategy from the onset that would allow me the means to analyse and write about emotional expressions in a non-individualizing and non-stigmatizing way (Hubbard et al, 2001). Uncovering emotional expressions in a field where they formally have no role could easily lead to unjustly implicating individual social workers or the social problems of the children and families in the cases. With the reframing, I developed practice-based solutions, attempting to avoid focusing on individual social workers. In the analytical stage, with multiple readings of the field notes, I sought to avoid individualizing emotions as belonging to specific social workers by focusing on the expression of emotions in concrete situations. Furthermore, by changing the name of the participants in my field notes when beginning the analysis, I sought to relinquish some of my familiarity with individual social workers and challenge my readings of the field notes, creating room for a new reading that focused on the contextual and shared characteristics of emotional expression. In my writing, I edited the multitude of notes, impressions and recordings in order to deal with specific aspects of understanding the emotional paradox pertaining to social work practice (see also Inckle, 2010).

Thus, my ethnographic engagement with the field led to unexpected emotions, which showed me the relevance of emotions in the decision-making processes of social workers. This realization directly influenced how I read my field notes, and it led to the development of a more critical ethical strategy. It also pointed to the need for a more careful analysis of the role that emotions play in the everyday practice of social workers in particular, and more generally, it pointed ahead to situational and cultural understanding of emotional life.

Emotions in everyday decision-making

To empirically unpack the role of emotions in the everyday practice of the meetings, I will return to the meeting and circumstance I used to introduce this chapter, in which the social worker, Karen, is angry and frustrated with a mother who she finds is not acting in the best interest of her two sons. Before this meeting, I had heard about the mother and her two sons, 16-year-old David and 12-year-old Mark, as they had been on the agenda of almost all the weekly team meetings that I had attended over the past two months. They had been a case at the agency for many years, and all the social workers knew them, either from working directly with the family or from hearing about them in the meetings.

The group of social workers present at the meeting was responsible for handling all cases with young people between the ages of 12 and 18. At the weekly meetings, the agenda consisted of three parts: 1) the assignment of new cases, 2) the discussion of complex cases (put forward by the social workers), and 3) the cases where new interventions might be needed. Karen's case with David and Mark was put on the agenda as both a complex case in need of discussion and one that required new interventions. This need for new interventions was a surprise for most of us because at the meeting two weeks before it had been decided that an intensive home-based intervention needed to be implemented. For the previous six months, Karen had worked hard to make the mother realize that she needed help structuring their everyday life so that the boys would get up in the morning, go to school and also go to bed before midnight. The mother was also said to be needing tools for handling the many conflicts in the home, both between the boys and between her and her sons. At the meeting, everyone agreed that Karen had exerted an enormous amount of effort to get the mother to accept the intensive help that was offered. In my notes from the previous meeting, I wrote:

> They appear almost happy. Yvonne, a family counselor, is stating: 'I never thought we would get in. It is such a turnaround for Mum. Maybe she's on something' [laughing]. Karen, smiling, says: 'Or rather, I think she may be *off* something. I never been able to get her to do urine tests but I just know that she has been using some kind of drugs, besides the alcohol'. Ann, the team manager, states: 'Now we, hopefully, we will know a lot more, also about the boy's difficulties'. Smiles around the table. Next case on the agenda. (Field notes)

At the meeting two weeks later, I noted how the smiles were all gone. All eight people around the big meeting table looked worried when Karen, in an angry voice, started to explain what had happened with David, Mark and their mother. I wrote:

> Karen says: 'Where should I start. It's all a mess now. David disappeared last week and we couldn't find him for two days. Mum blamed us, me and the family counselor, for being too much in their face, which apparently should have stressed David. He was located late Thursday night by the police, all high on something. They send him to the acute institution, and that's where he is now. Refusing to get out of bed and talk to anyone. Although, he declared, that he wouldn't move back home with Mum'. Karen paused, taking a breath.

Alex, another social worker, asks: 'What about Mum, what does she say?' Karen shaking her head from side to side says: 'Well yes, you see that is the problem. She won't have him back home and this weekend she turned up at the acute center with Mark, claiming that she could no longer handle him at home. So now he is also in acute care!' Yvonne exclaims, putting her hands to her face, 'Oh no!' Karen looks at her and continues in an angry voice: 'I feel so angry with Mum here. She should step up now and take responsibility, save her sons! Is there really nothing we can do? Are we completely powerless here?!'

Ann, the team manager, looks at Karen and says calmly: 'Yes, I know, this is the last thing we wanted to happen! But I think there is no way back now; the boys should be taken into more permanent placements'. Karen strongly opposes the idea, referring to the fact that home-based family work never had a chance. Everyone, except me, takes part in the following discussion about what to do next. It is agreed that Alex, who earlier had a good relationship with David, should contact him to find out what he is thinking. Mark should, as quickly as possible, be moved to a foster care. In the end Karen says: 'I just feel that we are letting them down big time'. Ann nods sympathetically and says: 'Yes, but we must follow the procedures and find out what is going on with Mum before we let the boys move back home'. Karen states: 'Then it's too late, she won't have them back'. Ann declares that it is time for a short break. (Field notes)

During the short break, Karen and Alex continued to discuss the case. I asked them what they thought would happen now? Karen explained that she thought they would lose Mum and so would the boys. She thought it was sad because she believed that Mum had some potential to be a better mother. Karen was not angry anymore, but her voice was strained, apparently because the team was not willing to go that way. Alex put an arm around Karen's shoulders trying to comfort her. He said: "But I don't think we can. We are obliged to put the children first, not Mum". Karen turned her eyes to the ceiling. "And working with Mum is not putting the children first? You know, they only have one Mum". The others returned and the meeting started again with discussions of new cases.

This case with David, Mark and their mother created emotional engagement, not only for Karen, but for the others who engaged with the case and with Karen's emotional struggles. I also felt unsettled by the turn in the case and worried about what would happen with the two boys. To my surprise, emotional concerns such as Karen's appeared to be widely accepted at the meetings, creating what Forsberg and Vagli (2006, p 26) call 'environments for emotions', allowing for shared reflections and ambiguity in discussions at the meetings. I had seen these kinds of emotional engagements in collegial evaluations and interpretations of client cases in many situations throughout the field study, and I saw them as being the result of a culture exceptionally open to the role of emotions, allowing for expressions of both despair and concern (Forsberg and Vagli, 2006).

In time, when rereading my field notes, I noted that although these negative emotions were visible and accepted, often they also created states of uncertainty and increased complexity at the meetings. Although uncertainty and complexity were key aspects of most of the cases, I recorded that only a limited amount of time was allotted during the meetings to sharing those feelings. After a while (a maximum of one hour), the uncertainty and complexity had to be addressed or, ideally, solved (Fahlgren, 2009). I found that uncertainty and complexity stood in the way of bringing the cases forward and reaching a decision about how to act next. When a decision was to be made at the end of the discussions, emotional arguments were often set aside, such as when Ann, the team manager, empathized with Karen's feelings that the mother had potential but did not see them as being valid in deciding the future cause of action.

When reaching the phase of decision-making at the meetings, I observed a preoccupation with how to legitimize a decision; at that stage, feelings and emotions played an insignificant role, ceding the stage to procedures and a focus on facts and certainty (Forsberg and Vagli, 2006). It was not that emotional argumentation played no role at this phase; however, it was clear that a more bureaucratic form of argumentation increased the chances of the decision receiving the approval of the management and meeting the legal requirements. Reading over my notes, I found that the practice of decision-making at the agency followed this pattern whereby emotions were welcomed at the beginning of the discussions but were almost always automatically set aside at the end of the discussion and rarely present when the decision for future actions was made. The paradox worked in this way, virtually systematically replacing its emotion-laden ethical side with the interactional pulses of its organizational side.

Controlling emotions

Although they were fairly evident, I did not question these phases of the decision-making process during the fieldwork. At first, I was surprised to find that the emotional expressions and argumentation were integrated and legitimized in the context of the meetings. I remember returning from the meeting and conveying to colleagues that the field of social work indeed had not been dehumanized by increased demands of documentation and regulation. Rather, the field was packed with feelings and emotional expressions, which also emerged in the decision-making processes. While analysing the material, I had to moderate my initial impressions. Yes, there was room for feelings and emotions but this room was mostly allocated to parts of the discussions and not allowed to be an active part of the final decisions. Thus, I slowly discovered that, contrary to my first impressions, feelings and emotions were also highly regulated and controlled in the agency.

Not only did the organization of the meetings control the space allowed for the social workers' feelings and emotions, more direct measures of control were implemented outside the meetings. I first noticed this one day when I was waiting in the corridor to conduct an interview with Alex, one of the social workers. At that time, I noticed a poster of a traffic light hanging on the wall. I took a photograph of it (see Figure 3.1).

I wondered what the poster was about and who it was meant for: the social workers, the families? When Alex approached me, I asked him what it was about. He shook his head laughing, saying: "I don't know. I guess it is to control us, so that we don't let our feelings take over [he continued laughing], thinking we can do as we like or something like that". I laughed with him because I also found it a bit ridiculous and out of sync with the many emotional expressions I had observed at the weekly meetings. I did not pay more attention to it at the time. Later, when I looked at the poster again, I saw that the text used to frame the decisions and responsibilities was written in a language devoid of any emotions, which puzzled me. The phrase 'domain of production' led me to think of the production and manufacturing of goods, and I wondered: What is produced in the child welfare agency? Was it the production of decisions? It did not make much sense to me.

The poster and its rigid wording did not have any visible effect on Alex, and when I asked some of the other social workers about it, I got the same dismissive reaction. To my disbelief, no one appeared to pay much attention to the poster, finding it superfluous and without much

Figure 3.1: Photo of poster taken by the author during fieldwork

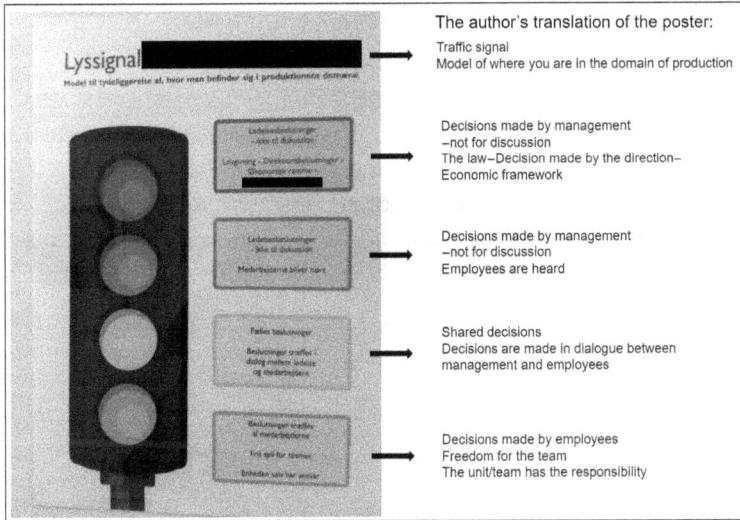

The author's translation of the poster:

Traffic signal
Model of where you are in the domain of production

Decisions made by management
–not for discussion
The law–Decision made by the direction–
Economic framework

Decisions made by management
–not for discussion
Employees are heard

Shared decisions
Decisions are made in dialogue between
management and employees

Decisions made by employees
Freedom for the team
The unit/team has the responsibility

meaning. Consequently, it was not the topic of critical discussion that I had anticipated it would be. Nonetheless, for me, it was a highly conflictual poster which made me feel uncomfortable with its direct and controlling wording that instructed the social workers how to behave in the 'domain of production'.

During the fieldwork, I succeeded in getting an interview with the head manager, Marianne, who apparently was the person who had suggested that the poster be created and displayed. Because the poster did not seem to have any direct impact on the social workers, I had not planned for it to be part of the interview. However, Marianne brought it up:

Interviewer: What do you think about the role of the law in social work? Does it limit or support the work?

Marianne: I think it is supportive because, in my world, it gives you a platform, it creates stability. But I know that many of the employees feel that it is a limitation because they are emotionally involved and [they] find it difficult to take a step back and look at what is actually going on. They can find it really difficult. And that is also why they get supervision. Everyone gets supervision because it is so incredibly important. It [the work] tears one's emotions, of course it does. Sometimes I'm a little rough [with them] and say that the brain is [the] biggest [organ] and sits at the top [of the body] because it needs to be used first, before the heart. I have tried to introduce [a model] of where you are in the area of the production domain. There are these posters of a traffic signal hanging around here.

Interviewer: Yes, I have seen them. They are very direct!

Marianne: [Laughing] Yes, they [the social workers] don't like them, but I have been over them many times [with them]. Especially in relation to the red sign, I have said to them: 'Here you have nothing to say. It is pure management. It is the law. It is the finances. It is political decisions'. There are so many areas where we can just say, 'Well, okay then', and that is the basis for our employment. It is what we have to comply with. Therefore, you can just forget about it. They [the social workers] use so much energy discussing if this or that is fair and right. And that is not working. I say, 'Go and talk about the things associated with the yellow and green lights where you have some influence'. That [point] I make clear all the time. You have to know where you are in the production domain, making sure that you are not sliding into something that you cannot control. Make sure that you always have a good explanation for doing what you do by referring to what is in the law. If you are emotionally out of control, then you cannot help.

My minimal expression of scepticism towards the poster during the interview did not disturb Marianne, just as the social workers' scepticism did not seem to disturb her. For her, the task appeared to be to make me, and the social workers, understand that the poster was a way to help the social workers handle their unavoidable emotional engagement with children and families in a productive, rather than an unproductive, way. It was an active attempt at controlling critical discussions about the fairness of the law, the legitimacy of management and the room for decision-making. Marianne's poster was directed at what Hochschild (2012, p 58) called 'display rules' by telling the social workers when and how they should express their feelings. In some ways, during the interview I felt subjected to similar display rules, by not fully revealing the depth of my scepticism.

I felt that the social norms guiding the interview did not allow me to critically question Marianne's imposing of display rules attempting to control the social workers' engagement. She had granted me an interview in her busy schedule *and* she was clearly proud of her poster and the thoughts behind it. This left me feeling that there was little room for letting her know that I found the poster and its message to be highly controversial and controlling (Hubbard et al, 2001). One could always consider what could have happened if I had shared my dislike and had been more critical of the poster in the interview. It could have led to an interesting and, most likely, a more emotional exchange of opinions. It could also have led Marianne to show me the door. In this situation, I held back and allowed Marianne the option to share her perspective.

Marianne was a key gatekeeper of my access to the meetings in the child welfare agency, so maintaining her support was a vital concern at the time. I also felt obligated, not only towards her but also towards her employees, which made me hold back. They had all so willingly led me into the 'backstage' of decision-making, sharing with me their thoughts, concerns and emotions, bypassing the formalities of written casework and interactions with children and families (Goffman, 1990). Consequently, I did not want to be overly critical of a poster that the social workers did not seem to care about and that Marianne took great pride in. Like many ethnographers before me, I wanted to be accepted and, if possible, blend in—which depended on my personal relationships with 'key individuals' in the field (Coffey, 1999). However, this choice to uphold field relationships also meant that it was difficult for me to deepen my understanding of the role the poster and its display rules had in the everyday power dynamics of emotions in decision-making.

Conclusion

My ethnographical engagement with emotions provided me with insight into the emotional paradox at the centre of much of the practice in human service provisions. At first, the expected rationality of the bureaucratic structures was overshadowed by my surprise that the emotional expressions of the social workers were a recognized and central part of their everyday practice. At the weekly meetings, I observed that emotional expressions were allowed time and consideration; they were recognized as an important part of the social work practices, and colleagues were empathetic and sympathized with each other. However, over time, I found that, although emotions were an accepted part of the process, they were only allowed to play a minor role in the final defining phases of the decision-making processes. In the final phase, emotions were pushed aside; primacy was given to the facts, the law and to identifying concrete solutions. I was only able to see this pattern in the role of emotions in the decision-making processes because of the exploratory nature of ethnography. I sat in on many meetings and took many notes that I did not know how I would use. Ultimately, it was the very experience of being present at the meetings at the child welfare agency that allowed my own emotionally-sensed knowledge to play a role in the analytical process. Nonetheless, to determine how and if emotional expressions inform the final decisions would require a stronger focus on emotions from the onset of the field work, leading to more detailed field notes and interviews, and would perhaps also require video recording of the meetings.

Likewise, it was fleeting ethnographic curiosity that led me to take a photograph of the poster in the hall—one that, afterwards, provoked me but apparently did not upset the social workers in the field. This led me to see the field as a culture wherein emotions are tolerated because they are seen as an unavoidable aspect of the work with children and families. It also showed me a culture wherein emotions are expected to be controlled to fit an overall idea of decision-making as a rationalistic, bureaucratic process. At the end of my ethnographic work, I found that the many negative emotions experienced by the individual social workers in relation to the cases were given little room when the final decisions were made. It was only possible to acquire these insights about the role of emotions in the field of human service provisions through my ethnographic engagement; few other methods would, to the same extent, recognize the ethnographer's own emotional engagement as being relevant for generating significant knowledge. While ethnography helped me to discover aspects not emphasized in research, it also lead to a new research interest in the need to better understand the role emotions play more generally in the decisions made in human service organizations where rational argumentation, legal support and systematic knowledge are paramount.

References

Barbalet, J. (2006) 'Emotion', *Contexts*, 5(2): 51–53.

Coffey, A. (1999) *The Ethnographic Self*, London: Sage.

Daly, M. and Lewis, J. (2000) 'The concept of social care and the analysis of contemporary welfare states', *British Journal of Sociology*, 51(2): 281–298.

Davies, K. (1994) 'The tensions between process time and clock time in care-work: The example of day nurseries', *Time and Society*, 3(3): 277–303.

Davis, B. (2001) 'The restorative power of emotions in child protection services', *Child and Adolescent Social Work Journal*, 18(6): 437–454.

Deery, R. (2008) 'The tyranny of time: Tensions between relational and clock time in community-based midwifery', *Social Theory and Health*, 6(4): 342–363.

Denzin, N.K. (2007) *On Understanding Emotion*, New Brunswick, NJ: Transaction Publishers.

Dickson-Swift, V., James, E.L., Kippen, S. and Liamputtong, P. (2009) 'Researching sensitive topics: Qualitative research as emotion work', *Qualitative Research*, 9(1): 61–79.

Ellis, C. (1999) 'Heartful autoethnography', *Qualitative Health Research*, 9(5): 669–683.

Emerson, R.M., Fretz, R.I. and Shaw, L.L. (2011) *Writing Ethnographic Fieldnotes*, Chicago, IL: University of Chicago Press.

Fahlgren, S. (2009) 'Discourse analysis of a childcare drama: Or the interfaces between paradoxical discourses of time in the context of social work', *Time and Society*, 18(3): 208–230.

Forsberg, H. and Vagli, Å. (2006) 'The social construction of emotions in child protection case-talk', *Qualitative Social Work: Research and Practice*, 5(1): 9–31.

Goffman, E. (1990) *The Presentation of Self in Everyday Life*, London: Penguin.

Gubrium, J.F. and Holstein, J.A. (1997) *The New Language of Qualitative Method*, Oxford: Oxford University Press.

Harrits, G.S. (2016) 'Being professional and being human: Professionals' sensemaking in the context of close and frequent interactions with citizens', *Professions and Professionalism*, 6(2): 15–22.

Hastrup, K. (1992) 'Writing ethnography: State of the art', in J. Okely and H. Callaway (eds) *Anthropology and Autobiography*, London: Routledge, pp 116–133.

Helm, D. (2016) 'Sense-making in a social work office: An ethnographic study of safeguarding judgements', *Child and Family Social Work*, 21(1): 26–35.

Hochschild, A.R. (2012) *The Managed Heart: Commercialization of Human Feeling*, Berkeley, CA: Univeristy of Califronia Press.

Holland, J. (2007) 'Emotions and research', *International Journal of Social Research Methodology*, 10(3): 195–209.

Holland, S. (2011) *Child and Family Assessment in Social Work Practice*, London: Sage.

Hubbard, G., Backett-Milburn, K. and Kemmer, D. (2001) 'Working with emotion: Issues for the researcher in fieldwork and teamwork', *International Journal of Social Research Methodology*, 4(2): 119–137.

Inckle, K. (2010) 'Telling tales? Using ethnographic fictions to speak embodied "truth"', *Qualitative Research*, 10(1): 27–47.

Ingram, R. (2013) 'Emotions, social work practice and supervision: an uneasy alliance?', *Journal of Social Work Practice*, 27(1): 5–19.

Jacobsson, K. and Meeuwisse, A. (2018) ' "State governing of knowledge": Constraining social work research and practice', *European Journal of Social Work*, 23(2): 277–289.

Mol, A. (2008) *The Logic of Care: Health and the Problem of Patient Choice*, Abingdon: Routledge.

Nussbaum, M.C. (2001) *Upheavals of Thought: The Intelligence of Emotions*, Cambridge: Cambridge University Press.

O'Connor, L. and Leonard, K. (2014) 'Decision making in children and families social work: The practitioner's voice', *British Journal of Social Work*, 44(7): 1805–1822.

Skotte, P.S. (2018) 'Colligation in child welfare work: Decision-making in a case on the tipping point', *Qualitative Social Work*, 17(1): 115–132.

Sparkes, A.C. and Smith, B. (2012) 'Narrative analysis as an embodied engagement with the lives of others', in J.A. Holstein and J.F. Gubrium (eds) *Varieties of Narrative Analysis*, Thousand Oaks, CA: Sage, pp 53–73.

PART II

Grasping empirical complexity

4

Sensitizing concepts in studies of homelessness and disability

Nanna Mik-Meyer

As valuable as they might be, observational data are not just informational but can inspire (re)conceptualization and a view to empirical complexity. Following a discussion of 'sensitizing concepts', this chapter discusses how observations conducted in ethnographic fieldwork on disability and homelessness contributed to developing ideas that further sensitized our understanding of field material. In illustration, the chapter draws on two studies: my research team's recent fieldwork on agency and authority in the circumstance of homelessness, and on my work on 'othering' as a process of marginalization in research on disability.

While it might seem contradictory, in the first case, sensitive observational work in video-recorded placement meetings led to an understanding of how homeless clients were perceived, unexpectedly, by service providers as *both* helpless individuals *and* active agents with authority. This spurred the team to be sensitive to the power held by the clients, not just to their helplessness in the circumstances (Mik-Meyer and Haugaard, 2020; Mik-Meyer and Silverman, 2019). In the second case, after visiting two research sites where employees with cerebral palsy worked, I discovered that the physical disability of the employees had profound effects on their relationships with their able-bodied colleagues. This discovery led me to investigate the research on othering conducted within gender studies as well as within the research field of disability. My analysis showed that able-bodied colleagues and managers wanted to avoid othering and marginalizing their co-workers with disabilities but nevertheless ended up contributing to exactly that othering and marginalization (Mik-Meyer, 2015a, 2016a, 2016b). Taken together, the studies illustrate an orientation towards empirical complexity otherwise undiscovered in observational studies bereft of analytic understanding.

From sensitizing concepts to empirical complexity

Herbert Blumer's (1954) classic work on sensitizing concepts, 'What is wrong with social theory?', early on emphasizes how analytical ideas and a related (re)conceptualization can spring from ethnographic data. Blumer distinguishes two phases when doing ethnographic work. In the first phase, the ethnographer explores practice and writes detailed descriptions, and in the second phase the ethnographer uses his or her field observations to conduct the analytical work, or 'understanding', as it might be described. According to Blumer, social theory is too separated from the empirical world, as the concepts of social theory are not based in the researcher's field observations. Put another way, field observations that are simply informational but not attuned to understanding hardly provide the kind of insight that ethnography can offer.

Blumer distinguishes between concepts viewed as definitive, that is, as concepts that refer 'precisely to what is common to a class of objects, by the aid of a clear definition in terms of attributes or fixed bench marks', and sensitizing concepts, which, according to him, are concepts that guide the researcher's work and 'suggest directions along which to look' (Blumer, 1954, p 7). This means that social theory concepts are not to be considered as fixated with just one meaning. For instance, the concept of othering suggested—to me as a researcher visiting Danish workplaces—a direction in which to look. So, othering is not a concept with just one meaning and a clear definition, as what it means to be 'othered' comprises different processes in different research fields and at different locations. In the field of disability, othering is closely linked to discourses of tolerance, equality and sameness (Mik-Meyer, 2017), whereas in the field of homelessness, othering is part of a discourse of agency and authority (Mik-Meyer and Haugaard, 2020; Mik-Meyer and Silverman, 2019). However, processes of othering encompass similarities across very different research fields as well.

According to Blumer and other interactionists such as Erving Goffman, the concepts of social theory must be sensitive not only to changes in theoretical understanding but also to a changing social world. This means that researchers, in their development and discussion of social theory concepts, have to include both theoretical and empirical discoveries. Otherwise, the social theory concepts risks 'feed[ing] on itself', as Blumer (1954, p 3) puts it. In such unfortunate cases, concepts from social theory are used to interpret the empirical world instead of investigating how the concepts actually fit the empirical world and how the empirical world ought to lead to theoretical changes.

Another shortcoming of social theory (in the 1950s), according to Blumer, was that concepts in then-current social theory did not provide adequate guidelines for how to conduct research inquiry, making it difficult for social scientists to test their theories. In his view, the lack of a careful empirical grounding for theoretical concepts meant that they were vague (for instance, concepts such as 'social class', 'social institutions' and 'cultural norms')—and this was the 'basic deficiency in social theory' (Blumer, 1954, p 5). Finally, Blumer (1954) pointed to the problem that social scientists rarely use the empirical facts provided by research. When concepts are vague, researchers do not know which questions to ask and what to examine, and this means that they are encouraged to stay in their own (theoretical) world. This led Blumer to suggest that social theory should develop what he referred to as sensitizing concepts, that is, concepts that give the social scientist 'a general sense of reference and guidance in approaching concrete empirical instances, [and] suggest directions along which to look' (Blumer, 1954, p 7), as seemingly contradictory as they might seem to be at first sight.

However, investigating and developing sensitizing concepts does not mean that they cannot be tested, improved or refined. Nevertheless, testing, improving and refining are more difficult with sensitizing concepts than with definitive concepts, because sensitizing concepts do not have a fixed meaning. For instance, the meaning of the concepts of othering and authority changes according to the research field investigated and its practitioners, which is why a refinement of the concepts should include empirical data. Social theory is about improving the perception of concepts such as othering and authority through the direct study of the social, empirical world, emphasizing its distinctive form. These basic ideas of Blumer's have inspired much ethnographic and observational research, including the studies discussed.

Analytical ethnography

More recent commentary along these lines shows how useful it is to base the development of concepts on complex ethnographic data, not least because 'inconsistencies [are] a central property of social life' (Deener, 2017, p 374). According to Andrew Deener, with more nuanced conceptual lenses, inconsistencies and ambiguities of social life can be shown to be the norm rather than disturbing factors the researcher should avoid or explain away (Deener, 2017, p 374). Observational data, in particular ideas of ethnographic complexity, give the researcher knowledge of the ambiguities of a field, as this 'softer' methodology enables the inclusion of all sorts of data in the research (Deener, 2017, p 360). The ethnographer's combining their role as an outsider to the field with their ethnographic authority, that is, their being able to combine insider knowledge from the field with outsider theory based on the researcher's academic training, is one way to develop a sensitizing approach to the field. Gary Alan Fine and Tim Hallet (2014) posit that the ethnographer, as an outsider, can see the processes that are taken for granted by the insider, and can use this outsider position to facilitate a development and fine-tuning of concepts from social theory based on his or her observational data. In line with Blumer's thoughts, the ethnographer brings a specific type of conceptualization of the field forward, which is different from the knowledge of the studied participants.

What this suggests is an 'analytical ethnography' (Lofland, 1995; Snow et al, 2003), wherein the researcher, through fieldwork, develops 'mini-concepts', extends the meaning of pre-existing theories or concepts to other fields and modifies pre-existing theories (Snow et al, 2003, pp 186–191). The point is to develop, extend and modify concepts through the lens of complexity, such as when Philip Strong (1979, 1988) refined Erving Goffman's theory of ceremony by studying a 'bunch of encounters' in the new setting of paediatric consultations in the United States and Scotland (Hillyard, 2010, p 425). By focusing on roles within the 'consultation etiquette' of the medical encounter, Strong found two 'equally central dimensions to the ceremonial order: The "technical competences of server and client" and "their moral character"' (Strong, 1988, p 240 cited in Hillyard, 2010, p 430). This strengthened focus on all of the participants morality meant that Goffman's theory was further developed to include an emphasis of 'etiquettes' rather than 'etiquette' (singular): Goffman's ideal model of ritual orders—the server-client relationship—was present in the consultations, but this ritual order was not the only one (Hillyard, 2010, pp 430–1).

As the key to developing, refining and modifying concepts is to immerse oneself in the field, quite a number of scholars have examined the importance of the relationship between the ethnographer and the participants in the field. For instance, Kathleen Blee (2019) shows how her work with concepts was shaped by her relationship to the people she studied; in one case, she studied white supremacists, and in another, she studied grassroots activists. The field relationship with the white supremacists was characterized by an 'expectation of mutual deceit', while the field relationship with the grassroots activists was characterized by honesty and a 'shared sense of politics' (Blee, 2019, p 743). By examining her vastly different field notes from the two studies, she found that 'field relationships shape theorizing by affecting not only what researchers can access but what they notice or find puzzling and what they regard as significant in a research setting' (Blee, 2019, p 754). Her field relationships pulled her in different theoretical directions even though she started out with a similar research question in each case about how the members' opinions become aligned with the ideologies of their groups. In the white supremacists study, she focused on how members adopted the group's ideas, but did not engage with the content of these ideas, whereas, in the grassroots activists study, she examined the content of their beliefs, but did not investigate how their perceptions had been developed in the group.

Similarly, Jadwiga Leigh (2019) retheorizes the concept of 'affective practice' by drawing on insights from ethnographic work on agency and conflicts stemming from a child protection service. Affect theory was first introduced by Baruch Spinoza, who distinguished between emotion and affect. Affect was seen as 'produced by the body, or the mind, when an interaction occurred with another body or mind' (Leigh, 2019, p 214). However, Leigh draws on and further develops Margaret Wetherell's (2012) concept of affective practice, and shows that although conflicts mainly unfold in the encounter between a social worker and a manager, everyone in the workplace ends up being engaged in affective and emotional work. In this case, ethnographic observation led to a nuanced adjustment of the perception of the social theory concept of affect.

Empirical complexity

Investigating social theory concepts in practice emphasizes the importance of scholars thinking about what Goffman might call methodological 'impression management'. This refers to the way they, as ethnographers, affect the research participants and hence the results of their research. Here, complexity is introduced in the empirical reflexivities of research relations in the field. The point is that research participants often have different understandings of what goes on in the field than the researcher. The goal of including observational data in a research project is hence to include otherwise hidden perceptions and patterns of understanding in order to gain a better perception of the studied participants' 'landscape of meaning' (Decoteau, 2017, p 72). Other researchers use 'shadowing' (Czarniawska, 2007) to gain a more 'holistic representation' of what goes on in the field (Gilliat-Ray, 2011, p 480). The point is that immersing themselves in the field affects the researchers' findings, just like various other methodological approaches inform the theoretical and conceptual work in different ways (Järvinen and Mik-Meyer, 2020).

A word of caution. The emphasis on empirical complexity does not mean, as is sometimes alleged/claimed, that the researcher is not well versed in theories pertinent to the studied phenomenon, which is a rather myopic critique of researchers conducting ethnography-based research (for instance, Huber, 1973). According to Huber, researchers should 'spell out in advance and in detail what is expected and why it is expected' (Huber, 1973, p 282) and use concepts and explicated assumptions to inform their observations. In a similar vein, Loïc Wacquant (2002) formulates a critique of an inductive approach to observation studies in a provocative review of Mitchell Duneier's *Sidewalk* (1999), Elijah Anderson's *Code of the Street* (1999) and Katherine Newman's *No Shame in My Game* (1999). According to Wacquant (2002), Duneier (1999) gets too close to the data without holding it against theory, whereas Anderson (1999) is too far away from his data and forces it into a theoretical framework, while Newman (1999) pushes theory aside, even though the data challenge it. Wacquant argues that doing ethnography without theory is impossible, and that ethnographers need to acknowledge this, using theory in every decision and step of the study and being transparent about it. His critique has led to counterarguments (for instance, Wilson and Chadda, 2009) in which Wacquant's top-down approach is criticized (see also Anderson, 2002; Duneier, 2002). However, without taking sides in this debate, what stands out is the need for researchers to be what might be called 'analytically reflexive' about the role of theory and concepts in working with observational data.

Empirical complexity in two observational studies

In my research, I combine observation data, interviews and documents. The reason for combining different kinds of data is not steered by an ambition to get closer to a 'real world' out there (Silverman, 2013; Mik-Meyer, 2020a). My reason for combining different methodologies is to qualify a sensitizing approach to my field of research as suggested by Blumer. By using observational data, I am able to get an insider's perspective on topics of importance seen from the research participants' points of view. Topics that may otherwise have fallen outside my research design and interest only because I would not have known that they existed. When researching the negotiations of marginalized identities in workplaces and in shelters, my on-site observations (Hammersley and Atkinson, 2019) or video-recordings of real-life encounters are optimal data (Heath et al, 2010) as they allow me to access the researched participants' perspectives on the social world that they are part of. In my case, I often supplement these observations with policy documents such as legislation and organizational scoring schemas guiding professional work, as this kind of data also gives me an insider perspective on the perceptions and joint understandings in the field that (often) guide the actions of the participants studied (Mik-Meyer, 2018, 2020). Open-ended interviews are obviously a third kind of data that will provide information on the thoughts of the participants. For instance, when examining the policy documents related to the fields of homelessness and disability, I quickly discovered the many dilemmas and ambiguities defining these two areas, which directed my attention to the patterns related to conflicts and disagreements between clients and staff. In many cases, the conflicts and disagreements reflected key structural dilemmas of housing (the scarcity of available apartments), economy (debt, for example) related to being homeless or disabled. For instance, staff would not explicitly state the letter of the law or the rules and procedures of staying at a shelter in their actual video-recorded encounters, but reading policy documents and interviewing staff revealed that such issues often affected these encounters. Therefore, knowledge gained from interviews and from reading policy documents added valuable insights when analysing what went on in the workplaces where employees with disabilities worked or in the video-recorded placement meetings at homeless shelters.

Homelessness, agency and authority

Our recent study of homelessness is based on 23 video-recorded placement meetings in three Danish shelters. Research emphasizes and problematizes the ambivalence of being homeless in a society that stresses that all citizens, including homeless individuals, should be active, responsible and in charge of their own life (Parsell, 2011; Parsell and Parsell, 2012; Farrugia and Gerrard, 2016; Parsell and Clarke, 2019). However, most studies do not provide *concrete* examples of how the ambivalence of being homeless—that is, the way in which homeless people are perceived as being in a challenging position and simultaneously perceived as people with resources—is negotiated in everyday organizational life. One of the major strengths of an ethnographic approach to recording real-life interactions in shelters is the possibility of providing analysis of what actually goes on in these placement meetings, that is, of explaining how the ambivalence of an identity of strength and weakness is negotiated during—in this case—placement meetings. Like any observational data, recordings can shed light on why participants often end up actively reproducing the practices from which they explicitly distance themselves (in, for instance, interview situations). In my research on homelessness, a key finding was that these encounters—most likely unintendedly—ended up reinforcing passivity in clients despite an effort of social workers to achieve exactly the opposite, namely, to help the homeless individuals become responsible for their lives, as they would stress in the follow-up interviews (Mik-Meyer, 2020b).

My recording of these real-life events resulted in my discovering new aspects of what it meant for homeless individuals to be 'active' and 'responsible' for their lives, showcasing the complexity of the rubric of 'homelessness'. One surprising aspect was, for instance, the unexpected effects of gender norms on these encounters, which was visible after reviewing the 23 real-life encounters several times. One of my publications uncovered how stereotypical gender norms of women affected staff's expectations of the way the homeless men should act and perceive their own situation (Mik-Meyer, 2020b). In placement meetings, service providers evaluated the ability of male clients originating from the Greater Middle East to cook, clean and do stereotypically feminine work in the home. The service providers' idea was that they had to learn these duties while living at the shelters if they were to succeed in living on their own after their stay at the shelter. This focus on stereotypically feminine household work in placement meetings was not a result of a preconceived idea of stereotypical gender norms being key in placement meetings. However, the recorded meetings displayed 'gendered stories' of housewives and cleaning ladies, which explicated the norms by which the staff evaluated the actions of the homeless men; whether these men's actions reflected a prototype of a well-functioning and responsible person or not. With this in mind when examining the video recordings for what was said verbally as well as what was bodily expressed (for instance, through stiffening, leaning forward, looking down, displaying an arrogant gaze and so forth), I was able to analyse the way the stereotypically gendered perspectives affected the staff's encounter with homeless men with ethnic backgrounds other than Danish at the placement meetings. This type of observational data provided a rich source of how organizational members mutually negotiated gendered expectations and the effects of this gendered negotiation (Mik-Meyer, 2020b).

The video recordings also displayed the relevance of investigating the negotiation of the key social theory concepts of agency and authority, as much of the participants' orientations toward each other had to do with negotiating agency and authority (Mik-Meyer and Haugaard, 2020; Mik-Meyer and Silverman, 2019). The placement meetings opened with pleasantries, that is, with friendly comments that at first would suggest equal power among the participants as well as display the policy-relevant goal of placing the client at the centre (so-called client centredness) (Mik-Meyer and Silverman, 2019). However, the structural constraint of an action plan, quickly introduced by the staff member structuring the conversation and topics of relevance, made it clear that the staff had a particular authoritative position. The staff represented the organization and its perceptions of what to consider as clients' 'troubles' or 'problems' (Gubrium and Järvinen, 2014), whereas the clients were positioned as the receivers of the organizational work defined by the action plan. The action plan was an 'obligatory passage point' (Clegg, 1989, p 205) that framed all the meetings and the (somewhat joint) perceptions of what would constitute a 'social problem' of the homeless. In other words, the action plan was concurrently a tool of agency and of power, as it provided both parties with expectations relative to the meeting and thus provided the base for negotiating agency and power. Both parties knew that the pleasantries and friendly comments that suggested equality existed vis-à-vis an organizational reality defining relevant social problems and—consequently—relevant actions to take in order to solve the problems.

One key contribution to and refinement of the social theory concept of authority was to exemplify how this concept is indeed a nuanced and negotiated phenomenon without a fixed meaning. We theorized authority as a right to speak, to be heard and taken seriously within a specific framework. The authority of service providers in shelters and municipalities was dependent on the organizational framework (the action plan and so forth), and they had—unsurprisingly—the authority to speak upon organizationally relevant issues. However, to jump to the conclusion that this meant that the homeless individuals did not display authority in the meetings would be wrong. The homeless individuals were expected to take on authority as citizens who knew what they wanted and who should correspondingly work strategically to achieve this goal. However, the homeless individuals were also expected to behave in the role of the (passive) client, which meant that they were expected to constantly juggle a double and mutually inconsistent pair of roles when trying to be heard and taken seriously.

Therefore, we concluded that the performance of authority was carried out on a scale. At one end, the service providers performed organizational authority, and at the other end the homeless individuals performed authority as, respectively, citizens (with resources) and clients (without resources). Although the two available positions for the clients were very different, respectively accentuating strengths and weakness, both positions could hypothetically (and did in real life) give them the right to speak and be taken seriously (Mik-Meyer and Haugaard, 2020; Mik-Meyer and Silverman, 2019). When the homeless persons were taken seriously and were heard by the staff, they displayed a practical knowledge of their situation. However, when the service providers rejected the homeless persons' perceptions of their situation, then it was typically because the staff perceived these perceptions as organizationally irrelevant. When different perceptions of what constituted a social problem were competing, the organizational authority of the staff would typically win. However, we also found that staff were reluctant to take the authority and define the solutions to clients' problems. Both parties deployed different resources which they perceived as meaningful to the contexts in which they interacted. Therefore, the authority of clients was measured up against how they succeeded in making their actions relevant to a number of organizational discourses. Authority was, in this study, a scalar phenomenon and not a command–obedience relationship (Weber, 1978, p 58) wherein social actors either had the authority to command or did not. In our work, authority was usually less than full command. Rather it had to do with the right to speak and be taken seriously.

In a co-authored article with David Silverman (Mik-Meyer and Silverman, 2019) on the negotiation of agency, we found an overall ambivalent discourse of client centredness ('My view matters') in the video-recorded placement meetings that comprised three positions that the homeless could adopt. They could adopt the position of someone in need and worthy of help ('I have had a troubled life, but am moral'), of a responsible person ('I take control of my life') and of a troubled and passive client ('I am dependent on the staff's decision'). This analysis, based on observational data, led us to suggest that the emphasized policy goal of client centredness had to be investigated in practice in order to understand what was meant by this goal. Taking centre stage as a client or being put at the centre of the work can be played out by actors in many different ways, which is why a normative model of client centredness must be treated as a research topic rather than as a concept with a fixed meaning that politicians can act on (Mik-Meyer and Silverman, 2019, p 18). When interactions did not deliver agency to any of the participants, this had consequences for everyone. Clients' failure of agency was usually related to practical matters, whereas service-providers' failure of agency was visible when they could not deliver in relation to the organizational action plan. As both parties' agency depended on the other party's actions, they turned to collaboration rather than conflict when in a tight spot. In this project, collaboration meant to work towards a shared perception of the clients' troubles—and hence a shared perception of what action to take to help solve the client's troubles (Mik-Meyer and Haugaard, 2020).

In conclusion, the video recordings were an especially good data-acquisition tool for me to use to get insights into topics of relevance for the research participants and to get real-life, detailed knowledge about joint expectations—knowledge that would have been difficult if not downright impossible to get through the methodology of interviewing or studying policy documents.

Processes of othering

My second example of how the complexities of observational data contribute to the development of more nuanced analytical thinking in a research project stems from an investigation of how colleagues and managers perceived their colleagues with visible disabilities. This study's data acquisition began with some weeks of field observations in two workplaces where employees with visible disabilities worked. In both workplaces, I immediately discovered a kind of childish interaction, that is, cases where colleagues and managers spoke to their colleagues with a disability as if they were children or people who needed extra attention and special care. Able-bodied colleagues and managers would greet their colleague with a disability with expressions such as "There comes the vacation child" and so forth. My observations furthermore included a (too) frequent use of their first names in conversations (Mik-Meyer, 2015). I soon discovered that the 'institutional identity' (Holstein and Gubrium, 2000; Gubrium and Holstein, 2001) available to these employees with disabilities was that of a child or a person in need of special care. When conducting interviews, talk about care was also predominant—even though the interview guide did not include questions on this topic (Mik-Meyer, 2016a). Additionally, observations included a stereotypically feminized approach to the employees with disabilities—who were predominantly male. Able-bodied staff members approached this group of employees as fragile, weak and in need of caregiving. In interviews with the employees with disabilities, they reflected on this caring approach—also without being asked questions on this particular matter.

All in all, it was clear that employees with disabilities were perceived as quite different than the able-bodied staff at the workplaces. In the interviews with able-bodied staff members, stories popped up regularly of other people who were considered different, but whose difference from the norm had no connection to physical impairments. Able-bodied staff members talked about homosexuals, persons with another skin or hair colour, individuals who wore strange clothes, had a different ethnic background than Danish, who were drunks, transvestites, old, pregnant, in grief and so on (Mik-Meyer, 2016b). The commonality of these stories was exclusively these people's 'different' appearances, which spurred my interest in why most able-bodied interviewees chose to talk about *other* different people when being asked questions about their colleague with a disability. I systematically searched for these stories in my interviews and examined why and how they popped up in the interviews. They were typically the result of spontaneous, slip-of-the-mind kind of answers to questions about what they first thought when they met their new colleague with a disability (see Mik-Meyer, 2016b for a complete analysis).

These findings indicated that the processes of othering of employees in Danish workplaces included a different kind of marginalization than what is typically found in disability research. Collectively, my project showed that discrimination practices could take a different form than what research in the field of disability typically focuses on, namely, lower wages, poor career opportunities, bullying and ill-treatment and so on. My study found that to discriminate against ones colleague could include more subtle practices, which the social theory's sensitizing concept of othering stimulates an investigation of. Othering of employees with disabilities was an everyday practice that could not be changed or controlled by, for instance, focusing predominantly on economic matters, policy reports or changing the formal culture at the work place (Mik-Meyer, 2016a). To discriminate against or 'other' your colleague with a disability was related to a dominant discourse of ableism, which automatically made employees with visible disabilities different. Processes of othering were also related to dominant discourses of tolerance and inclusiveness, which automatically made it wrong to talk about difference. The result was a subtle process of othering in which co-workers tried to refrain from explicitly talking about the difference of their colleagues with disabilities even though ableism at their workplace made this group of employees stand out. However, this subtle process of othering was surely not a process that able-bodied staff members appreciated or wanted to be part of. As such, the findings support one of the key qualities of observational data, namely, that observations on site can help explain why research participants may end up reproducing practices that in interviews they explicitly distance themselves from.

Conclusion

The focus of this chapter has been on the way observational data can help tease out key empirical complexities, here within two different research fields. In both instances, sensitizing concepts from social theory along with observational data helped shed light on topics in social theory centred on questions of gender norms, agency, authority and othering. Blumer's (1954) point that researchers should approach concepts of social theory as having fluid meaning allows for empirical data to affect and develop concepts of social theory that are otherwise too general and weakly empirically grounded. Observational data are in this respect ideal for discovering new aspects of the social world that no other methodology can provide access to.

As grounded in the flux of reality as they are, observational data should of necessity be brought on board as part of the goal to investigate the way that formal social policy—for instance, the policy of client centredness—plays out in real life situations. Basing research on observational data allows for discussions of different topics than the ones that a formal social policy approach would suggest. For instance, wage gaps or the career trajectories of employees with disabilities rather than the everyday process of othering (which might be experienced as being equally as problematic as receiving lower wages than your colleagues). Immersing themselves in the field, the researcher will be confronted with different and timely aspects of the social world that other, less nuance-centred methodologies cannot capture. In that sense, observational data are key if the goal is to expand one's knowledge of particular research fields, as well as if one wants to help fine-tune and give credence to empirically complex social theory.

Acknowledgements
I would like to thank the editors, Jay Gubrium and Katarina Jacobsson, for very helpful comments. I would also like to thank the Independent Research Fund Denmark for financing the two empirical projects mentioned in the chapter.

References
Anderson, E. (1999) *Code of the Street: Decency, Violence, and the Moral Life of the Inner City*, New York: W.W. Norton & Co.

Anderson, E. (2002) 'The ideologically driven critique', *American Journal of Sociology*, 107(6): 1533–1550.

Blee, K. (2019) 'How field relationships shape theorizing', *Sociological Methods and Research*, 48(4): 739–762.

Blumer, H. (1954) 'What is wrong with social theory?', *American Sociological Association*, 19(1): 3–10.

Clegg, S.R. (1989) *Frameworks of Power*, London: Sage.

Czarniawska, B. (2007) *Shadowing: And Other Techniques for Doing Fieldwork in Modern Societies*, Malmö: Liber.

Decoteau, C.L. (2017) 'Learning to see otherwise', *Ethnography*, 18(1): 68–75.

Deener, A. (2017) 'The uses of ambiguity in sociological theorizing: Three ethnographic approaches', *Sociological Theory*, 35(4): 359–379.

Duneier, M. (1999) *Sidewalk*, New York: Farrar, Straus and Giroux.

Duneier, M. (2002) 'What kind of combat sport is sociology?', *American Journal of Sociology*, 107(6): 1551–1576.

Farrugia, D. and Gerrard, J. (2016) 'Academic knowledge and contemporary poverty: The politics of homelessness research', *Sociology*, 50(2): 267–284.

Fine, A.G. and Hallett, T. (2014) 'Stranger and stranger: Creating theory through ethnographic distance and authority', *Journal of Organizational Ethnography*, 3(2): 188–203.

Gilliat-Ray, S. (2011) '"Being there": The experience of shadowing a british Muslim hospital chaplain', *Qualitative Research*, 11(5): 469–486.

Gubrium, J.F. and Holstein, J.A. (2001) 'Introduction: Trying times, troubled selves', in J.F. Gubrium and J.A. Holstein (eds) *Institutional Selves: Troubled Identities in a Postmodern World*, Oxford: Oxford University Press, pp 1–20.

Gubrium, J.F. and Järvinen, M. (eds) (2014) *Turning Troubles into Problems: Clientization in Human Service*, London: Routledge.

Hammersley, M. and Atkinson, P. (2019) *Ethnography: Principle in Practice*, Abingdon: Taylor and Francis.

Heath, C., Hindmarsh, J. and Luff, P. (2010) *Video in Qualitative Research: Analysing Social Interaction in Everyday Life*, London: Sage.

Hillyard, S. (2010) 'Ethnography's capacity to contribute to the cumulation of theory: A case study of Strong's work on Goffman', *Journal of Contemporary Ethnography*, 39(4): 421–440.

Holstein, J.A. and Gubrium, J.F. (2000) *The Self We Live By: Narrative Identity in a Postmodern World*, Oxford: Oxford University Press.

Huber, J. (1973) 'Symbolic interaction as a pragmatic perspective: The bias of emergent theory', *American Sociological Review*, 38(2): 274–284.

Järvinen, M. and Mik-Meyer, N. (2020) 'Analysing qualitative data in social science', in M. Järvinen and N. Mik-Meyer (eds) *Qualitative Analysis: Eight Approaches for the Social Sciences*, London: Sage, pp 1–28.

Leigh, J. (2019) 'Atmospheres of mistrust and suspicion: Theorising on conflict and affective practice in a child protection social work agency', *Qualitative Social Work*, 18(2): 212–228.

Lofland, J. (1995) 'Analytical ethnography: Features, failings, and futures', *Journal of Contemporary Ethnography*, 24(1): 30–67.

Mik-Meyer, N. (2015) 'Gender and disability: Feminising male employees with visible impairments in Danish work organisations', *Gender, Work and Organization*, 22(6): 579–595.

Mik-Meyer, N. (2016a) 'Disability and "care": Managers, employees and colleagues with impairments negotiating the social order of disability', *Work, Employment and Society*, 30(6): 984–999.

Mik-Meyer, N. (2016b) 'Othering, ableism and disability: A discursive analysis of co-workers' construction of colleagues with visible impairments', *Human Relations*, 69(6): 1341–1363.

Mik-Meyer, N. (2017) 'Disability, sameness, and equality: Able-bodied managers and employees discussing diversity in a Scandinavian context', *Scandinavian Journal of Disability Research*, 19(2): 129–139.

Mik-Meyer, N. (2018) 'Organizational professionalism: Social workers negotiating tools of NPM', *Professions and Professionalism*, 8(1): 1–15.

Mik-Meyer, N. (2020a) 'Multimethod qualitative research', in D. Silverman (ed) *Qualitative Research*, London: Sage.

Mik-Meyer, N. (2020b) 'Organisational dilemmas, gender and ethnicity: A video ethnographic approach to talk and gestures in homeless shelter consultations', in R. Mir and A.L. Fayard (eds) *The Routledge Companion To Organizational Anthropology*, London: Routledge, pp 319–336.

Mik-Meyer, N. and Haugaard, M. (2020) 'The performance of citizen's and organisational authority', *Journal of Classical Sociology*, 20(4): 309–334.

Mik-Meyer, N. and Silverman, D. (2019) 'Agency and clientship in public encounters: Co-constructing "neediness" and "worthiness" in shelter placement meetings', *British Journal of Sociology*, 70(5): 1640–1660.

Newman, K.S. (1999) *No Shame in My Game: The Working Poor in the Inner City*, New York: Alfred A. Knopf and Russell Sage Foundation.

Parsell, C. (2011) 'Homeless identities: Enacted and ascribed', *British Journal of Sociology*, 62(3): 442–461.

Parsell, C. and Clarke, A. (2019) 'Agency in advanced liberal services: Grounding sociological knowledge in homeless people's accounts', *British Journal of Sociology*, 70(1): 356–376.

Parsell, C. and Parsell, M. (2012) 'Homelessness as a choice', *Housing, Theory and Society*, 29(4): 420–434.

Silverman, D. (2013) *Doing Qualitative Research* (4th edn), London: Sage.

Snow, D.A., Morrill, C. and Anderson, L. (2003) 'Elaborating analytic ethnography: Linking fieldwork and theory', *Ethnography*, 4(2): 181–200.

Strong, P. (1979) *The Ceremonial Order of the Clinic*, London: Routledge and Kegan Paul.

Strong, P. (1988) 'Minor courtesies and macro structures', in P. Drew and A. Wootton (eds) *Erving Goffman: Exploring the Interaction Order*, Cambridge: Polity, pp 228–249.

Wacquant, L. (2002) 'Scrutinizing the street: Poverty, morality, and the pitfalls of the urban ethnography', *American Journal of Sociology*, 107(6): 1468–1532.

Weber, M. (1978) *Economy and Society: An Outline of Interpretive Sociology* (vol 1), edited by G. Roth and C. Wittich. Berkeley, CA: University of California Press.

Wetherell, M. (2012) *Affect and Emotion: A New Social Science Understanding*, London: Sage.

Wilson, W.J. and Chaddha, A. (2009) 'The role of theory in ethnographic research', *Ethnography*, 10(4): 549–564.

5

Grasping the social life of documents in human service practice

Emilie Morwenna Whitaker

Checklists, memos, reports and other standardized forms take up much space on organizational ethnographers' desks and pervade the lives of their research respondents. Some researchers say that writing and documentation are the heartbeat of organizational ethnography (Atkinson, 2019). Yet, despite the preoccupation with documents and writing, until recently it was common to find ethnographic accounts of professional worlds that barely referred to documentation or writing practices (Atkinson and Coffey, 2004; a rare exception is Buckholdt and Gubrium, 1979). In part this has been a consequence of the predominance of studies of what has come to be called 'talk-in-interaction'. These 'talkie' ethnographies have revealed useful insights about the social production of organization and order-making in various human service sectors, including social work (for example Housley, 2000; Griffiths, 2001).

Yet, human service work of all kinds is full of documentation; it is central to the creation and maintenance of the work itself and to stabilizing local professional cultures and identities. To understand the everyday work of human service provision, we need to take seriously the routine tasks of filing, recording, assessing, form filling and case building. If we wish to understand how those organizations work and how people work in them, we must attend to their status as authors and readers of documents (Atkinson and Coffey, 2004). Research need not artificially demarcate and separate out talk-in-interaction from textual practices, because the social worlds (Strauss, 1978; Becker, 1982) of human service are constructed and maintained through both modalities—oral and textual—in tandem.

The approach informing the ethnographic research considered in this chapter is very different from approaching documents as unproblematic 'outputs' or 'evidence' of institutional or professional practice. Rather, researchers are attending to what Prior (2003) calls the 'vitality' of forms and paperwork, alerting us to the *social life* of documents. Riles' (2006) edited volume, for example, brings together studies that illuminate how paperwork practices are embroiled in the circulation and production of knowledge, authority and governance (Gupta, 2012; Hull, 2012). Ethnographic work on cases and their construction points to the work documents do in actively producing practices and subjects of attention (Messick, 1993; Jacob, 2007). Alongside this is the kindred turn to materiality in the humanities, which has shed light on the practices, processes and consequences of documentation (Kafka, 2009; Kang, 2018). Collectively, such studies demonstrate that documents are not autonomous entities separate from but internal to the social or bureaucratic worlds in which they are embedded but play active roles in constructing their subjectivities and processes (Cavanaugh, 2016: Atkinson, 2017).

This chapter takes up Prior's (2003) call to attend to the vitality of documents in everyday social work practice, in this case with disabled children and their families. The chapter does not provide a guide to 'uncovering meaning' or norms inscribed within texts (compare Lester, 2009: Brodwin, 2013). It deliberately avoids the temptation to become 'bedazzled by content' (Prior, 2004, p 77). Rather, documents are treated as practical accomplishments, a sensibility not dissimilar to Garfinkel and Sacks' (1970) 'ethnomethodological indifference'. The focus is on a single documentary form—the core assessment—and follows it across a number of ethnographic episodes. The analysis identifies three distinct ethnographic approaches for studying documentation: tracing the material and graphical impact of the form itself; puzzling out practices of inscription and the work this does; and utilizing our scope for roaming to explore how people use forms in everyday interactional practices with others.

The ethnographic field

The data discussed draw upon an ethnographic study of social work practice with disabled children and their families at a time of change (Whitaker, 2015; Whitaker, 2019). The fieldwork consisted of 400 hours of observations. These included everyday activity in the team office, team meetings, management meetings, group supervisions and one staff training day. Lunch breaks were shared with team members when possible. I engaged in informal conversations in the office, attended meetings and shared car journeys to and from events. My observations were combined with semi-structured interviews with all staff. I collated a significant number of professional and bureaucratic texts including case files, case notes, costing and auditing forms, flowcharts, guidance notes, organizational charts and support plans. Paperwork pervaded the site. It was a ball kicked around in the mêlée of the office; to speak of it was to bond workers, critique management and to defend professional status.

Initial accounts become 'cases' as they move through statutory and professional processes. They accumulate additional textual marginalia as they move along, among them case notes, correspondence from other professionals, service reports and guidance notes. It is the creation of the paperwork, the aggregation of disparate forms—notes and documents—that identifies and denotes a topic or domain as a recognized and legitimate object of government attention and activity (Messick, 1993: Riles, 2006; Hull, 2012). This is why, almost instinctively, we balk at our documents being lost. Whether it's a planning application or joining the electoral roll, when documents are lost we are affronted not only by carelessness but by the implicit rejection that our appeal or account will not be heard.

In this team, the starting point for practice is the professional identification, documentation and justification of need. Needs must be placed into context, given a history and biography. But needs are not uncovered like stones, nor are they diagnosed through tests and lab work. Rather, in practice, they are constructed as cases are constructed. Not all needs are deemed worthy of professional attention. Some needs trigger a stronger institutional response than others. To successfully account for the identification, meeting and reporting of children's needs, social workers engage in the production of series of paperwork chains that begin with the core assessment. The core assessment record provides a structured framework for social workers to record information from a variety of sources. It is intended to provide evidence for social workers' judgments, decision-making and planning. It is one of the key sources of evidence among the multiple types of information available within such an organization (compare Gubrium and Buckholdt, 1979).

Assessing need

Core assessments were detailed, descriptive and lengthy. Descriptions of home visits and conversations with parents sat alongside correspondence from schools and health visitors. Relevant records from general practitioners and hospital consultants were noted next to information about household income and housing status. This collation of documentation needed to be distilled and ordered around 'The Triangle'—three domains that must be 'assessed' and recorded. These were: the developmental needs of the child; parenting capacity; and family and environmental factors. I was given examples of core assessments shortly after arriving in the field; managers thought it would help me understand the context of the work a little better. Within the office space, social workers would repeatedly centre the identification and articulation of needs as the heart of their work. They would refer to 'digging out', 'identifying' and sometimes even 'diagnosing' needs.

'Needs-talk' looped over and between the oral and textual practices of social workers as they sought to produce credible and justifiable accounts of practice. In Nancy Fraser's (1989, p 9) original formulation, needs-talk provides 'institutionalized patterns of interpretation'. It offers a framework for constructing the case while setting the parameters of institutional response. In other words, needs-talk helped to construct and classify cases. Needs-talk was capable of bestowing responsibility to 'meet needs' on the family or on the state. Needs-talk was used to evaluate the quality of relationships surrounding the child—to ask who was meeting these needs and how well, in order to form a judgment. Yet I was struggling to square the detailed, often evocative and intimate case-talk with the box-led, lengthy digital form, as the following reconstructed exchange from field notes on day 20 indicates. Amy is the social worker:

Amy: It's really important we get these core assessments right, because that's where we start to shape it all. But there are so many things to cover now, and you've got to cover them all because you can't submit the assessment unless you've written something under each section. Not everything is that relevant, and sometimes the really important stuff you have to sneak in, in a way.

EMW: So you feel you've got to shoehorn things in?

Amy: Precisely. So there's a case that has come over to us from the short-breaks teams. The core assessment looks a lot at what we call 'environmental factors' and part of that is background on the parents, including awkward things like income and education level. Well, his parents, really lovely, articulate, income-wise you'd think fine. But mum was telling me they've remortgaged and only last weekend they had a mini garage sale. They wanted to get the boy a scooter. They have spent so much money getting the downstairs retrofitted that they remortgaged. No help, the PCT [primary care trust] were useless. So I've found a way to get that into the assessment but it cuts across loads of the boxes. (Field notes)

The formulaic nature of the document itself, with headed boxes to complete, disrupts the conventional storied nature of professional welfare accounts (Pithouse and Atkinson, 1988; White, 2003). The core assessment begins the process of carving up family biographies into subsections and byways. It puts up lines of demarcation where in the flux of everyday life there are none. By subdividing, underscoring and classifying facets of family biography they become more orderable. It is a directed form of order-making and knowledge 'gathering' (Peckover et al, 2008; Hall et al, 2010). The whittling down of narrative and biography into more digestible chunks enables the institution to carve out specific, worker-identified 'needs' and therefore to meet them with pre-existing organizational resources. Forms render some things visible, while actively masking others, leading to professional workarounds and resistances, as Amy's account identifies. The justification for forms of this kind is that the targeted and deliberate identification of 'need' is apparently 'evidence based', whereas the narrative form of years past was mere contextual waffle (Cleaver et al, 2004). Like many organizational formats, the core assessment imposes a uniform frame on social workers' understandings, clients' narratives and other sources of information. It thus inscribes what Gubrium et al refer to as 'the descriptive demands of forms' (Gubrium et al, 1989, p 198). As Amy makes clear, the form 'shapes' the case, and demands 'completeness' so that every section is completed. At the same time, its formulaic imperatives potentially exclude what might otherwise be deemed relevant information. The documentary frame determines what shall be available and will count as 'evidence'.

Inscribing need

The following reconstructed exchange is from field notes on day 12 of observation. Megan is the social worker, who has just returned to the office after a home visit. The child in question is an autistic boy of 7 already known to social services as was his mother. Prior to Megan's visit, the family had been on the caseload of a different team, one used to supporting children with less complex family circumstances. The home visit was to follow up on a call from the school and to work up a core assessment:

Megan: It was like a house of horrors. Carpet all threadbare; the smell; mattresses on the landing. Mum is not well, at all. She's only 36, but looks mid-50s. The place really stressed me out, dark and curtains half falling off the poles. I could do without the additional clothes wash after work tonight, already got enough piled up at home. Hey ho. Not surprised we got the call from the school, in terms of appearances it's bad. But the kids were talkative and engaging. Their sleeping arrangements were fine, weirdly, like, tidy? I think despite the younger one's autism, and mum knows about what that's likely to mean as he gets stronger; she showed me a leaflet the GP...Anyway she has booked in with the support group I checked. (Field notes)

Until Megan burst into the office with her 'house of horrors' tale, I had only encountered cases on the page, in isolation or in slivers in everyday chat. With Megan's dramatic entrance, an opportunity emerged to 'follow' the case. I arranged to meet up for lunch with her a few days after the incident. The following extract relates to the same case, in a follow-up interview:

EMW: It sounded pretty dramatic the other day, that house of horrors visit! Are you ok?

Megan: [laughs] Yes, yes I'm fine. Overreacted a bit, I think, it had been a long day and I've had a chance to speak to Helen in mental health and the two schools. Needed time to digest really, it was just, well, eerie at the time. Too much coffee maybe!

EMW: How are you going to include the home visit in the assessment? That's what the visit was about, right?

Megan: Yes. We say cores are about need and of course we are there for the child. It is their assessment, their needs. But the flipside of need is risk, isn't it? So we try to nod to the potential of that, even if we don't precisely use that language. It's a bit wishy-washy, but with a core, yes, it's about detail and description, painting a picture of family life. But with this one, we don't know really where it's going yet, so you don't want to pre-judge anything beyond that. I always make sure I use as much stuff from everybody really—school, GP, health visitor. This is just the beginning really, you don't want it to read as the be all and end all in case something else happens. I know that the core is like the foundation, as it were, for everything else. I'll be spending quite some time on it. Don't get me wrong though, if I thought those kids were at risk cos mum was unstable or the house was actually unsafe, they'd be out of there. I just don't think that's the case here. (Field notes)

In our conversation, Megan is highlighting the artfulness of constructing a case. She takes a notable step back from the 'house of horrors' tale she entered the office with, while underscoring her credibility in identifying risk and protecting the child's interest. She hints at the importance of ambiguity in completing some elements of the core assessment: "It's a bit wishy-washy…yes, it's about detail and description, painting a picture of family life. But with this one, we don't know really where it's going yet, so you don't want to pre-judge anything". This scope for ambiguity was borne out in the core assessment document which she shared with me a fortnight later, as the following extract indicates.

I have concerns about cleanliness of the property—cat detritus was found upstairs, there was a lack of proper sleeping arrangements for Miss X—a mattresses on the floor was found which Miss X said was a temporary fix for her until a new bed arrived. The house does need some care and attention, so I am recommending our in-house domestic team coordinate with the housing team to do a deep clean and tidy. Miss X would benefit from extra support so I have referred her back to her GP and to the local autism network. (Extract from Section 17 Core Assessment)

In the written assessment, the evocative and sensorial 'house of horrors' descriptors were reworked. In the core assessment, social workers were tasked with providing accounts and making judgments they knew would inform future prescriptions for action. Had the 'house of horrors' been written as such, with cat faeces documented forensically, dirty mattresses mapped, a picture of chaos painted, the trajectory for this case would likely turn from one concerned with 'need' to one of 'neglect'. Most obviously what is written has significant consequences for the child and family. What needs are demarcated will influence what services and support are provided. What context is given will firm up the 'official' view of the family, what the institution 'thinks' about them. As such, the core assessment helps to construct and firm up the subject at hand—this is a competent parent or a vulnerable parent or a risky parent. Official documents are accounts that make things happen in the world: the sifting of entitlement claims; the inscribing of subjectivity; and the 'laying of foundations' for future action.

Following the form

The second ethnographic strategy concerns the mobility of the record, as it travels in organizational space and time, as does the ethnographer herself. Documents enable institutions to act over time and space, to collapse and expand both. The completion of an assessment and its bureaucratic representation condense the temporal dimensions of the client's problems, but render the account available for future inspection. The forms reorder the present and immediate past while projecting possible organizational futures. Megan was tasked with constructing a case in the present, utilizing accounts and evidence from the near past. The assessment would have future consequences dependent on the account provided in the present. In her own words, because "we don't know really where it's going yet", the door needed to be kept open to alternative possibilities, at least for a while, lest the case be "pre-judged" and set on a very different path. The function of the document is to present past action to future inspection, while also being conscious that the prescription makes it possible in future to refer to what was agreed in the past. The effect of the form, meanwhile, is to synchronize, to make the different times (and spaces) equivalent. (See Gubrium et al, 1989 on the chronotypes of organizational forms and records.)

Further, the document reinforces the abstraction which distinguishes written from oral communication (Goody, 1977; Cicourel, 1985). In most instances of oral communication, we have a specific sense of who we are speaking to—we can call this a 'case sense'. Written communication, because it is made over time and at a distance, is more often made in general terms, and directed at an unknown reader— constructed in a 'category sense'. Megan's tempered phraseology is written within the register of a category sense. The core assessment, once written, enables unknown others to take it up, to pass it along, to make it more of a fact, while aligning it firmly with the author's ownership and judgment (compare Latour and Woolgar, 1979: Latour, 1987). The core assessment turns the local production of knowledge into an artifact that can be loosened from its local context. As such, writing allows specific forms of knowledge to become 'mobile'. It is the combined *immutability* and *mobility* of these inscriptions that render them peculiarly functional, while multiplying their effects for professionals and families.

In attending to paperwork as actively constructed, mutable and mobile we are jolted out of easy presumptions that these are finished, static and representative things. By following paperwork, we are confronted with chains of relations, power and discourses invoked and constructed on the page. They provide written accounts of justification and (in)action while at the same time constructing the very subjects of that justification. Paperwork 'makes the case' in both senses of the term (Atkinson, 1995). Documents, case notes and audits coexist in alliances that reconstitute agency and interactivity. The file, thus, does not just report and represent. It also involves and constitutes an extended nexus of those present and absent.

Contesting need

The third ethnographic perspective turns to the practical use of documentary materials. Documentary sources, like the core assessment, feature prominently in social workers' professional meetings. Such records, as we have seen, constitute the 'evidence' that can be consulted in order to establish the facticity of events and to justify particular interpretations.

In much professional human service work there is a symbiotic relationship between meetings and documents. Entire ceremonies can be devised to assess professional practice through a forensic examination of case paperwork (Housley, 2000; Whitaker, 2019; Whitaker and Atkinson, 2019). Case assessments are pored over in supervisions, discussed and contested between team members, referred to in multi-agency meetings. Documents do not remain sealed in folders—digital or otherwise. They become ripe for rereading in utterly different contexts serving different ends. Documents regularly find new audiences at meetings (Freeman, 2008; Whitaker, 2019). They may be circulated in advance, proffered as an example, slammed down in frustration. Meetings, like documents, are also aimed at future actions: they are 'symbolic encodings' (Weick, 1995) which enables them to be used or acted upon by others, later, elsewhere, 'at a distance'. Paperwork can be dusted off and redeployed when a challenge is made. It has a role in interpersonal and embodied interaction. It very much 'gets off the shelf'.

The following extract is taken from my research diary. In it I reflect on a meeting wherein the core assessment was used as 'evidence' to contest need. This meeting was a regular institutional event; ordinarily between 8 and 10 team leaders and managers would attend. This particular instance referred to a case of twin boys:

> Major drama at the meeting today. Team leader incandescent after a parent requested a review of her support. Parent writes a private letter that was so intimate and personal it must have taken real courage to send. I can't believe it was read out, I just can't. Then to dig out the core assessment as though it was an arbiter of truth, when its 2 years old, flipping through it like a school report. The most awkward and upsetting thing I've been party to so far. There was something in the tone of the reading that implied the idea of 'not wanting to parent'. (Research diary)

The 'major drama' began with a letter from the parent. In the meeting, the team leader took to her feet to read it to the assembled staff. The parent had written to complain about the 'bureaucratic nightmare' of the system as she tried to support twin boys with complex support needs. In it she asked for additional support and an urgent review of their support plan. I made an ethical decision not to explicate the specific contents of the letter in my field notes, my thesis or elsewhere.

After the letter was read, the manager concluded with:

> 'You know, you're her mother! I'd do that for my child! I would expect families to be doing that for their children. What do you want me to do?! We've created this sort of extraordinary expectation I think.' (Research diary)

"I'd do that for my child" was a reference to the requirement that every four hours one of the boys had to take a variety of medicines for different problems. The mother was struggling to do this on her own. She was tired. She was struggling to cope. She felt that a review was needed urgently. She was seeking overnight support from the sleep service and 'an extra pair of hands'.

Next, the team manager brought out the core assessment. Or rather, she raised it from the table in front of her and proceeded to treat it as a prop for a sermon. For all the high drama, this moment was clearly planned. She continued, flipping the pages as she went: "The core assessment 'does not identify any needs associated with mum's ability to parent.'" She turned the page, "The home was 'smart, kept well, clean and ordered.'" "The family support network was 'small but local.'" Silence was propped up by supportive knowing nods from those present.

The mother's letter was met with incredulity, and her moral standing as a parent was called into question. The construction on paper was of someone 'coping', and here was someone in her own words 'not coping'. Paperwork shapes and stabilizes subjectivities from the perspective of the organization; this contestation challenged that. Documents are also 'part of the way in which the organisation *talks to itself*...[and] about itself' (Harper, 1997, p 129) (emphasis in original). The organizational warrants for intervention are destabilized when the accuracy of its own accounts of sense-making are troubled.

The document does not compete with face-to-face interaction, but anchors and frames it. In this process, social work texts and social work talk are transformed, producing a new situation that cannot be reduced to any simple combination of either the text itself or practice without text. The ethnographic design holds both in tension by moving back and forth between the inside and outside of specific episodes, tracing and tracking their origins and futures (Clifford, 1983). This is an important methodological point. This moment of workplace drama encourages us to think about practices of unfolding, making and contestation. Organizational life is series of continuous, situated and contingent processes geared to defining and stabilizing the present situation (Altheide, 2000). Ethnographic work enables forms, cases and people to be followed as part of the micro-politics of organizational life. There is a rhythm and flow to the episodic nature of ethnographic work as there is to organizational life.

Ethnographic work draws attention to the *context* of speech and writing acts. The competent social worker is a 'stressed out' (not 'burnt out') social worker, like Megan returning from her 'house of horrors'. The credible team manager is one who valiantly stands by the organizational account in meetings, but concedes to a review in private. What is significant is that stress or incredulity is not hidden but *carefully* displayed. That Megan referred to a 'house of horrors' and her stress in talk and not in print is less about the accuracy of that descriptor and more about the work that phrase is doing. Her talk shores up a sense of professional identity and competency; she is confirming to another who 'we' are and what we 'go through' and how that makes 'us' special and distinctive from others.

I was only able to spot the local potency of needs-talk as a discursive repertoire of how the organization talks to itself because I kept bumping into it in the course of my fieldwork. I followed it across modalities of talk and text into management meetings, along car journeys and over coffees. Had I encountered any of these episodes in isolation, it is unlikely I would have identified the importance of it as a prism for thrashing out micro-sociological dramas about how accounts become claimed, validated or rejected.

Conclusion

Ethnographic work can do things with documents that other methodologies struggle to do. Three have been identified here. Firstly, we can trace the material and graphical impact of the form itself. This was important in order to establish institutionally granted parameters of knowledge and action. They provide a directed form of order-making and knowledge 'gathering', whittling down complexity into more digestible chunks. Workers could find workarounds to this directive—Amy found creative ways to 're-storify' her case work. The form 'shapes' the case, and demands 'completeness' so that every section is completed. At the same time, its formulaic imperatives potentially exclude what might otherwise be deemed relevant information. Secondly, the ethnographer can analyse forms for various kinds of inscription. Inscription does not only refer to content. Analyzing inscription also requires identifying forms of address (is this document inscribing a 'case' or 'category' sense), mapping the range of potential audiences and routes through which documents flow and plotting what the potential consequences of that trajectory will be. The ethnographer can follow the life course of a document in close to real time, and can attend to the settings it arrives in. An ethnographic take on practices of inscription involves attending to how a given document becomes mutable and mobile, what its career might be. Finally, the third ethnographic approach focuses on how people use forms in everyday interactional practices and how they leverage ethical and professional dilemmas with and through documentation. This is explicated in the case of the twins. Here, the ethnographer is drawing attention to the intimacies between talk and text in organizational settings.

The rich fruits of ethnographic fieldwork—field notes, naturally occurring talk, interview data and extracts from documents—speak to the richness that ethnographic work generates in terms of our 'own' writing. Insightful conversations about practice, informal quips about colleagues and the observation of the grind of paperwork materialized because we were undertaking immersive ethnographic fieldwork. As we observe and write and follow up and observe and write, the imperceptible and iterative loops of description/analysis help us to align with the rhythms of our fields. Noticings and events duly find their way written up as notes or memos, considered in diaries, drawn as maps to be picked up and reworked later. In-situ and post-hoc writing help to firm up an understanding of what was going on as it occurred and unfolded (Atkinson, 2019).

Ethnographers have the luxury of going back and asking questions, seeking out examples or clarification and finding another case to follow. The iterative and multimodal nature of ethnographic work (talk, text, embodied interaction, observation) helped me to 'see' the field in infrastructural and architectural terms. This was important in order to understand indigenous modes for making sense of the work, in this place at this time. Quips and frustrations mentioned in passing in a corridor helped to shore up important aspects of the context of the place and work. My gradual familiarization with team members meant that asking to see an example of an assessment or a form was not an imposition. Over time they would proffer examples without request, and I too built up a healthy pile of paperwork. I read files, took notes and asked questions in real time. Cases were discussed and debated as part of the natural ebb and flow of the setting, illuminating the challenges of contemporary social work practice with children and families. I began to understand the registers team members used to persuade and cajole in the process of case building. I could plot the institutional enclosures and regimes through which they and the families they worked with had to pass.

The document itself is a practised thing: more akin to a corridor than an arrow, it is something through which other things flow. It plays an important part in constituting social realities and coordinating activity. It is contingent, because it could always have been otherwise, and is produced through what Dorothy Smith (2002, p 3) calls 'back and forth work' among and between writers and readers, authors and editors. This is evident in the 'working up' of the case assessment. Ideas, suggestions, frustrations and characterizations were tried on and tried out in talk before being stabilized temporarily in print. Yet, an interview alone would not reveal the number of hands involved and iterations made before an account is encoded in text. It would miss the 'house of horrors' tale and its artful reworking. Equally, being handed a pile of core assessments to 'read' would mask the contestations, deliberations and real skill that lay behind the text. Reading case files in isolation would not reveal the degree of self-referential work involved in paperwork. Such a strategy would fail to notice how discursive formations trail between paperwork and interaction, and how tropes found in one are carried over into other contexts and settings. An ethnographic approach to paperwork involves following these documents as they travel across the site, asking how, where and by whom they are produced, edited, revised or filed. By following a documentary career across a number of episodes, the suppleness and potency of paperwork reveals itself. Instead of asking what documentary practices produce in terms of rationality and coherence, ethnographic attention revels in their indeterminacies, conditions and possibilities. It can stumble across that which goes unwritten but said, ending up slammed on desks or read like a sermon.

References

Altheide, D.L. (2000) 'Identity and the definition of the situation in a mass-mediated context', *Symbolic interaction*, 23(1): 1–27.

Atkinson, P. (1995) *Medical Talk and Medical Work*, London: Sage.

Atkinson, P. (2017) *Thinking Ethnographically*, London: Sage.

Atkinson, P. (2019) *Writing Ethnographically*, London: Sage.

Atkinson, P. and Coffey, A. (2004) 'Analysing documentary realities', in D. Silverman (ed) *Qualitative Research: Theory, Method and Practice*, London: Sage, pp 77–92.

Becker, H.S. (1982) *Art Worlds*, updated reprint. Berkeley, CA: University of California Press, 2008.

Brodwin, P. (2013) *Everyday Ethics: Voices from the Front Line of Community Psychiatry*, Berkeley, CA: University of California Press.

Buckholdt, D.R. and Gubrium, J.F. (1979) *Caretakers: Treating Emotionally Disturbed Children*, Thousand Oaks, CA: Sage.

Cavanaugh, J.R. (2016) 'Documenting subjects: Performativity and audit culture in food production in northern Italy', *American Ethnologist*, 43(4): 691–703.

Cicourel, A. (1985) 'Text and discourse', *Annual Review of Anthropology*, 14: 159–185.

Cleaver, H., Barnes, J., Bliss, D. and Cleaver, D. (2004) *Developing Information Sharing and Assessment Systems*, London: Department for Education and Skills.

Clifford, J. (1983) 'On ethnographic authority', *Representations*, 2(1): 118–145.

Fraser, N. (1989) *Unruly Practices: Power, Discourse, and Gender in Contemporary Social Theory*, Minneapolis, MN: University of Minnesota Press.

Freeman, R. (2008) 'Learning by meeting', *Critical Policy Analysis*, 2(1): 1–24.

Garfinkel, H. and Sacks, H. (1970) 'On formal structures of practical actions', in J.C. McKinney and E.A. Tiryakian (eds) *Theoretical Sociology: Perspectives and Developments*, New York: Appleton Century Crofts, pp 338–366.

Goody, J. (1977) *The Domestication of the Savage Mind*, Cambridge: Cambridge University Press.

Griffiths, L. (2001) 'Categorising to exclude: The discursive construction of cases in community mental health teams', *Sociology of Health and Illness*, 22(4): 453–476.

Gubrium, J.F. and Buckholdt, D.R. (1979) 'Production of hard data in human service institutions', *Pacific Sociological Review*, 22(1): 115–136.

Gubrium, J.F., Buckholdt, D.R. and Lynott, R.J. (1989) 'The descriptive tyranny of forms', in J.A. Holstein and G. Miller (eds) *Perspectives on Social Problems: A Research Annual*, Greenwich, CT: JAI Press, pp 195–214.

Gupta, A. (2012) *Red Tape: Bureaucracy, Structural Violence, and Poverty in India*, Durham, NC: Duke University Press.

Hall, C., Parton, N., Peckover, S. and White, S. (2010) 'Child-centric information and communication technology (ICT) and the fragmentation of child welfare practice in England', *Journal of Social Policy*, 39: 393–413.

Harper, R. (1997) *Inside the IMF: An Ethnography of Documents, Technology and Organizational Action*, San Diego, CA: Academic Press.

Housley, W. (2000) 'Story, narrative and team work', *The Sociological Review*, 48(3): 435–443.

Hull, M. (2012) *Government of Paper: The Materiality of Bureaucracy in Urban Pakistan*, Berkeley, CA: University of California Press.

Jacob, M.A. (2007) 'Form-made persons: Consent forms as consent's blind spot', *PoLaR:Political and Legal Anthropology Review*, 30(2): 249–268.

Kafka, B. (2009) 'Paperwork: The state of the discipline', *Book History*, 12: 340–353.

Kang, H.Y. (2018) 'Law's materiality', in A. Philippopoulos-Mihalopoulos (ed) *Routledge Handbook of Law and Theory*, London: Routledge, pp 453–474.

Latour, B. (1987) *Science in Action*, Cambridge, MA: Harvard University Press.

Latour, B. and S. Woolgar (1979) *Laboratory Life: The Construction of Scientific Facts* (2nd edn), reprint, Princeton, NJ: Princeton University Press, 1986.

Lester, R. (2009) 'Brokering authenticity: Borderline personality disorder and the ethics of care in an American eating disorder clinic', *Current Anthropology*, 50(3): 281–302.

Messick, B. (1993) *The Calligraphic State: Textual Domination and History in a Muslim Society*, Berkeley, CA: University of California Press.

Miller, G. (1994) 'Toward ethnographies of institutional discourse', *Journal of Contemporary Ethnography*, 23(3): 280–306.

Peckover, S., White, S. and Hall, C. (2008) 'Making and managing electronic children: E-assessment in child welfare', *Information, Communication and Society*, 11(3): 275–294.

Pithouse, A. (1987) *Social Work: The Social Organisation of an Invisible Trade*, Aldershot: Avebury Gower.

Pithouse, A. and Atkinson, P. (1988) 'Telling the case: Occupational narrative in a social work office', in N. Coupland (ed) *Styles of Discourse*, Beckenham: Croom Helm, pp 183–200.

Pithouse, A., Hall, C., Peckover, S. and White, S. (2009) 'A tale of 2 CAFs: The impact of the electronic Common Assessment Framework', *British Journal of Social Work*, 39(4): 599–612.

Prior, L. (2003) *Using Documents in Social Research*, London: Sage.

Prior, L. (2004) 'Doing things with documents', in D. Silverman (ed) *Qualitative Research: Theory, Method and Practice* (vol 2), London: Sage.

Riles, A. (2006) *Documents: Artifacts of Modern Knowledge*, Ann Arbor, MI: University of Michigan Press.

Smith, D.E. (2002) *Texts, Facts and Femininity: Exploring the Relations of Ruling*, New York: Routledge.

Strauss, A. (1978) 'A social world perspective', in N.K. Denzin (ed) *Studies in Symbolic Interaction* (vol 1), Greenwich, CT: JAI Press, pp 119–128.

Weick, K.E. (1995) *Sensemaking in Organizations*, Thousand Oaks, CA: Sage.

Whitaker, E.M. (2015) 'Personalisation in children's social work: From family support to "the child" budget', *Journal of Integrated Care*, 23(5): 277–286.

Whitaker, E.M. (2019) '"Bring yourself to work": Rewriting the feeling rules in "personalized" social work', *Journal of Organizational Ethnography*, 8(3): 325–338.

Whitaker, E.M. and Atkinson, P. (2019) 'Authenticity and the interview: A positive response to a radical critique', *Qualitative Research*, 19(6): 619–634.

White, S. (2003) 'The social worker as moral judge: Blame, responsibility and case formulation', in C. Hall, K. Juhila, N. Parton and T. Pösö (eds) *Constructing Clienthood in Social Work and Human Services*, London: Jessica Kingsley, pp 177–192.

6

Debating dementia care logics

Cíntia Engel, Janaína Aredes and Annette Leibing

Although around the world Brazil's image is of a youthful nation, population aging is happening there in a highly accelerated way: currently there are more than 28 million older Brazilians (IBGE, 2020). The soaring number of people with dementia has become a major public health problem: Brazil has one of the highest prevalence rates of dementia in the world, reaching a mean of 7.6 percent (Prince et al, 2015). Dementia care is extremely challenging, especially considering that in Brazil care happens mostly at home, making families responsible for their older family members' well-being. Care resources (home care, medications, housing infrastructure, and so forth) are widely lacking (Burlá et al, 2013), except for richer as opposed to poor people. Without a well-functioning social net, most Brazilians rely on a 'patchwork of care'—a notion that describes uncertain and ongoing negotiations required of people so as to be able to provide care—the tinkering of individuals mobilizing multiple sources of help, on which they cannot always rely (see Leibing et al, 2016).

How can this complex landscape of care be captured methodologically? Based on ethnographies carried out in a Brazilian metropolis—the Federal District—we propose focusing on 'logics of care' in order to get closer to what is at stake in care work. Here we follow Annemarie Mol (2008), who claims that processes that involve care have their internal logics and that we can approach them by observing—from concrete situations—what is done in the way of care. Alternatively, as proposed by Pols (2015), we look at the intra-normativity of these practices, what is considered good care and what is understood as a challenge, dilemma or as negative practices. More concretely, by juxtaposing two ethnographies of dementia care—one situated in a geriatric outpatient clinic, one at home—our aim is to show that the two logics that emerged from comparative fieldwork are at the same time distinct and specific but also interconnected.

In the first ethnography, care is provided within the public health system—the *Sistema Único de Saúde* (SUS)—by a multidisciplinary team.

This kind of care is based on what we want to call the 'ensemble logic'. The second case, which we describe as homecare, shows how care is carried out in households based on what we call a 'routine logic'. The terms 'ensemble' and 'routine' are emic terms borrowed from our interlocutors.[1] They do not represent obvious and unified meanings, but they lead us to dialogue comparatively with the reflections of our interlocutors and how they define what must be done to provide good care.

We also do a comparative exercise in relation to the two logics of care. We monitor what are the main problems and how these problems are situated in both logics, how they influence action and value systems. We pay attention to the fact that the logics are interrelated, not restrained to one ethnographic setting, and therefore deepen our understanding of situated dementia care, but equally enlarge debates by providing data that is lived and debated from different perspectives. Mol's notion of a 'politics-of-what' is helpful here: 'A politics-of-what explores the differences, not between doctors and patients, but between various enactments of a particular disease' (Mol, 2002, p 176). And although one of our ethnographies at first sight is about doctors and one is about patients, what is at stake here is the 'distinct complementarities' found in the complex processes and technicalities of care. We finally combine this with the notion of 'care ecology' proposed by Das and Das (2006) and Das (2015) in order to think about the articulations of places, specialties, prescriptions and ways of using medicines—and about how responsibility is assigned for what goes wrong.

Care is not a simple or obvious term for anthropologists who study dementia. For this chapter, we understand care as a type of practice that engages a multiplicity of elements—technological, economic, technical and affective—and that involves decision-making processes and the constitution of a variety of skills: it means ' persistent tinkering in a world full of complex ambivalence and shifting tensions' (Mol et al, 2010, p 14). As stated by Pols (2015), such a perspective radicalizes the relationality of care, because acts of care cannot be reduced only to questions of dependency and power. In addition to being a practice with particular logics and normativities, we also understand care as a process that unfolds alongside political, economic and health infrastructure issues—all of which are included and articulated in the practices. As Thelen (2015) would say, care can be understood as an open-ended process, directly connected with social organization or, as Das (2015) suggests, relying on local 'care ecologies' (Das, 2015) that add to the bigger-picture vectors, like places, people and policies of care.

Comparative ethnography

The data discussed in this chapter come from a comparative ethnography carried out by one of the authors, Cíntia Engel. The study formally lasted one year and six months and was divided into two main research circles, which maintained intense dialogue with each other. For nine months, the researcher observed, conducted interviews, read medical records and followed the clinical routine in the multidisciplinary geriatric centre of a university hospital. It is a centre of excellence (located within a public university hospital) and specializes in the treatment of dementia. The centre was chosen because it is a place that combines the function of assisting patients with training professionals, and its senior geriatricians are involved in knowledge transfer and even policymaking at the local and national levels.[2]

For another nine months, Cíntia visited the homes of three different families, following their daily routines—their processes of making food and cleaning the house, their ways of caring and consuming medicines—and moving with them through health centres, pharmacies, consultations with different doctors and interactions with neighbours, friends and relatives.

We opted for narratives of two 'typical' cases from each context. Our intention is not to debate the particularities of each case, but rather to constitute a description that brings us closer to the articulations, the processes, the type of logic that connects several experiences that emerged in the field. As already mentioned, we work with two emic notions to help us in this comparison: the 'ensemble' and 'routine' categories.

'Ensemble logic': care at a specialized public geriatric unit

One of the first expressions we heard in the field referred to the fact that, when taking care of someone with dementia, it is necessary to pay attention to the 'ensemble' (o conjunto). Many people arrived at the geriatric health unit with multiple health problems—the cases they attended, doctors told us, were complex. And although, as we will see, a major part of a treatment involves medications targeting specific symptoms, health professionals are very aware of the circumstances, the big picture—or the ensemble—that includes the socioeconomic situation of each family. We decided to call this type of approach the 'ensemble logic'.

The ensemble logic doesn't only involve the recognition that patients' health conditions are complex; there is also an attempt to deal with this ensemble of problems through ongoing discussions around reading multiple signs and proposing various interventions that are easily questioned and adjusted when the bundle of (physical and social) symptoms shift due to pathological, pharmacological and social circumstances. Ultimately, as we will see, treating the ensemble is to stabilize relationships.

Mr João arrived at the centre already diagnosed with Alzheimer's disease in an intermediate phase—between moderate and severe.[3] Prior to his visit to the centre, he was being treated by two doctors, a private psychiatrist and a public cardiologist. He began to pass out frequently and eventually became more aggressive towards his wife. One of his doctors thought that, given the complexity and variety of symptoms and the large number of medications he was taking, it was best to refer him to a geriatrician.

In a first consultation at the centre, the professionals heard the complaints of Mr João's daughter and wife. He said little. The daughter mentioned that Mr João was fighting a lot with his wife; he was insisting on having intimate relations with her without her consent and was calling her ugly names. The wife, a lady in her late eighties, was visibly tired, cried a few times during the consultation and reported her difficulties in daily life, especially because of her difficult coexistence with her husband.

Furthermore, what was worrying everyone was the fact that Mr João twice—or three times—lost consciousness and fell, without anyone being able to help him. They were waiting for the results of an exam ordered by the cardiologist to find out how his situation was, given that Mr João had already had heart problems.

Mr João was already using some medications: donepezil[4] and memantine[5] to treat Alzheimer's disease; clonazepam[6] to help him sleep at night; citalopram,[7] an antidepressant, because Mr João had complained about being sad as the result of being sick. Additionally, he was taking two drugs to deal with his heart condition.

In this consultation, without having the results of the examination on the cardiac condition, the geriatricians decided to stop the clonazepam. The geriatric doctors disapproved of the use of certain drugs, which, following guidelines from the Ministry of Health, they conceived of as 'unsuitable for the elderly', including clonazepam and some antidepressants, such as fluoxetine and amitriptyline. But it was very common for people to arrive at the centre having used those drugs for years and resistant to giving them up.[8]

The doctors explained to Mr João's wife that his actions were not 'malice', that they were part of the disease process. They offered the wife the chance to participate in a group of caregivers, where she could discuss her problems and 'accept' this new condition of her husband's. Mr João's daughter, however, explained that her mother knew that the problems at home were related to the disease, but knowing would not prevent her being tired and upset. In addition, she had severe mobility problems due to osteoporosis and it would be very difficult for her to go to the groups alone, while the daughter and her brother could not miss work to take her by car.

In such groups we observed that, similar to issues raised in caregiver groups abroad, members are informed about how the disease develops and tips are given on how to deal with daily life. An important recommendation is to follow a regular routine, avoiding conflicts and not pointing out forgetfulness or mistakes to the person with dementia; it is equally important to create spaces of rest for the caregiver, including by their asking for help with daily activities. A central idea at the centre was that by establishing good care relationships it is possible to improve daily life, which then positively influences the treatment and eventually leads to slowing down the decline due to dementia. The treatment, then, targets to a great extent the care relationship. Medications are not only meant for cognitive impairment: treatment depended a lot on good home care.

In the case of Mr João, the health team decided, in addition to counselling on how to care for and deal with daily life, to prescribe an antipsychotic, a controversial intervention because of the risk of serious side effects. The justification given by the prescribing resident was that 'the family was suffering' from Mr João's behaviour. The team also called his wife for an individual appointment, arguing that she was 'burdened by care' and that she also needed to take care of her own problems, such as osteoporosis and several other health problems. 'Burdened by care' is a category that gained diagnostic status at the centre. It is understood that, if the responsible person becomes overloaded, they can get sick and be unable to provide good care. The antipsychotic, therefore, did not only target Mr João's body; it became a medication prescribed to help the husband and wife coexist, so that care at home could be improved.

At a subsequent appointment, the geriatrician looked at the cardiac exam and noticed that Mr João's heart rate was alarmingly low. In a team meeting, the health professionals then debated whether the drugs prescribed for dementia could be responsible in part for the cardiac problem. All these drugs slowed the heart rate, and became riskier when prescribed in combination. As one geriatrician explained, antipsychotic drugs might interact with one of the drugs for Mr João's cardiac condition. Thus, the drug treatment that was supposed to reorganize the family dynamic was interfering with Mr João's treatment for his heart.

In a debate about what to do, one of the doctors suggested cutting all dementia drugs and focusing only on the heart condition. Another doctor, however, was concerned about family relationships and the health of Mr João's wife. The wife's condition could worsen and, if she reached her limit, perhaps Mr João would be left without any assistance and could be admitted to an institution—a last resort solution for most Brazilian families. They ended up cutting most of the dementia drugs and the antipsychotic drug, believing that the danger in maintaining them was too high.

The team considered that if the wife lost her ability to care, one of the children would have to take over, or would still have to hire a private caregiver. The centre's social worker was called in to mediate the situation. The social worker's function was as much to convince the children to participate more often in daily care as to guide the family in looking for all the benefits provided by law to help with the family's expenses. In this way, they would avoid another category that was used at the centre like a diagnosis: 'family insufficiency'. This term would be applied when a family was unable to share care among its members or when there was not enough income for hiring a professional caregiver. In consultation with Mr João's wife, the team decided to prescribe an antidepressant for her, imagining that this way the couple's life together might improve.

We want to draw attention to some points which stand out with respect to Mr João's care. The 'ensemble' includes everything, from drug interactions to family relationships. Geriatric care, even when only based on medications, is therefore a relational mode of care. Ideal care here involves an emotionally stable primary caregiver, a large family engaged in care, financial resources to hire professional caregivers (in order to put less pressure on the family) and the use of properly administered medications. However, such an ideal constantly runs up against a number of challenges.

One challenge, for example, arises when an overburdened caregiver insists on more medications for the person with dementia. Another is that a family may not organize itself in the expected way: conflicts occur, and siblings might even end up in court. Another is that medicines can cause unwanted effects, accrue high costs, or there might be difficulty attaining them at a nearby pharmacy, thereby undermining good care. For all these reasons, treatment demands constant corrections and adjustments of doses but also of relationships, what we call elsewhere 'a constant fine-tuning' of drugs and relations (Leibing et al, 2019).

This type of geriatric therapy depends largely on a counterpart from families and caregivers being involved, and older people without families are rarely seen at the centre. Geriatric treatments depend on family members constantly observing the uses of medications, on their knowing how to report good and bad effects, on chasing after exam results, on pushing against bureaucracies to access rights to get free medications, on organizing family care. It is this counterpart that we will talk about in the next section, but from another perspective: that of families caring at home.

Establishing and maintaining routine: care within households

At home, a fundamental category used by the research interlocutors to talk about care was the 'routine'. Phrases such as 'You have to get the routine', 'It got in the way of my routine', 'I miss our routine' were common sayings. The use of the term routine, however, has a specific meaning. It is different from routine used in the caregiver groups, where a common recommendation is always conducting the same activities at the same time of the day—something that provides a feeling of security and orientation to those living with dementia. It is also different from what is usually called routine when talking (critically) about care in institutions: standardized and rigid organizational ways of caring (Kitwood, 1997; Chatterji, 1998).

To some extent, the elaborations of the interlocutors about the routine relates to the idea of managing everyday life, or daily life, as elaborated by Pols et al (2018) and by Das (2015). Routine is an intense space of reflexivity, testing and adjustments. Or it can also mean, as we have learned from our interlocutors, a certain rhythm of the days, weeks and months that allows for organization—without major disruptions—of the handling of multiple relationships, doctors and medicines, of time spent on public transport and of the ability to pay for most care expenses.

Establishing and dealing with routines is not a state of regular repetition; it is rather a constantly changing and intense challenge that involves reflexivity, experiments and adjustments. It involves engaging people, family members, neighbours—even the researcher—on a daily basis: a patchwork of care.

Mrs Aparecida, an eighty-year-old woman who lived in a city around the Federal District and who had lived with Alzheimer's for seven years, started experiencing some loss of consciousness. The first few times, her daughters took her to the emergency room of a public hospital near her home. On these occasions, doctors, when measuring Mrs Aparecida's blood pressure, noticed that it was high and prescribed her a medication to lower it. However, on one of the days when Mrs Aparecida was sick again and went to the emergency room, a very young doctor decided that she had labyrinthitis and prescribed a medication for this condition. After taking the medicine, Mrs Aparecida became very ill. First she was agitated, then drowsy, and complained a lot about her malaise. The family decided to stop the medication. Mrs Aparecida was supposed to have an appointment with the geriatrician, but not for another three months. So the family looked for another doctor, a family doctor from the local basic health unit—which is responsible for primary care. This family doctor understood the repeated loss of consciousness as resulting from seizures and prescribed a drug for it: phenobarbital.

One of the daughters, suspicious and resentful after the experience with the emergency doctor, took a letter to the geriatrician's health centre. The geriatrician, a doctor with a post in a Federal District institution, agreed with the hypothesis about seizures, but decided to prescribe another drug: phenytoin. This medication could be had free in Mrs Aparecida's home municipality, at the so-called popular pharmacy. However, although this city was connected to the Federal District as part of the wider metropolitan area, it belonged to another Brazilian state, Goiás. Therefore, in order to get the medication in Mrs Aparecida's home municipality, it was necessary to have a prescription from a doctor that worked there, or at least a prescription made in the same state. They used to solve this bureaucratic imbroglio with the doctor at the basic unit, who took the prescriptions from the geriatric doctor and rewrote them with the forms of the municipality where they lived. The problem in this case, however, was that this doctor did not agree with the change of prescription made by the geriatrician—in his conception the two drugs were 'the same thing'.

The family ended up buying the medicine prescribed by the geriatrician in a private pharmacy where they had to pay, because when trying the one prescribed by the doctor at the basic unit, Mrs Aparecida became very sleepy. When they finally had the consultation with the geriatrician three months later, they learned that he had chosen phenytoin because it was a 'preference among geriatricians': it causes less drowsiness—despite the expected benefits being the same. However, the medicine did not solve the problem of the seizures, which actually increased. After augmenting the dose, Mrs Aparecida became sleepy and disconnected; she looked 'doped', as her daughter observed.

Mrs Aparecida used to get very agitated around lunchtime, and she would move things like furniture and household items around—something that bothered her daughters, especially because that used to upset the process of preparing lunch. When they complained about it to the doctor, they received a prescription for an antipsychotic medication. But this medicine left Mrs Aparecida 'seeing things'. They tried to manage this agitation with still other drugs, but it was difficult, and she was constantly very doped. Observing these situations, one of the daughters complained about doctors and medicines, saying that they could not find a middle ground: they either made Mrs Aparecida very agitated, or very doped. When she was that way, the daughters admitted that they even missed her former state, when she was moving everything around the house.

With time, the daughters ended up creating some strategies for coping with this agitation. They learned to let Mrs Aparecida do whatever she wanted and move things around as she desired—but with supervision. This improved their coexistence. The supervision was oriented toward not letting Mrs Aparecida get hurt. Which was easier to do if two people were around.

This attempt to keep more people at home was a constant challenge. At a certain point this was resolved by hiring a professional caregiver. This external caregiver received her salary from Mrs Aparecida's retirement pension. One of the daughters, the one who lived with Mrs Aparecida, was unemployed and therefore stayed at home. The rent, food and credit payments were provided by Mrs Aparecida's granddaughter, who also lived in the house, and from the retirement pension of Mrs Aparecida's husband, Mr Sérgio—who until now has been absent from this narrative of care. The problem was that he hated living in that city; they came from another region of Brazil, and Mr Sérgio wanted to return, he was missing his home. In addition, his daughters didn't have a good relationship with him. The crises of coexistence intensified and the solution that the unemployed daughter came up with was that she returned to work. Thus, Mr Sérgio's income would not be essential for the household anymore.

After some months of job searching, she was hired as a lunch cook at a public school in the region. But then she noticed that the hired caregiver at home was overwhelmed. She realized this only because Mrs Aparecida stopped eating. First, they thought that it could be due to the progress of the disease, but she only avoided meals that were made by the hired caregiver; food made by her daughters was still eaten.

Another daughter, who lived nearby, started to spend more time with her mother. Even with this change, things took time to settle.

This daughter also used to deal with the bureaucracy of the public health system, the SUS: she was responsible for picking up medicines and making appointments with doctors. And that was not a simple job. In order to access all the locations that involved Mrs Aparecida's care, she needed to take illegally operating vans for transport or arrange rides with neighbours since their neighbourhood had almost no public transport. That was when the researcher became engaged in the 'routines' by proving rides with her car.

In addition, there were many other steps and more bureaucracy to overcome in order to be able to make appointments and access medications, not to mention long hours of waiting. Often, entire days were lost just to get one medication. This daughter repeated several times the sentence: "They play with our time!" Having also been responsible for some of the days caring at Mrs Aparecida's home, it became increasingly impossible for her to manage her time. For this reason, it was not uncommon—even though they could access medicines or other technologies, such as diapers and wheelchairs, free of charge in specific, though far away pharmacies—that they ended up buying them at the expensive pharmacy in order to save time. This private investment involved negotiations and financial sacrifices and the mobilization of more distant family members. And family members used multiple credit cards, running up high debts.[9]

The situation became even more complicated when the doctor at the basic health unit stopped attending. Investments in basic care were increasingly constrained by then-current ultra-neoliberal policies, and he was dismissed. There was no longer a local doctor who would fill geriatric prescriptions, so getting public access to medicines became an even more time-consuming process. Buying drugs at the expensive pharmacy became more common and the family's debts increased. In addition, the daughter's contract as a lunch cook was only temporary. Her uncertain future in relation to employment and income meant that further changes would need to be made.

All these highly complex and complicated negotiations to establish a routine were part of taking care of someone with dementia. Providing a more constant rhythm of everyday life was fundamental for Mrs Aparecida's well-being and for interpersonal relations—on this doctors and family members agreed. Perhaps that is why the term routine was used so often by the family. 'Getting a routine', therefore, involved much more than just following a schedule of activities or following learned patterns. It meant constantly trying to create a rhythm that was challenged on a daily basis.

'Ensemble' and 'routine' as care logics

How do these two kinds of care logics relate to each other? We have seen that the ethnographies produced several analytical categories through which we were able to highlight a number of issues that are at stake in dementia care. These categories not only map specificities of home care versus that of a geriatric outpatient unit, they also mirror a strong overlap of the two worlds. This is why a multi-site (or the juxtaposition of more than one) ethnography is so powerful: it is a methodology that is able to highlight interconnectedness—an interdependency of milieus, theories and value systems seen from different vantage points (see also Chapters 7–9 in this volume).

Medications in both worlds are central for good care; they are desired and, at the same time, dangerous objects. They sometimes do not work for the symptom they were prescribed for; they create other symptoms; they change relationships; they require adjustments and intense dialogues with doctors. Both families and doctors expressed doubts and uncertainty on this subject: it is difficult to know what the effect of one drug among many others is and to follow its long-term effects. The dialogue about the effects and the decision to continue or interrupt a certain medication are sometimes even more complex, since they can involve more than one specialist (geriatricians, clinicians and neurologists among others), different levels of action (such as emergency, basic and specialized care) and different perspectives on prescriptions and what symptoms to treat. In addition, such processes also involve dealing with the performance limits of each professional and, above all, building skills to deal with possible divergences.

From the different positions regarding dementia care, the obstacles to what would be 'good care' change. Some challenges cross both logics: excessive symptoms, accumulation of diseases, damage of networks, economic restrictions and instability of drugs in relation to each other all challenge dementia care.

However, these are problems that cannot simply be attributed to one of the parties, blaming, for example, caregivers who do not know how to provide care, do not judge effects well, are not interested in caring or are part of dysfunctional families—which seems to be the strategy of the ensemble logic. This way of looking at problems ends up corresponding, at least partly, to the notion of 'guilt geography' suggested by Das and Das (2006). According to that perspective, some groups, such as, for example, the urban poor, are classified as responsible for the bad use of biomedical technology. That perspective often puts the guilt exclusively on those groups, although the way that medical technologies are put into practice often involves relationships within the care environment, institutional cultures and even the preferences of doctors for certain prescriptions. From interviews with health professionals we also learned that the government is perceived as guilty in not providing enough resources for good care, and health professionals are therefore forced to juggle two kinds of insufficiency (as well as guilt).

Conclusion

When following the two categories, ensemble and routine, we relate to certain logics of care that are not necessarily opposed, nor are they simply to be analysed separately and then compared. Analysis involves, above all, considering porous relationships and care with tenuous limits. Looking at the logics that emerged in our ethnographies, we rethink and nuance certain truths found in the dementia literature: for example, we are unable to narrate the common opposition between desiring more holistic care and criticize malignant drug care, as is often found among critical social scientists (for example Ballenger et al, 2009; Moreira, 2010; Lock, 2013). We also do not conclude, like some authors do, that biomedical care deals only with the physicality of diseases without considering other factors that mark the daily lives of people and families, often subsumed under the category of care (as a moral obligation) (Kleinman, 1989; Maluf, 2018).

When we, as researchers, opened ourselves up in order to understand the precepts of the studied logics, our initial concepts about care and the use of medications were shifted to some extent, largely due to the intensity of the practice of complex ethnography. By attentively studying practices and relations in two groups, a transformation of our initial hypotheses occurred (Wagner, 2010). We put forward, as Peirano (2004) has argued happens, our own concepts, expectations and choices, at the risk of reshaping them. Ethnography, in this sense, is not only a privileged method for researching care but also a space of powerful theoretical composition regarding care practices.

Notes

[1] Those logics are debated in a more detailed way in Engel (2020).

[2] One part of this research became part of a wider project on dementia coordinated by Annette Leibing, who had also done fieldwork at the same centre. Janaína Aredes contributed to this chapter with her experience of fieldwork in geriatric care in the city of Belo Horizonte.

[3] All names are fictitious.

[4] A controversial medication with limited effect, prescribed for slowing down dementias (Ballenger et al, 2009).

[5] A medication prescribed for more advanced stages of dementia, but with no aim of curing the disease.

[6] A medication prescribed to deal with sleeplessness and agitation. Although its use is not indicated and the excessive use of the medication by the elderly is even considered a public health problem in Brazil, its consumption remains very common for elderly people with or without dementia.

[7] An antidepressant widely used to deal with 'behavioural' symptoms of dementia. To learn more about such behaviour-related medications, and to categorize such types of dementia symptoms, see Leibing (2009).

[8] The history of extensive prescription of psychotropic drugs for a variety of symptoms in Brazil is widely debated by local social scientists (Maluf, 2018). The frequency of such prescriptions relates to greater patient demand for these drugs, circulation of them among acquaintances and addiction processes.

[9] Han (2012) also describes in her work how daily care is entangled in financial relationships and in the creation of debt.

References

Ballenger, J.F., Whitehouse, P., Lykestsos, C.G., Rabins, P.V. and Karlawish, H.T. (eds) (2009) *Treating Dementia: Do We Have a Pill for It?*, Baltimore, MD: Johns Hopkins University Press.

Burlá, C., Camarano, A.A., Kanso, S., Fernandes, D. and Nunes, R. (2013) 'Panorama prospectivo das demências no Brasil: um enfoque demográfico', *Ciência & Saúde Coletiva*, 18(10): 2949–2956.

Chatterji, R. (1998) 'An ethnography of dementia', *Culture, Medicine and Psychiatry*, 22(3): 355–382.

Das, V. (2015) *Affliction: Health, Disease, Poverty*, New York: Fordham University Press.

Das, V. and Das, R. (2006) 'Pharmaceuticals in urban ecologies the register of the local', in A. Petryna, A. Lakoff and A. Kleinman (eds) *Global Pharmaceuticals: Ethics, Markets, Practices*, Durham, NC: Duke University Press, pp 171–205.

Engel, C. (2020) *Partilha e cuidado das demências: entre interações medicamentosas e rotinas*, Doctoral thesis, University of Brasilia.

Han, C. (2012) *Life in Debt: Times of Care and Violence in Neoliberal Chile*, Berkeley, CA: University of California Press.

IBGE (Instituto Brasileiro de Geografia e Estatística) (2020) 'Idosos indicam caminhos para uma melhor idade', *Censo 2020*, 19 March, available at: https://censo2020.ibge.gov.br/2012-agencia-de-noticias/noticias/24036-idosos-indicam-caminhos-para-uma-melhor-idade.html

Kitwood, T. (1997) *Dementia Reconsidered: The Person Comes First*, Buckingham: Open University Press.

Kleinman, A. (1989) *The Illness Narratives: Suffering, Healing, and the Human Condition*, New York: Basic Books.

Leibing, A. (2009) 'From the periphery to the center: Treating noncognitive, especially behavioral and psychological symptoms of dementia', in J.F. Ballenger, P. Whitehouse, C.G. Lykestsos, P.V. Rabins and H.T. Karlawish (eds) *Treating Dementia: Do We Have a Pill for It?*, Baltimore, MD: Johns Hopkins University Press, pp 74–97.

Leibing, A., Guberman, N. and Wiles, J. (2016) 'Liminal homes: Older people, loss of capacities, and the present future of living spaces', *J Aging Studies*, 37(1): 10–19.

Leibing, A., Engel, C. and Carrijo, E. (2019) 'Life through medications: Dementia care in Brazil', *ReVista: Harvard Review of Latin America*, 19(2): 1–6.

Lock, M. (2013) *The Alzheimer Conundrum: Entanglements of Dementia and Aging*, Princeton, NJ: Princeton University Press.

Maluf, S. (2010) 'Gênero, saúde e aflição: políticas públicas, ativismo e experiências sociais', in S.W. Maluf and C.S. Tornquist (eds) *Gênero, saúde e aflição: abordagens antropológicas*, Florianópolis: Letras Contemporâneas, pp 21–68.

Maluf, S. (2018) 'Biolegitimidade, direitos e políticas sociais: novos regimes biopolíticos no campo da saúde mental no Brasil', in S. Maluf and E.S. Quinaglia (eds) *Etnografias comparadas*, Florianópolis: Editora da Universidade Federal Santa Catarina, pp 15–44.

Mol, A. (2002) *The Body Multiple: Ontology in Medical Practice*, Durham, NC: Duke University Press.

Mol, A. (2008) *The Logic of Care: Health and the Problem of Patient Choice*, New York: Routledge.

Mol, A., Moser, I. and Pols, J. (2010) 'Care: putting practice into theory', in A. Mol, I. Moser and J. Pols (eds) *Care in Practice: On Tinkering in Clinics, Homes and Farms*, Bielefeld: Transcript Verlag.

Moreira, T. (2010) 'Now or later? Individual disease and care collective in the memory clinic', in A. Mol, I. Moser and J. Pols (eds) *Care in Practice: On Tinkering in Clinics, Homes and Farms*, Bielefeld: Transcript Verlag.

Peirano, M. (2004) 'A teoria vivida. Reflexões sobre a orientação em antropologia', *Ilha Revista de Antropologia*, 6(1,2): 209–16.

Pols, J. (2015) 'Towards an empirical ethics in care: Relations with technologies in health care', *Med Health Care and Philos*, 18: 81–90.

Pols, J., Krause, K., Driessen A. and Yates-Doerr, E. (2018) 'Thinking with dementia: An introduction to the series', *Somatosphere*, 10 September, available at: http://somatosphere.net/2018/09/thinking-with-dementia-an-introduction-to-the-series.html

Prince, M., Wimo, A., Guerchet, M., Ali, G.-C., Wu, Y.-T. and Prina, M. (2015) 'World Alzheimer report 2015: The global impact of dementia', Alzheimer's Disease International, 21 September, available at: www.alz.co.uk/research/world-report-2015

Thelen, T. (2015) 'Care as social organization: Creating, maintaining and dissolving significant relations', *Anthropological Theory*, 15(4): 497–515.

Wagner, R. (2010) *A Invenção da Cultura*, São Paulo: Cosac Naify.

PART III

Challenges of multi-sitedness

7

Social worlds of person-centred, multi-sited ethnography

Aleksandra Bartoszko

Human services are conducted in a *place*, but places are not always separated entities with solid boundaries. Rather, places form and are part of cultural, social, political, economic and academic networks that depend on and/or conflict with each other. The place-bound understanding of human services is partially due to the dominant academic and political focus on professionals and institutions that deliver services and on their specific meetings with singular clients, users or patients. Usually, however, the service recipients move from one place to another as they must relate to multiple institutions. I argue that the study of human services must account for this physical and conceptual movement *between* places. In particular, the relations between these places need ethnographic attention.

One way to focus attention on the relations that shape human services and experiences with them is through *person-centred, multi-sited fieldwork*, terms I use to describe my research on addiction treatment in Norway (Bartoszko, 2018c). This type of ethnography emerged as I followed (not shadowed—a point I will return to later) one person I call 'Siv' through arenas of care (for example, the hospital, her general practitioner's office, the social services office, her lawyer's office and a patient ombudsman's office) while she negotiated her right to individualized treatment and appropriate medication in opioid substitution treatment (OST).[1] The relationships and trajectories that I traced around Siv as she pursued her preferred treatment became my 'field', consisting of her family, friends, policymakers, health professionals, research institutions, patient and user organizations, professional organizations, pharmaceutical companies, the media and political parties. The OST patient's social world mirrors the relations and dependencies in the realm of human services.

Person-centred, multi-sited fieldwork offered me an ethnographic lens through which to view the multidisciplinary substitution treatment of opioid addiction *and* facilitated examination of patients' lived experiences of the pharmaceutical interventions through their political, epistemic, moral and clinical dimensions. The ethnographic focus on the relations between places of human service where decisions about this patient's life were made revealed the mutual constitution of the social, medical and legal in this particular form of therapeutics, and in human services in general. This chapter describes how my ethnographic approach allowed me to examine the state, the experts and the medical and legal reforms related to addiction treatment and policy.

The Norwegian context

My study emerged in the aftermath of the Substance Treatment Reform in 2004, under which the responsibility for all types of addiction and rehabilitation services (including health, psychosocial and social educational aspects) was transferred from the county level to state-owned regional healthcare enterprises. These enterprises were given the statutory responsibility to ensure that all people in their catchment areas have access to specialized healthcare services. In addition, responsibility for treatment shifted from social welfare services to specialized healthcare; therefore, drug treatment was defined as part of specialized health services along the same lines as somatic and psychiatric care. However, other services provided to substance users remained the responsibility of local municipalities.

The main goal of this reform was to improve the health of drug users through guaranteed access to multidisciplinary specialized treatment for substance addiction (Tverrfaglig spesialisert behandling av rusavhengighet, TSB), standardization of treatment and referrals to treatment through general practitioners (previously, only social services could make such referrals). TSB services focus on comprehensive and individual approaches, with equal importance given to social welfare and health perspectives. In addition, all interventions are meant to be knowledge-based (Helsedepartementet, 2004). Nevertheless, by moving the responsibility for treatment to the health service, the Norwegian government chose a 'medical' approach to addiction, which largely increased the role and influence of medicine and doctors in the treatment field (Skretting, 2005). What is more, persons diagnosed with dependence syndrome (avhengighetssyndrom) were granted patients' rights.

Meeting Siv

Initially, I planned to study how the Substance Treatment Reform unfolded in patients' lives, with these questions in mind: What does it mean to be *a patient* with substance addiction, and what does it mean to have patients' rights or, more precisely, *to receive* patients' rights? Do these rights matter to patients? How do patients understand, apply and negotiate their rights?

Before starting my fieldwork, I presented my project idea to a friend who suggested that I speak to someone she knew who was a 'heroin addicted' patient invoking her patients' rights to continue treatment with morphine.[2] In early November 2013, I was sitting on a train on my way to meet someone who would provide a direction for the rest of my fieldwork; I was on my way to meet Siv. Our first meeting was at Siv's mother's place, where Siv was living in order to help her mother recover from a broken hip. Siv met me at the train station and warned me that we would have to go into the kitchen or her bedroom to talk about 'these things' (drugs, her past and current situation) because her mother did not like to hear about them. After a nice chat with her mother over cinnamon rolls and a cup of tea, we went to Siv's little room where we talked so late that I had to run to catch the last train back to Oslo.

Thereafter, I spent many hours and days in Siv's little room—a room filled with smoke from Tiedemanns Rød 3 tobacco and the smell of instant coffee that we sometimes enjoyed with lemon zest biscotti Siv had baked or with sweets her mother brought us. Cold wind often blew through the window, rustling piles of documents from her treatment team, health reports, printed bills of rights, library books and tufts of dog fur. On that first evening, however, I had no guarantee I would ever meet Siv again. Uncertainty, waiting and sudden engagements and disengagements are a natural part of doing ethnography. A few days after our first meeting, Siv sent me a text message asking if I would join her at her next treatment team meeting. I did so, and thereafter I accompanied her to all these meetings.

Following Siv

Forty-nine-year-old Siv had been an OST patient for three years. One day, the OST doctors discontinued her morphine treatment despite acknowledging statements in her medical records that the 'patient functioned well during her treatment with morphine.' As an alternative, they offered her buprenorphine—a semi-synthetic, long-acting opioid recommended as a first choice by national OST guidelines. Siv had had negative experiences with buprenorphine; however, if she rejected the change, she would be excluded from the program. She invoked her patients' rights and filed a complaint with the relevant entities. Pending a decision, her doctors continued the morphine treatment. For over two years, through negotiations in the clinic, legal complaints and attempts at political pressure, she struggled for what she perceived to be a good quality of life.

While my overall research objective was to explore OST patients' experiences within the context of the Substance Treatment Reform and the granted patients' rights, after meeting Siv I narrowed my focus to patients' experiences with a change of treatment modalities that appeared to be contentious. Patients who wish to switch or keep their prescribed drugs must negotiate with OST staff. The length and intensity of the negotiations vary depending on the patient's situation, preferences, negotiating capital and relationship to the treatment team, as well as the prescribing physician's preferences. Informed and led by Siv's case, I became interested in how patients and practitioners interpret, understand and negotiate user involvement and patients' rights in the context of choosing a medication. By tracing these negotiations, I wanted to explore how local healthcare policies and technologies shape the experience of being a patient and a citizen with opioid drug dependence. Thus, the project moved between social analyses of the institutional practices that shape Norway's response to opiate addiction and of the stories and lives of those affected by those practices. As I was eager to understand Siv's experiences as well as the logics of addiction treatment in Norway, person–centred multi-sited fieldwork came in handy.

Siv was not only my first interlocutor but also the one with whom I spent most of my fieldwork time, and thus, a prominent guide in the field. Since she lived outside Oslo, where I was based, every visit with her substantially limited my other field activities and the possibility of meeting other interlocutors. For instance, to join her for 15-minute doctor's appointment meant four hours of travel time, which prohibited my attending meetings in Oslo the same day. As Siv's case genuinely triggered my interest, I prioritized time with her, and rather quickly decided to take these impractical round trips to get to know Siv and her world better. Another trade-off was that I was rarely able to join her as spontaneously as I could the interlocutors in Oslo or nearby. Nevertheless, I also quickly realized that Siv and her case were rich enough material for my study, and focusing on her story also had methodological and analytical advantages.

During the fieldwork, I witnessed the life Siv had organized for and around herself, particularly in the context of OST treatment. I closely followed her through her daily arenas of care from November 2013 to December 2014. I accompanied her to meetings with OST consultants and appointments with her general practitioner. I attended her meetings with the health and social services ombudsman, supporting doctors and patient organizations. I accompanied her on her weekly visits for urine sample deliveries and to the pharmacy to pick up medications.

However, as anthropologist Todd Meyers (2013) has emphasized, *following* does not mean *shadowing*. I did not shadow Siv's every move. Following includes:

> conversations with concerned family members, friends, parole officers, clinicians, and social workers—often in the absence of the 'study participant'. Rumour, too, was a form of *following*. ...*Follow* would include documenting the work of clinicians and the material administrative traces that remained after someone would disappear—a *file itself*. ...*Follow* would also need to account for and blend the moments of impaired and unimpaired interaction with [my interlocutors]. (Meyers, 2013, pp 5–6)

Anthropologists Eugene Raikhel and William Garriott have noted that this approach involves 'attending not only to lived experience but also to the material out of which lived experience is made: the relations, knowledges, technologies, and affects, as well as the recursive impact of subjectivity itself' (Raikhel and Garriott, 2013, p 10). In my understanding, this implies expanding the network of interlocutors continuously during the fieldwork without giving epistemological priority to any of them. As anthropologist Steffen Jöhncke wrote in his work about a methadone clinic in Copenhagen, 'If there are any "natives" in this account, it is not the users in particular, but all of the people in general who participate in this field' (Jöhncke, 2008, p 7).

Configurations of worlds and organizations

Theoretically and methodologically, I drew inspiration from Raikhel and Garriott's (2013) idea regarding trajectories. They combine the approaches of both interpretative and critical social science, focusing on individual experiences, historical processes and structural conditions. They suggest looking at addiction through the lens of movement: 'movement of people, substances, ideas, techniques, and institutions along spatial, temporal, social, and epistemic dimensions' (Raikhel and Garriott, 2013, p 2). In other words, the study of drug use and addiction should include objects, subjects and the process of meaning exchange between them in different social and cultural contexts. I have used these concepts as a way to approach the life of people with opioid addiction and dependence (and those others involved in their lives) while applying them as heuristic tools in my general analytical thinking.

In practice, to follow networks and study addiction and dependence as trajectories means visiting social worlds embedded in networks of people and organizations. Siv not only made these contacts but mentioned them in conversations with me or others. She frequently referred to patients, professionals and politicians to whom she had spoken by phone or sent emails, or who she simply had heard about. I followed these references conceptually and physically. Through her friendships, including those on the internet, I met other patients in similar situations who contributed comparative insights. These contacts broadened my understanding of Siv's network and the relations that influenced her knowledge of available human services and of herself as a patient, citizen and friend. The snowballing ethnography quickly revealed patients in substitution treatment to be a heterogeneous group that included those leading very 'stable' mainstream lives, those actively engaged in open drug scenes and those in between these two extremes. Siv's friends and acquaintances, and others I met while exploring Siv's world, belonged to all categories, fluctuating among them. Depending on their situation and geographical location, they used different combinations of medications. They also used and switched between different human services: pharmacies, low-threshold sites, specialized clinics, rehabs, detoxification units and urine collection sites, social welfare centres and child protections services, lawyers and dentists. In all these arenas, their status as former, current or future patients in addiction treatment dominated their experience with the services and revealed in more or less explicit ways the relations between these places.

As Figure 7.1 outlines, I travelled to the places where the people to whom Siv referred lived or worked. I sought to have conversations with them and to get a sense of the relationships they shared with Siv. Sometimes these relationships were direct; sometimes not but were important to Siv's understanding of her situation. For instance, I visited representatives of the Directorate of Health not only because she had mentioned them several times but also because these officials were responsible for making and disseminating the national guidelines central to her case. I wanted to understand the logic and process

Figure 7.1: Siv's social world. The arrows indicate types of relations significant for Siv's case. Solid lines indicate relations with direct contact (physical, digital or by phone). Dotted lines indicate relations with actors or institutions that Siv mentioned, for example through reading an article in an addiction journal and referring to a researcher from a Norwegian institution. Double arrows indicate relations which the various actors mentioned and which impacted Siv's case, for example a physician in opioid substitution treatment (OST) referring to the directorate guidelines, or bureaucrats from the directorate mentioning scientific experts they collaborate with.

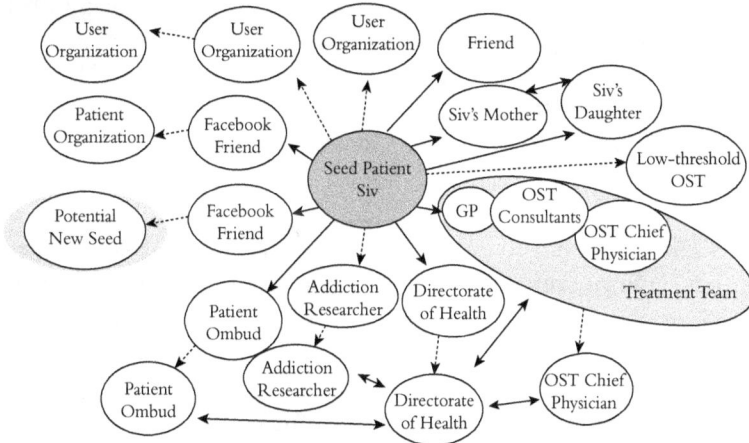

behind the creation of the guidelines and to discuss relevant issues and challenges. I travelled to other cities to speak to doctors who had helped Siv's case by tapping relevant contacts and institutions or by advising on medical issues. I interviewed representatives of the office of the health and social services ombudsman where Siv had filed her complaint. All these persons shaped how Siv understood her situation and how she organized her life at that point in time. In turn, they shaped my understanding of and sharpened my focus on the social relations constituting the field of addiction treatment in Norway.

During discussions and negotiations with her treatment team, Siv frequently mentioned 'current research'. Following the thread, I spoke to addiction researchers, quite a few of whom happened to be OST clinicians serving also as policy advisers, and I gained insight into the linkages between research, clinical practice and policy. With this knowledge, I was in a better position to identify Siv's place in among all these arenas as well as to map the consequences of various connections and relations. When speaking with researchers, clinicians and state bureaucrats, I paid particular attention to the language they used and how they positioned OST patients in relation to other patients and the dependence diagnosis in relation to other diagnoses. I asked OST doctors and consultants how they perceived and defined their work, and I questioned them about the cases I was working on or reading about in the public texts. I was interested in how they navigated the complex landscape of addiction medicine, the challenges they confronted and the possible solutions they had identified. To understand the language of the OST staff and clinical researchers, I took courses in addiction medicine at the Oslo University Hospital (OUS), arranged by the Norwegian Centre for Addiction Research (SERAF), a course that many OST consultants have taken. I participated in OST conferences, workshops and seminars organized by the Norwegian Institute for Alcohol and Drug Research (SIRUS), SERAF and OUS, to mention a few.

Through Siv's relationships, including those with the health and social services ombudsman, patient interest organizations and the county medical officer, I enhanced my understanding of the social world of OST patients. I came to realize that this world is composed of families, friends, policymakers, health providers, research institutions, patient and user organizations, professional organizations, pharmaceutical companies, media and political parties. The network of encounters, relations and trajectories, which I traced around Siv, became my 'field'. Through this multi-sited fieldwork, focusing on the logic of relations, associations and translations between all these actors, places and arenas, I acquired a broad insight into 'emergent discourses' or oppositional practices, not just those that were dominant (Marcus, 1998, p 53). Nevertheless, the important focus was on the person herself. I do not assign any analytical privilege to the networks, as opposed to the human beings, with whom I interacted.

Connecting artefacts, times and spaces

In the early stage of my research, I contacted various user and patient organizations in order to accelerate my fieldwork and identify project participants. I spoke to people with the Norwegian Association for Human Drug Policy (Foreningen for Human Narkotikapolitikk, FHN), local divisions of FHN and the Interest Organization for Substance Misusers (Rusmisbrukernes Interesseorganisasjon, RiO) along with OST patient organizations, such as LAR-NETT and Pro-LAR. I also visited numerous low-threshold organizations and institutions including drug injection rooms (Sprøyterommet), day centres and food distribution facilities. I travelled west to Bergen for a user-initiated protest action, and north to Trondheim to participate in establishing a new patient organization.

These arenas and engagements gave me insights into the complex worlds of people with opioid addiction and dependence in Norway. For instance, as I accompanied Lasse (pseudonym), a fieldworker from the FHN, which distributes sterile equipment to users on the streets in Oslo, I became familiar with the city's 'drug scene', its rituals, people and services. I learned about the life that Siv and my other 'patient interlocutors' had left behind and I could better understand their stories. Lasse became my conversation partner, and these walks facilitated my meeting people who had either 'dropped out' of treatment or who had never applied to it. Even after establishing my own network of patients, I continued to accompany Lasse and to visit the organizations regularly to follow their work.

This multi-sited, multi-temporal approach led me to collect various material cultural productions including texts, pictures and movies. I used this diversity of sources to show how they spoke to each other. For instance, my interlocutors often read and actively used texts that had significant political and social power. I observed how my interlocutors, both patients and professionals, used OST guidelines to negotiate treatment. I wondered: How does Siv read these guidelines? What significance do they have for my interlocutors' lives? What exactly are the guidelines?

As many of my interlocutors, including Siv, spent much of their time online, *netnography* (see Caliandro, 2014; Kozinets, 2015) became an important part of my fieldwork. I followed social media debates and the relations established through them. How did Siv use social media to share her story, and with whom? How did she use social media to learn about patients' rights and treatment possibilities? I read posts in Facebook groups that Siv and other interlocutors joined, participated in through discussions, or simply followed.

I also read medical records and archival files that Siv had collected. They helped me to fill 'gaps of knowledge' and gaps in Siv's memory. I looked at how Siv's life was defined in these records. How did she read and react to these professional and clinical stories? All these texts helped me to understand Siv's life from different angles and perspectives.

I followed the news and read newspaper articles. I looked at the public atmosphere around drug-related issues. Which articles did my interlocutors read and comment on? How did they react? What sense were they making of these readings? Studies within the OST field in Norway often present patients as if they exist on a desert island (for example, Havnes et al, 2014; Nordbø, 2014; Granerud and Toft, 2015; Grønnestad and Sagvaag, 2016), isolated from society, neither reading nor meeting other people beyond the clinics. After one of my interlocutors had read a newspaper article on an action conducted against an open drug scene in Bergen, she exclaimed, "Look what they do with us in Bergen!" I realized then that her attitude and experience with the treatment could not be limited to happenings at the OST office. She filtered her experience through things that were happening to people with whom she identified. This situation illustrates 'the inadequacy of conceptualizing worlds or spaces—such as those of the clinic or of the "street"—as separate from one another' (Raikhel and Garriott, 2013, p 10; see also Meyers, 2013).

Challenges of dissemination

Focusing research presentations on one person brought challenges related to the anonymity of interlocutors (Bartoszko, 2018a, 2018b, 2018c). Some of my interlocutors were well known among other patients, therapists and health agencies because of their diagnoses, non-traditional medication or public disclosures of their histories. Siv was one of these, and the 'uniqueness' of her story was what had triggered my research interest. To use radical anonymization and alter the details of her struggle would mean losing much of the point of her story and our cooperation. Additionally, I would have to construct the research data and risk not meeting the requirements of material reliability and credibility. Researchers who avoid 'unique cases' get standard responses and standard stories from standard patients, rarely gaining insights into nuanced experiences and unconventional choices. Therefore, I weighed the value of anonymity against the value of the knowledge that extensive person-centred fieldwork could create. Since my objective was to explore the significance of the unique, the idiosyncratic and the sometimes provocative in the treatment of addiction in Norway, I decided to anonymize Siv's story only partially. I changed her name, family relations, places and times, and I altered clinical relations and identities of third parties. Nevertheless, some people in the OST field may recognize parts of her story. Siv agreed to my choice and she is familiar with my writing style and the closeness of my presentation to her story.

Another challenge of studying and writing through the lens of one person is the accusation—particular from OST professionals—of being 'partial'. Opioid substitution treatment is part of a charged social and political landscape that links diverse actors and stakeholders, including researchers, health professionals, regulators, policymakers, police, patients, consumers and private industry investors. It is a landscape of hopes, losses, benefits, profits, risks, trust, suspicion and of life and death. My gradual involvement in patients' lives, particularly Siv's life, following their struggles, enabled me to share their frustrations, impatience and feelings of unreasonability on the part of clinicians and of systemic injustice. This kind of involvement and empathy with interlocutors is both a professional blessing and a curse. To detach completely from these feelings is an impossible task and an undesirable one. Yet, it is possible to transform such feelings into analytical creativity, and thus, in my publications I have tried to write with care about all the actors I have met during my fieldwork. Therefore, even if my work critically explores the OST and the Norwegian response to opioid addiction, it is not 'anti-OST', nor is my intention to undercut the social value of the treatment program, medicine or social policy. Rather, I address the various meanings produced by and around these institutions as I explore the unintended consequences met with at the various crossroads that make up a singular human life. Throughout my project, I explored the perspectives of patients, doctors, consultants, researchers and state agents. Nevertheless, my primary goal was to understand patients, their situations and experiences. What challenges do they encounter, and how do they cope with the complex issues of addiction treatment and the polyphony of clinical and political voices?

Conclusion

According to the methodological literature, Siv could be described as my 'key informant' (see Lavrakas, 2008). Nevertheless, I choose not to use that term because doing so would imply, in some ways, that Siv's expertise was more valid than that of others I met during my fieldwork. That is not the case, and in fact, none of my interlocutors fit this category. Although I spent more time with some, I believe it is impossible to create any hierarchy of my interlocutors in relation to their knowledge of local conditions. I did not approach Siv, or others, as an 'expert witness' or as someone 'knowledgeable about local custom and behaviours' but rather as 'an object of systematic study and observation in herself' (Hollan, 2005, p 463). I considered Siv to be my flashlight in the field of addiction (treatment) and related human services in Norway. In the diagram (Figure 7.1) I label her the 'seed' from which the field emerged.

That being said, in publications I often chose to emphasize Siv's subjectivities and the significance of her experience in the field my research had created. I argue that by focusing on her lived experience we get a sense of what was at stake for her in the local, moral and social world that she inhabited. That kind of approach facilitates an experience-near level of analysis. Despite some great person-centred ethnographies having been published and widely recognized as valid scholarship (for example Wadel, 1973; Crapanzano, 1980; Biehl, 2005; Wikan, 2008), many scholarly colleagues still ask what we can learn from the study of a singular person. What is the significance of Siv's story? Pondering his own work, Meyers has written, 'Does *one* symptomatic body—its physiology and psychology, the registers upon which healing and cure are mutually judged, the status and placement of local moral worlds on the individual, and so on—hold meaning for others?' (Meyers, 2013, p 13). I find an answer in his own words as well:

> The focus on the individual is essential not because it privileges singularity over collectivity, nor because it affords—however strangely—uncertainty, but because such a focus simply has the ability to show that generalizations are sometimes unrecognizable when held up against the individual experience of disorder. (Meyers, 2013, p 13)

In other words, complexities are hidden in the larger numbers. My project's methodological and analytical focus aimed to contribute, thus, to the current field of addiction treatment, particularly in Norway, which privileges generalizations over individual experience, certainty over uncertainty and being over becoming.

At the same time, however, by following one patient, my project shapes the field through significant insights into how addiction treatment in Norway works, as I have shown. Person-centred, multi-sited fieldwork gave me access to relations in the field that were based on empirical experiences, not theory. I was able to trace how care happens and how institutions interrelate based on the lived lives of people who must navigate between them all in search of better living. What is more, I was able to explore the specific relations between the state, the research field, the clinic and the law that *matter to the individual*. Such insights are, I argue, crucial for developing policies that account for the lived experiences they aim to address.

Notes

[1] In opioid substitution treatment (OST), an opiate-dependent patient receives a (preferably) long-lasting opioid under controlled conditions as a substitute for illegal opiates. In Norway, the treatment is organized as a multidisciplinary programme, which includes social service centres, general practitioners and specialized healthcare, in which the latter has authority to assess the need for treatment and is responsible for medications. OST national guidelines emphasize user involvement

in treatment and choice of medication. Three medications are recommended for treatment, but guidelines allow others if soundness of treatment is documented.

[2] A short-acting morphine sulphate is usually prescribed to patients in Norway undergoing pain. For treating opiate addiction, morphine is used in countries like Austria, Denmark or Switzerland. It is, however, administered as an exception in Norway, where the most commonly prescribed medications for treating opiate addiction are buprenorphine (Suboxone or Subutex) and methadone.

References

Bartoszko, A. (2018a) 'From hope to §3–1: Legal selves and imaginaries in the wake of substance treatment reform in Norway', *Journal of Legal Anthropology*, 2(2): 1–25.

Bartoszko, A. (2018b) 'The lethal burden of survival: Making new subjects at risk and the paradoxes of opioid substitution treatment in Norway', *Contemporary Drug Problems*, 45(3): 208–226.

Bartoszko, A. (2018c) 'The pharmaceutical other: Negotiating drugs, rights, and lives in substitution treatment of heroin addiction in Norway', PhD dissertation, OsloMet–Oslo Metropolitan University.

Biehl, J. (2005) *Vita: Life in a Zone of Social Abandonment*, Berkeley, CA: University of California Press.

Caliandri, A. (2014) 'Ethnography in digital spaces: Ethnography of virtual worlds, netnography, and digital ethnography', in R. Denny and P. Sunderland (eds) *Handbook of Anthropology in Business*, Walnut Creek, CA: Left Coast Press, pp 658–680.

Crapanzano, V. (1980) *Tuhami: Portrait of a Moroccan*, Chicago, IL: University of Chicago Press.

Granerud, A. and Toft, H. (2015) 'Opioid dependency rehabilitation with the opioid maintenance treatment programme: A qualitative study from the client's perspective', *Substance Abuse Treatment, Prevention and Policy*, 10(1): 10.

Grønnestad, T. and Sagvaag, H. (2016) 'Stuck in limbo: Illicit drug users' experiences with opioid maintenance treatment and the relation to recovery', *International Journal of Qualitative Study of Health and Well-being*, 11(1), doi:10.3402/qhw.v11.31992.

Havnes, I.A., Clausen, T. and Middelthon, A.-L. (2014) 'Execution of control among "non-compliant", imprisoned individuals in opioid maintenance treatment', *International Journal of Drug Policy*, 25(3): 480–485.

Helsedepartementet (2004) *Bedre behandlingstilbud til rusmiddelmisbrukere. Perspektiver og strategier-Strateginotat*, Helsedepartementet.

Hollan, D. (2005) 'Setting a new standard: The person-centered interviewing and observation of Robert I. Levy', *Ethos*, 33(4): 459–466.

Jöhncke, S. (2008) 'Treatment trouble: On the politics of methadone and anthropology', PhD dissertation, University of Copenhagen.

Kozinets, R. (2015) *Netnography: Redefined* (2nd edn), Los Angeles, CA: Sage.

Lavrakas, P.J. (2008) 'Key informant', in P.J. Lavrakas (ed) *Encyclopedia of Survey Research Methods*, Thousand Oaks, CA: Sage.

Marcus, G.E. (1998) *Ethnography through Thick and Thin*, Princeton, NJ: Princeton University Press.

Meyers, T. (2013) *The Clinic and Elsewhere: Addiction, Adolescents, and the Afterlife of Therapy*, Seattle, WA: University of Washington Press.

Nordbø, K. (2014) 'Unge LAR-pasienter; erfaringer om muligheter for endring', MA dissertation, University of Oslo.

Raikhel, E. and Garriott, W. (2013) 'Introduction', in E. Raikhel and W. Garriott, *Addiction Trajectories*, Durham, NC: Duke University Press, pp 1–35.

Skretting, A. (2005) 'From client to patient', *Nordic Studies on Alcohol and Drugs*, 22(1): S167–173.

Wadel, C. (1973) *Now, Whose Fault Is That? The Struggle for Self-Esteem in the Face of Chronic Unemployment*, St. John's, Newfoundland: Institute of Social and Economic Research, Memorial University of Newfoundland.

Wikan, U. (2008) *In Honor of Fadime: Murder and Shame*, Chicago, IL: University of Chicago Press.

8

'Facting' in a case
of concealed pregnancy

Lucy Sheehan

The chapter explores the processes and practices involved in what I refer to as 'facting' in a social work case. Facting refers to the 'doing' of facts, that is, the discovery and use in practice of what are referred to and taken to be the facts for all practical purposes by those concerned (see Garfinkel, 1967; Holstein, 1993; Liberman, 2018).[1] Using work shadowing as an ethnographic method and the unique exploratory mobility it facilitates, data from the case presented allows us to attend to the processes involved in finding, accepting and losing facts across different domains of child protection social work practice. The institutional and analytic mobility described here may be instructive for those engaging in human service ethnography across settings.

Following the story of baby Parker or, more accurately, his social worker Stella as she works with his parents and other professionals to make a plan to care for him safely, I draw upon ethnographic data to illustrate how key facts are situationally organized.[2] I consider the practical organization and utilization of court-centred 'findings of fact'—the term for when a judge determines the facts of a case through trial of evidence—in shaping interactions relating to Parker. In the process, the unique and individual nature of each case, the professional mandate of those involved, the weight given to types of knowledge and expertise in different settings and the role of categories in accomplishing specific work in a given context are made apparent. This gestures towards the need to understand the processual basis of knowledge claims in social work practice, with special attention to the moral and practical work that accompanies them.

The ethnographic shadowing described here shows how seemingly neutral facts are bound up with the communicative practices of people, and with contingent social meanings. The very notion that facts can be 'found' suggests that they exist independently of the processes that organize them, that in effect they are *waiting* to be found. As baby

Parker's story unfolds, it becomes evident that notions of objectivity and neutrality linked with such conceptions of "fact" are themselves resources drawn upon in the practical accomplishment of organizing and sustaining meanings. In that regard, the term facting makes explicit the *practices* involved in turning something (accounts, past actions or inactions, assumed motivations, professional expertise) into 'found' facts, which vary across domains and in their consequences. Such insights reflect back on debates about the practical and epistemological grounds for valuing specific forms of knowledge in social work research, policy and practice.

Extending shadowing into the court setting

Ethnographies of practice recognize that child protection social work involves being on the move and that mobile methods are necessary to attend to practice encounters across the varied spaces that make up the everyday world of social work (Longhofer and Floersch, 2012). As related studies indicate, these include car journeys, home visits and community settings (Ferguson, 2008, 2009, 2016a, 2016b, 2017, 2018; Jeyasingham, 2018). Taking inspiration from these studies, I shadowed social workers in a child and family social work team in a local authority in Wales, moving with them as they worked.[3] I spent seven months with the team, observing practice up to five days per week. To see the journey that families made through Children's Services, I followed social workers as they worked with six families whose stories I came to know well.

Work shadowing as an ethnographic method follows the assumption that it is not a single situation but the predictable rhythm of situations that defines the lives of the people (Trouille and Tavoury, 2019). Shadowing enabled me to take an exploratory approach to observing how social workers accomplish their everyday work with families in specific interactions and how this work unfolds over time. It afforded me institutional mobility in that I was able to shadow social workers in the office, on car journeys, to home visits, meetings and into the court setting. Although court attendance for social workers occurs less frequently than home visits, for example, it requires significant professional time and attention. This is due to the potentially life-changing consequences for families subject to proceedings and the stress experienced by social workers as they are held accountable for professional judgment in a formal, adversarial setting.

The absence of ethnographic studies of child protection social work that have included observations in the court setting suggests that the court remains relatively invisible in social work research.[4] Shadowing over a long period of time enabled me to build a relationship with families and social workers which meant that when they were faced with court proceedings, they consented to my continued shadowing. I did not have the same existing relationships of trust with the legal representatives involved, and my credentials as a child protection social worker, alongside the consent of families, were key to negotiating access to legal meetings and to the court room. Work shadowing enabled institutional mobility which in turn afforded me the analytic mobility to explore how facts are negotiated and put to particular uses in different domains of practice, especially how facts in practice relate to court-centred findings of fact.

Baby Parker

Pertinent events of baby Parker's story unfold in relation to two key facts of the case: a previous finding of fact that Parker's mother Jacqui caused 'non-accidental injuries' to her older child, which shapes how Parker's parents are categorized and treated; and a 'concealed pregnancy' as a fact in the making, which shifts across domains as members discuss whether Jacqui and Parker's father Bob did or did not know she was pregnant. Data excerpts that follow draw primarily on field notes, expanded upon where possible by returning to audio recordings of social work with Parker's family. The excerpts illustrate how key facts are situationally accomplished in mundane negotiations, differing between: a) a car journey, b) a looked-after children's review (LAC review), c) a pre-court meeting and d) within the formal setting of the court. Each scenario begins with data excerpts, followed by an exploration of the interactional practices through which facts are discovered and used in each setting.

Making sense of uncertainty: travelling to Parker's first LAC review

I travel with Stella, Parker's social worker, in her car on the way to Parker's first LAC review, a regular statutory meeting in which family members and relevant professionals meet to discuss the day-to-day care of the child and their care plan. Stella asks me about my experience as a social worker, we briefly discuss our professional backgrounds. Stella tells me she is a newly qualified social worker just entering her second year in practice and that she feels overwhelmed with court work. Keen to find out about Parker's family, I then ask who we are going to see today:

> 'Now we've got baby Parker, born on [date], mum concealed the pregnancy, we were notified by the ambulance service 'cause it was early hours in the morning. I was already working with the mother since her other children are going through proceedings at the moment. I had suspicions but because I was still building my relationship with mum it felt awkward for me to challenge her and ask her that direct question, 'Are you pregnant?', on the first engagement session with me. In my head I was building up trust with mum, she'd finally agreed to see me and have supervised contact and next time, I thought, I'll ask that question [laughs]. But by the next time the baby had dropped. We had to seek immediate interim care order given the risks previously.' (Field notes)

I ask Stella what the risks were and she explains that Jacqui's older children were removed as the youngest was found with numerous unexplained injuries. Jacqui denied that she caused the injuries, instead implicating the father. However, the court made a finding of fact that she caused the injuries. Jacqui is now seeking to appeal the finding which she continues to dispute. I ask Stella what her view is and she explains:

> 'It's really difficult. My view is that she's gone through those assessments in the past, it's not only the professionals' word against hers but there's been a paediatric assessment, a psychiatric assessment for mum and there's different professionals who've been involved and they all seem to believe that, because there'd been a period of time where mum did care for those children. So, it's a difficult one really to overrule professional opinion from the past. It could be that she wants to be given an opportunity to care for this new baby and that is what she is challenging but it could be that she has been telling the truth all along. But how can we know that?' (Field notes)

Troubles-talk between social workers

The social worker specifies two defining elements of Parker's case: a concealed pregnancy and a finding of fact that Jacqui injured her older child. These accounts, the warrants for them and their use in

136

delineating the issues the social worker has to work with create two factual objects, with moral and practical consequences for the account worked up of the mother and for the social worker's account of doing her job properly.

Stella describes herself as a 'newly qualified social worker', a category which a fellow social worker knows comes with the expectation of a protected caseload and support and guidance through any initial court cases. This works as a category that legitimates Stella feeling overwhelmed with court work. It is in this context of telling her troubles that Stella orients to the 'concealment' of the pregnancy as problematic for her professional identity, carefully explaining why she did not 'challenge' Jacqui. The notion of failing to 'challenge' families was highlighted by the review into the death of 17-month-old Peter Connelly who died from severe abuse, with the news coverage that followed associating it with 'bad' social work practice (Haringey, 2009). Stella draws on the social work language of strengths-based practice ("building my relationship", "building up trust") to justify her decision not to verbalize her suspicions to Jacqui. Strengths-based practice brings with it the association of a practitioner seeking to balance their professional authority with collaboration with the family (Oliver and Charles, 2016), and can be interpreted as Stella doing 'good social work'. Taken together, Stella's descriptions of her professional experience, confidence and values do important identity work in this interaction. This moral accounting for a potential failing must be seen in the context of the practical implications of 'concealment' for Stella.

In using the word 'building', Stella makes clear she believed she would be able to address her suspicions about the pregnancy in her ongoing work with Jacqui, that she had more time. Stella laughs when she explains "the baby had dropped", which can be heard in the context of 'troubles-talk' (Jefferson, 1984), in which a person may laugh when telling their troubles but the other party recognizes that this is a serious comment. I understood that Stella's account of not asking about the pregnancy, set against the immediacy with which she describes seeking an interim care order, meant that this resulted in a stressful professional situation. Stella was unable to engage in the pre-proceeding's element of the Public Law Outline process with the family, which she oriented to as problematic, and will thus have to complete her assessment and support work with the family alongside the court process.[5] This account highlights the practical implications of 'concealment' for Stella, linking it with a temporal emergency, which in turn serves as a legitimate reason not to have completed pre-proceedings work that would be accepted by the court.

Concealment and balancing evidence in social work

As Stella works up the fact of concealment, she links it with certain questionable actions taken by Jacqui. These include Jacqui not informing social services of the pregnancy despite already working with Stella in relation to the risks she posed to her older children. This is moral work, in which a mother, who a court deemed responsible for injuring her child, had the opportunity to inform a social worker that she was pregnant again, but instead chose to conceal it, leaving it to the ambulance service to inform the local authority. It is notable that it is Jacqui who is deemed to have concealed the pregnancy, not Parker's father, highlighting the social worker's concern with maternal responsibility. It is possible to draw links between the category of the 'responsible' pregnant woman and the 'good mother' who puts the needs of her foetus and child first (Lupton, 2013; Milne, 2019). This moral account of concealment, linked to maternal responsibility, is bound up with Stella's assessment of Jacqui's past behaviour and the professional assessments underpinning the finding of fact.

Uncertainty is apparent as Stella talks about the finding of fact that Jacqui caused non-accidental injuries to her older child. Stella expresses uncertainty as to whether Jacqui's challenge is motivated by maternal responsibility and a wish to care for Parker or by a quest for justice as her consistent denials that she caused the injuries were truthful. This uncertainty is set against Stella's account of the consistent judgments made by a long list of allied professionals who all believed Jacqui caused the injuries. Stella differentiates between the 'word' of professionals and their 'assessments', placing the latter in higher esteem. Stella's evaluation of the uncertainty underpinning Jacqui's motivations alongside the certainty of past professional assessments links to the weight she places on each source of information. This becomes evident as Stella notes the intractability of past professional judgment. The finding of fact is worked up as credible, holding the authority of a previously mandated course of action, which is used as a resource by the social worker to discursively organize Jacqui and create continuity between past and present (de Montigny, 1995). Knowledge from the past is translated from its original site of production into something more solid, which is used to weigh up and understand the possible intentions and motivations of Jacqui. This in turn has implications for

Stella's assessment of Jacqui, who is painted as a deviant parent who caused injuries to her child.

The practical and moral consequences of facting

The concealment in question is worked up as having moral and practical implications for the social worker and the mother. It is treated for practical purposes as fact, a thing that unquestionably happened. In talking through the finding of fact, the social worker assesses the relative weight to give competing accounts. She privileges the certainty of the medical knowledge bound up in the production of the existing finding of fact over the uncertainty of the mother's account. The moral work that Stella does in accounting for her professional judgment and the uncertainty she works up about the mother's motivations for challenging the findings must be seen in the context of this interaction being reflexively organized as being between two social workers. If Stella had oriented to me as an 'outsider', or had the family been present, it is unlikely that she would have engaged in such accounting or left room for uncertainty as she engaged in facting. Thus, a cautious approach is necessary to the generation of decontextualized statements about research and practice.

Facting here employs the existing finding of fact as a resource to work up the new fact of concealment. Concealment is inextricably tied to the categorization of Jacqui as a deviant parent, already working with a social worker following the court making a finding of fact that she caused 'non-accidental injuries' to her older children. There could be no discussion of concealment without these moral and institutional categories tied to Jacqui's behaviours and intentions. 'Good mothers' do not need to conceal pregnancies. Each category is developed with associated activities that do moral and practical work. As Parker's story unfolds, it becomes clear how these moral and institutional categorizations have practical consequences for how Jacqui is considered by professionals, and for how the long-term plan for Parker develops.

The collaborative management of interactional troubles: attending Parker's LAC review

As we arrive at the venue where the LAC reviews take place, I follow Stella and the independent reviewing officer (IRO) into a room and Stella provides an update about the case, noting that Jacqui is seeking to challenge the finding of fact that she injured her older child. When the IRO is satisfied that she has a handle on recent developments, she shows us into the meeting room where the LAC review will take place. Jacqui and Bob are running slightly late as they have just come from a supervised contact with Parker. The IRO says she's pleased Jacqui and Bob are both here as it is important that they understand how decisions are being made and the things that are being spoken about so they can give their view too. She continues:

"So, I'll just give you a little bit of information, my understanding is that it was a concealed pregnancy so Parker was born quite quickly".

Jacqui and Bob shake their heads in disagreement and the IRO notes this: "Not a concealed pregnancy? What, what was it then, 'cause you tell me what happened and then then I'll hear from Stella then what we've been told". Jacqui explains that they didn't know she was pregnant, and Bob agrees, noting that Jacqui still had her period and that none of his family noticed that she was pregnant either. The IRO asks: "Okay so when was the first time you were aware that you were pregnant?" Jacqui and Bob explain that they found out that Jacqui was pregnant three weeks before Parker was born. The IRO asks if they told anybody at that time and Jacqui explains that she did not because she panicked. The IRO responds with her assessment: "Right okay, so I think that's why it is thought that it was concealed. So, I think, because you found out three weeks before and I understand your anxieties around it because of what happened before, because you didn't tell anybody then that's why it's classed as concealed, okay?" Stella says she agrees, and Jacqui nods.

Collaborative facting between professionals and parents

The IRO makes the fact of concealed pregnancy relevant as she sets out the starting point for the meeting. The mother and father orient to 'concealed pregnancy' as a problematic category requiring immediate work, treating it as an incorrect fact and later offering a mitigation that the pregnancy was concealed because Jacqui 'panicked'. Jacqui and Bob appear aware of the specialist term 'concealed pregnancy' and respond in a manner suggesting they understand the consequentiality of the term for the type of parents they are categorized as, for the purposes of the interaction and more generally.

Responding to this interactional trouble, the IRO adopts a safer interactional strategy. She seeks the parents' opinion before producing her own assessment which takes their opinion into account. This is akin to what Maynard (1989, p 91) terms a 'Perspective Display Sequence', but it is also a strategy that allows Jacqui and Bob to be heard in the meeting. The IRO proceeds with delicacy and caution using neutral language ('What was it then?') as she asks Jacqui and Bob to account for their view of concealment, following up with a statement that she already holds knowledge of what happened passed onto her by the social worker. The parents respond with a denial of any knowledge of the pregnancy, providing grounds for the irrelevance of and resistance to the category. The IRO seeks clarification of when exactly Jacqui and Bob became aware of the pregnancy, making temporality a relevant resource in defining the activities associated with the category of concealment. In seeking detail about when the parents knew and whether they told anyone, the IRO makes explicit the moral consequences of knowing and not telling.

The IRO then gives her diagnosis that it was indeed a concealed pregnancy. In doing so she incorporates Jacqui and Bob's account of 'three weeks' as well as her own understanding of their motivation for not telling, while also distancing herself from the diagnosis ("That's why it's classed as concealed, okay?"). The fact of concealment is established, with the social worker and mother's agreement, allowing all parties to move onto the rest of the meeting in which Parker's care and his care plan are discussed. The IRO works to do facting by cautiously drawing on the accounts provided by the parents while upholding the professional account in a manner that manages potential interactional trouble and allows her to achieve her professional aims in moving on with the meeting. This is achieved as the parents collaborate with the IRO's incorporation of their perspective into her diagnosis, a strategy which serves to mitigate interactional trouble and parental shame.

Tracing the practices through which concealment becomes a fact for the purposes of this interaction makes it possible to see that the members of the meeting are concerned primarily with the management of interactional trouble, which is in turn associated with the moral categorization of the parents and the professional necessity of establishing institutional categories on which to base interventions that follow. The occurrence of the LAC review makes explicit a relationship between the social worker, IRO and 'clients' that works as the context for the interaction. The 'clients' here are parents, but not just any parents, they are deviant parents with a vulnerable child who the court ordered to be taken into care, and the IRO and the parents themselves orient to this identity as they speak. Concealment is associated with timing ("when you knew") and telling ("did you tell"). The parents respond as though they are aware this category has moral implications for this interaction and beyond in the context of an asymmetrical relationship between themselves and the social work professionals. Jacqui, Bob, Stella and the IRO work to align their perspectives for practical, local purposes, and 'concealed pregnancy' becomes a factual object towards which each person orients themselves, even if the meaning remains unsettled.

Negotiating evidence in the solicitor's domain: preparing for a case management hearing

A few weeks later, I accompany Stella to court for Parker's case management hearing (CMH). The purpose of the CMH is to ensure all assessments, statements and reports are set to be completed in advance of a final decision about the child's care. We meet Stella's practice lead, who is a senior social worker supporting Stella with court work, and we wait for the local authority solicitor. We are in a small meeting room adjacent to the court. It is the norm before entering court for parties to proceedings to meet with their legal representatives so they can provide advice and take instructions. The local authority solicitor comes into the room and notes that this case is not about basic care but is about whether Jacqui poses a risk of causing any further injuries on the basis of what happened to her older child. He notes:

> 'I know you shouldn't pre-judge but the background's horrific.'

The solicitor tells his audience that Jacqui's statement about the concealed pregnancy is unclear:

> 'I've asked their solicitors, I want further statements from them about what they say about whether they knew about the pregnancy. It's not quite clear in mother's response... 'cause her statement is poorly drafted. She doesn't accept that she knew three weeks before but then in another one of her responses she says something like she accepts she hasn't been open and honest during the pregnancy but will be open and honest moving forward, but it doesn't say open and honest for three weeks. 'Cause she said she only knew for three weeks but it reads as though she knew for the whole pregnancy.'

The solicitor for the Cafcass guardian for Parker comes into the room to say they are ready to go into court now, and then leaves to find another solicitor.[6] The local authority solicitor continues, asking the social worker and the practice lead if they have seen any statements yet. They have not. The social worker explains that Jacqui remains "fixated on the three weeks before giving birth" as the time that she found out. The solicitor responds:

> 'There is no way on this earth she only knew three weeks before, on baby number three.'

The practice lead agrees, explaining that even the paramedics said in their notes that it is doubtful that the parents didn't know. The guardian's solicitor comes in once again and asks the group if they are coming.

Facting in the solicitor's domain

The solicitor holds the floor for the majority of this interaction as he prepares to go into court. He immediately sets up what the cases is 'about', that is, whether Jacqui is likely to cause physical harm to Parker, given she had been found to have done so to her older children. The discussion of concealment that follows happens in relation to these reported actions. The solicitor's work here entails passing on information about Jacqui's position on concealment, gleaned via her solicitor and via legal statements, establishing inconsistency. He does this by highlighting the discrepancy in the statement to present the concealed pregnancy as a cut and dried issue to the table. He is the only party in the interaction to have had access to the statements and uses this knowledge alongside his critique of the professional competence of Jacqui's solicitor ("Her statement is poorly drafted") to set out his position. In making explicit his plan to establish the facts of concealment in writing in relation to Jacqui's knowledge and the timing of that knowledge, he is doing particular work. He is outlining the information he will seek in the imminent hearing, the type of information upon which the 'fact' of concealment rests, while also making the social worker and her practice lead aware that he is performing his role as their legal representative.

Jacqui's statement, as detailed in the interaction, links the issue of concealment with knowledge, timing and Jacqui's openness and honesty or trustworthiness. This suggests that category of 'open and honest' is important in the context of court work and that Jacqui and her solicitor are aware of the relevance of an assessment of her moral character for the interactions that follow. This moral work can also be seen as the group move on to discuss their assessment of concealment, which serves as a proxy for establishing Jacqui's trustworthiness. In response to the solicitor's description of a discrepancy in Jacqui's account, the social worker puts forward her own account, gleaned directly from Jacqui, that she has been consistent in saying that she only found out about the pregnancy three weeks prior to Parker's birth. The solicitor rejects the credibility of the social worker's formulation by linking Jacqui's prior experience of pregnancy with an expectation of knowledge of what pregnancy feels like, thus linking her 'not knowing' to a breach of the normal expectations of motherhood and to her trustworthiness. The practice lead supports this assertion by drawing in the views of the ambulance service as further evidence.

As the group discuss concealment, they draw upon the artefact of the statement and moral categorizations of Jacqui to create order through the seeming alignment of their perspectives. The different resources drawn upon by the solicitor (the statement, other solicitor's comments) and the social worker (Jacqui's verbal account) to make claims about concealment highlight the differences in the forms of evidence valued in their professional roles. The solicitor's dominant right to speakership makes explicit that the court is his professional domain. The fact of concealment is a matter that the solicitor is gearing up to have settled via the court. This preparation for the hearing is also visible in the frequent interruptions of the guardian's solicitor, hurrying along the interaction. The working up of concealment here relates to professional expertise and competence, alongside moral categorizations of Jacqui. Importantly, the accounts given by Jacqui in previous interactions with the social worker, and reiterated by the social worker here, are of little consequence. The solicitor privileges written evidence, amenable to examination in court, above all. Once again, the collaborative facting practices accomplishing the object of 'concealed pregnancy' do work specific to the interactional and institutional context, and create and sustain order.

The fact of concealment and considerations of care

Attending an issues resolution hearing

The next court hearing I attend with Stella is Parker's issues resolution hearing (IRH). The IRH aims to resolve key issues of contention and set a timetable for the final hearing and any work to be completed. Each legal representative sits before the judge and outlines the position of their client in the order that they sit. The local authority solicitor speaks first:

> 'The parents accept that threshold is met but do not accept
> there was a concealed pregnancy. The local authority is

therefore seeking a finding that the parents concealed the pregnancy. The midwife has provided a statement that supports this and is available to attend the final hearing to give evidence.'

The legal representatives for Bob and Jacqui provide an update to the judge. Bob's barrister questions the proportionality of seeking a finding in respect of concealment. Parker's guardian's solicitor comments:

'The guardian believes seeking finding in relation to the concealment of pregnancy is sensible as likely to be helpful in future considerations of care.'

The judge responds by noting that she will hear arguments on the issue of concealment and outlines the evidence she requires to make a finding:

'I suspect parents don't have much to challenge the midwife, there is perhaps something in the language in the midwife's statement [with a raised eyebrow]—that she was "astounded" that parents didn't know about the pregnancy, but she's the professional. I may need her medical expertise before a finding. The midwife and parents will be witnesses in relation to a finding of fact.'

Finding the fact of concealment

The local authority solicitor brings the issue of concealment to the judge's attention, seeking a finding of fact based on the rationale that it is one of the final issues of contention that requires resolution before Parker's case can be concluded. She offers the midwife's statement and her time as a witness in support of her request. Bob's barrister invokes the term 'proportionality' to support his counterargument.[7] The guardian's solicitor offers further support for the local authority's request, highlighting the valuable role that a finding of fact will play in any future considerations of care. Future care can be heard as being in relation to Parker's care as well as decisions about the care of any children Jacqui and Bob go on to have in the future, thus making explicit the role that a finding of fact about concealment will have in setting limits on the parents in the future. A parallel may be drawn between this and the ways in which the original finding of fact worked to delimit interactional (moral and practical) possibilities with and in relation to Jacqui in the earlier excerpts.

The organization of rights to speakership in the courtroom, with each legal representative speaking directly to the judge, creates a particularly formal interaction, in which there are no verbal utterances that work as continuers and no overlaps in the talk. The statements made by each of the legal representatives must be heard in the context of them seeking to influence the judge's decision. The judge concludes that there is value in making a finding as to whether the pregnancy was or was not concealed, noting her reservations about the parents' disputation of concealment. She makes explicit the written evidence she will accept: the midwife's statement, as well as oral evidence from the midwife and the parents. She also makes explicit the type of medical witness she expects in her court, one who is 'professional', which can be read as meaning one who is factual and neutral in their language, when set against the emotive term 'astounded'. Through this process, concealment becomes something that did or did not happen, and while the judge has her views, the fact must be established through assessing the account provided by the parents against written and oral medical evidence.

The arguments in the IRH and the judge's decision work to set up a plan for evidence about the purported concealed pregnancy to be heard and weighed up at the final hearing. The grey area of motive with which the social worker grappled in the first excerpt does not feature. The practical accomplishment of a plan for the assessment of evidence in the court requires specificity about what will and what will not be considered sound evidence. The notion of 'future care' draws in Parker and any children Jacqui and Bob may go on to have in the future as warrants for the need to establish whether the pregnancy was or was not concealed, whether the parents did or did not know, and therefore whether the parents did or did not conceal information from social services. These warrants also make explicit the professional orientation to the consequences of formally finding the fact of concealment as spanning beyond this interaction, potentially working to delimit Bob and Jacqui's opportunities to care for their children in the future.

Losing the fact of concealment

Attending the final hearing

The last court hearing I attend with Stella is the final hearing for Parker in which a judgment about his long-term care is made. I sit in a meeting room adjacent to the court with Stella, the local authority solicitor and barrister and the barrister for Bob. The legal representatives for Jacqui and Parker's guardian come in and out of the room to discuss key points throughout. Bob's barrister raises the issue of concealment. The local authority solicitor notes that the midwife is unable to attend to give evidence today "and so the family got away with it". Bob's barrister responds in a friendly tone:

'I wouldn't say they got away with it but it's about what the local authority can prove to the court.'

The professionals continue to discuss the case until they are called into court. In court, the usual ritual takes place as each legal representative outlines the position of their client to the judge in the order that they sit. The barrister for the local authority speaks to the judge first, noting that she sent her the amended threshold document:

'The local authority considered proportionality in relation to the concealed pregnancy and will not pursue a finding. The midwife is unable to attend court to offer evidence and waiting on her availability would cause unnecessary delay.'

The legal representatives for the other parties are in agreement. The judge notes that Bob and Jacqui made the 'right' decision not to contest the local authority's plan given their 'difficulties', and agrees with the local authority's plan to place Parker in the care of his aunt.

In the preceding sections, 'finding' the fact of a 'concealed pregnancy' was central to the interactions and to the attendant moral and practical consequences. And then it was 'lost'. In the institutional context of a final hearing in which a decision about Parker's long-term care must be made, the barrister for the local authority draws on the legal concepts of 'proportionality' and 'unnecessary delay' as warrants for the shift in position to not pursuing a formal finding of fact that Jacqui concealed her pregnancy. The term proportionality can be heard to invoke the pressing need to make a decision about Parker's care, which outweighs the support a finding might offer in "future considerations of care" as argued at the IRH. Though the fact of concealment has been 'lost' in the formal sense, attempts to 'find' it and use it as an object to orient to collaboratively were central to shaping, practically and morally, the interactions preceding the final hearing.

Conclusion

Tracing how two key facts—non-accidental injuries and a concealed pregnancy—were worked up and utilized in Parker's case was made possible by shadowing the social worker as she interacted with the parents and other professionals in different domains of practice over time. This enabled an analytic exploration of the relational, contextual and situated nature of the accomplishment of facts as practical objects and their use in collaboration.

The story began with a fact already established via the court, that Jacqui had injured her older child. The moral consequences of this fact painted Jacqui as a deviant parent, a representation of her worked up in different ways across interactions as the case unfolded. The new fact of a concealed pregnancy, which had not yet been formally found via the court, and which thus held greater uncertainty and was ultimately 'lost', worked for all practical purposes as the defining fact of the case. The category of 'concealed pregnancy' was used repeatedly throughout this case, and each time the category and associated activities of the mother and of professionals were re-established with particular local consequences. Facting worked to link parental and predominantly maternal actions (historical and recent) with moral categorizations which had consequences for how the parents worked with and were viewed by professionals in different domains, and therefore for considerations of their capacity to work with social services and to care for their children. The practices employed to 'find' and 'lose' the fact of concealment were tied to their situational context, the task at hand, and the types of knowledge relied upon by different professionals in producing and using such facts. Nonetheless, the fact was treated as a neutral object, existing independently of the task at hand, and was used for the practical purpose of collaboration.

These analyses relate to a few locally situated instances of social work practice with one family, and are used to show how the 'same' fact of 'concealed pregnancy' is negotiated and managed across different domains and through different knowledge systems. Although it may be practical for social workers and fellow professionals to think of the facts of a case as ontologically stable and independent of their particular moment of use, this obscures the practicalities of accomplishing and sustaining meanings. In these excerpts the pregnancy is always referred to as 'concealed', but the work that categorization does changes depending upon the context of its use. Careful thought is needed to understand the basis of knowledge claims in social work practice, with special attention paid to the moral work and practical work that accompanies them. Work shadowing offers a unique combination of institutional and analytic mobility that opens up possibilities for such humanistic and context-sensitive ways of understanding practice.

Notes

[1] Taking inspiration from Garfinkel's (2002) inquiries into the neglected objectivity of social facts, this chapter is concerned with the artful, reality-producing practices through which people produce and sustain social order. Studies exploring this concern include Holstein's (1993) *Court-Ordered Insanity* which deals with facticity in court-related settings, and Liberman's work on Objectivation Practices (2018) which deals with the practices by which we turn our thinking or activities into *objects* (for example, facts) that are publicly available for people to use to order their affairs.

[2] This chapter draws on data from a larger ethnographic research study into social work practice under the Public Law Outline (PLO). The PLO sets out the rules that the local authority and thus social workers must follow when considering whether to apply to the court to make an order to protect a child. The way in which social workers go about their daily practice is likely to differ considerably from that envisioned by legislators. Studies into the PLO process that have drawn on observations have focused on pre-proceedings meetings (Broadhurst et al, 2012; Mason et al, 2013) and on threshold talk in edge-of-care cases (Doherty, 2017). Yet how facts are negotiated and unfold through PLO remains a topic in need of exploration. Describing 'facting' in social work practice with families as it unfolds, grounding descriptions of social work practice in members own understandings and orientations, contributes to this.

[3] The team worked with families with children in need and with child protection concerns. They took referrals, visited family homes, attended multi-agency meetings, completed assessments and developed plans with families to support them in safely caring for their children. The support and interventions offered to families followed a gradient of risk, from 'care and support' and 'child protection' to 'PLO' cases.

[4] Exceptions include de Montigny's (1995) account of producing a report to the court and attending a hearing, based on examples with 'imaginatively elaborated case details' drawn from his practice as a social worker.

[5] The Public Law Outline (PLO) 2008 and 2014 brought into effect the practice of formal pre-proceedings work with children and families, wherein parents are entitled to legal advice as they work with the local authority to make life safer for their children. The aim was to divert cases away from court where possible, and to ensure those that reached the court could be resolved quickly. The 26-week time limit for the conclusion of proceedings under PLO is based on the reasoning that decisions must be made within the developmental time frame of the child, and that the child's social worker and Cafcass guardian have sufficient expertise to comment upon this.

[6] The Children and Family Court Advisory and Support Service (Cafcass) Cymru is an organization in the Welsh government that provides a voice for any child in Wales that is involved with the family justice system. Parker is a party to proceedings and is represented by a Cafcass guardian, who in turn has legal representation.

[7] Proportionality is an important term in care proceedings. It is linked to the European Convention of Human Rights (EC Article 8) and requires that the

level of intervention corresponds with pressing need, and is proportionate to the legitimate aim of the intervention. Welfare evaluations that concern the 'best interests' of the child go hand in hand with proportionality evaluations in which the starting point is the principle of least intervention.

References

Barfoed, E.M. and Jacobsson, K. (2012) 'Moving from "gut feeling" to "pure facts": Launching the ASI interview as part of in-service training for social workers', *Nordic Social Work Research*, 2(1): 5–20.

Broadhurst, K., Holt, K. and Doherty, P. (2012) 'Accomplishing parental engagement in child protection practice? A qualitative analysis of parent-professional interaction in pre-proceedings work under the Public Law Outline', *Qualitative Social Work*, 11(5): 517–534.

De Montigny, G. (1995) *Social Working: An Ethnography of Front-Line Practice*, Toronto, ON: University of Toronto.

Doherty, P. (2017) 'Child protection threshold talk and ambivalent case formulations in "borderline" care proceedings cases', *Qualitative Social Work*, 16(5): 698–716.

Featherstone, B., Morris, K., White, S. and White, S. (2014) *Re-imagining Child Protection: Towards Humane Social Work with Families*, Bristol: Policy Press.

Ferguson, H. (2003) 'Outline of a critical best practice perspective on social work and social care', *British Journal of Social Work*, 33(8): 1005–1024.

Ferguson, H. (2008) 'Liquid social work: Welfare interventions as mobile practices', *British Journal of Social Work*, 38(3): 561–579.

Ferguson, H. (2009) 'Performing child protection: Home visiting, movement and the struggle to reach the abused child', *Child and Family Social Work*, 14: 471–480.

Ferguson, H. (2016a) 'How children become invisible in child protection work: Findings from research into day-to-day social work practice', *British Journal of Social Work*, 47(4): 1007–1023.

Ferguson, H. (2016b) 'What social workers do in performing child protection work: Evidence from research into face-to-face practice', *Child and Family Social Work*, 21(3): 283–294.

Ferguson, H. (2017) 'Researching social work practice close up: Using ethnographic and mobile methods to understand encounters between social workers, children and families', *British Journal of Social Work*, 46(1): 153–168.

Ferguson, H. (2018) 'Making home visits: Creativity and the embodied practices of home visiting in social work and child protection', *Qualitative Social Work*, 1: 65–80.

Garfinkel, H. (1967) *Studies in Ethnomethodology*, Englewood Woods Cliffs, NY: Prentice-Hall.

Garfinkel, H. (2002) *Ethnomethodology's Program: Working out Durkheim's Aphorism*, Lanham, MD: Rowman and Littlefield.

Hammersley, M., and Atkinson, P. (2019) *Ethnography: Principles in Practice* (4th edn), Abingdon: Routledge.

Haringey LSCB (2009) *Serious Case Review: Baby Peter*, London: Haringey LSCB.

Holstein, J.A. (1993) *Court-Ordered Insanity: Interpretive Practice and Involuntary Commitment* (vol 757), Piscataway, NJ: Transaction Publishers.

Jeyasingham, D. (2018) 'Place and the uncanny in child protection social work: Exploring findings from an ethnographic study', *Qualitative Social Work*, 17(1): 81–95.

Jefferson, G. (1984) 'On the organization of laughter in talk about troubles', in J.M. Atkinson and J.C. Heritage (eds) *Structures of Social Action: Studies in Conversation Analysis*, Cambridge: Cambridge University Press, pp 346–369.

Liberman, K. (2018) 'Objectivation practices', *Social Interaction: Video-Based Studies of Human Sociality*, 1(2), https://doi.org/10.7146/si.v1i2.110037.

Longhofer, J. and Floersch, J. (2012) 'An example of social work practice ethnography', in S. Becker, A. Bryman and H. Ferguson (eds) *Understanding Research for Social Policy and Social Work*, Bristol: Policy Press, pp 305–307.

Lupton, D. (2013) 'Infant embodiment and interembodiment: A review of sociocultural perspectives', *Childhood*, 20(1): 37–50.

Masson, J.M., Dickens, J., Bader, K. and Young, J. (2013) Partnership by law? The pre-proceedings process for families on the edge of care proceedings, available at: https://papers.ssrn.com/sol3/papers.cfm?abstract_id=2281146

Maynard, D.W. (1989) 'Perspective-display sequences in conversation', *Western Journal of Communication*, 53(2): 91–113.

Milne, E. (2019) 'Concealment of birth: Time to repeal a 200-year-old "convenient stop-gap"?', *Feminist Legal Studies*, 27(2): 139–162.

Oliver, C. and Charles, G. (2016) 'Enacting firm, fair and friendly practice: A model for strengths-based child protection relationships?', *British Journal of Social Work*, 46(4): 1009–1026.

Trouille, D. and Tavory, I. (2019) 'Shadowing: Warrants for intersituational variation in ethnography', *Sociological Methods and Research*, 48(3): 534–560.

Wastell, D. and White, S. (2017) *Blinded by Science: The Social Implications of Epigenetics and Neuroscience*, Bristol: Policy Press.

9

Ethnographic challenges of fragmented human services

Tarja Pösö

Child protection—as with many other types of human services nowadays—takes place in many locations: public administration buildings, family homes, children's homes and courts, just to mention some. Such locations have provided the context for many well-known, child protection ethnographies (for example Pithouse, 1998; Dingwall et al, 2014). More recent ethnographies examine movements between these different locations: moving from an agency to the family home or to the court, or having discussions with children while driving from one location to another (Ferguson, 2016). As more and more social work is done virtually and different forms of online technologies influence social work practices and interaction therein (Boddy and Dominelli, 2017), even virtual spaces have become a research interest.

As a result, ethnographic research in human services should not take for granted that the choice of location as the field of study is straightforward. Increasingly, the idea of the field in ethnography as concretely sited does not coincide well with the variety and dynamics of the fields where human services function. Fieldwork carried out in a child protection office provides a different view on the legitimacy of decision-making than ethnographic work on social media sites where service users advocate for their rights in child protection. Nevertheless, both sites could be interesting for a researcher studying decision-making.

From the point of view of fields and locations, the fragmentation of child protection is an important contextual factor to take into consideration. An important broader context is that fragmented service production is seen as related to the impact of neoliberal ideology on public administration, dividing child protection and services into tasks (for example the assessment of needs, service plans, decision-making, in-home services vs out-of-home care services vs after-care services) carried out by different practitioners in different organizational settings.

Procedural matters have gained in importance. Some statutory services are outsourced to for-profit or non-profit organizations and their 'locations'. This means that children and families need to go between different agencies, locations, service providers and practitioners. Practitioners need to spend more time in multi-agency cooperation and information exchange and on the move between different locations. The fragmentation of service provision has caused concerns that the care and service trajectories of children, parents and families are guided more by organizational imperatives than by the families' needs and rights to services (Featherstone et al, 2014).

The multiple locations and functions of service provision and shattered care trajectories of child protection pose a challenge to ethnographic research design as the key elements for ethnography are 'being there' ('thereness') and providing a holistic description of the field. Methodological issues are not isolated but rather inevitably integrated in what and how we know about child protection (for example Andenaes, 2014). That is why the way in which we understand and define the field and the locations to be studied becomes an integral part of the findings and meaning of the study. When the 'field' is understood as a social construct, according to Streule (2020, p 428), 'the ethnographic field-site transforms into a research object of its own, multiply related with local, regional and global processes and not delineated by administrative boundaries'.

The ethnographic challenge

The challenge nowadays is that ethnographic studies on/in child protection (and many other similarly organized forms of service provision) should recognize their present forms of organization and, accordingly, use that understanding to inform methodology. Self-evidently, the forms of service provision should not determine how ethnography is carried out; instead, methodological knowledge should be constantly reflected on and contrasted with knowledge about the nature and form of the human services under study and vice versa. In a word, the challenge is to be 'reflexive'.

The following discussion builds on a variety of empirical studies of child protection that used a range of ethnographic approaches and that were carried out by myself in Finland and by other researchers in Finland and elsewhere. Texts about ethnography are typically written by those who have done ethnography or by those who write about ethnography as a method among other qualitative methods (Cunliffe, 2010), and sometimes by those who hold both positions. Writing this chapter, I hold both positions but also take on a third one, that of a speculator: I muse over ideas of what ethnographic research could be like in the current, fragmented child protection situation and reflect on the empirical definition of the 'field' as a location in the process. The study by Dingwall, Eekelaar and Murray (2014), described in the following section, has been path-breaking and inspired me to think about what this study, originally carried out in the early 1980s, would be like in the present child protection context.

Dingwall, Eekelaar and Murray's ethnographic field

It would be an overstatement to say that child protection research has acknowledged the many sites of services only recently. In Dingwall, Eekelaar and Murray's (2014) classic research, consisting of the original study from 1983 and updates in 1995 and 2014, a team of law, sociology and social work researchers studied the identification and screening of problems of children and families in frontline practice in a variety of organizational settings: child welfare agencies, home visits, health clinics and hospital admissions as well as court hearings. The particular UK agency context is described in detail and its particularities are drawn up in contrast with the US context (Dingwall et al, 2014, pp 10–17). At the sites, observations were made, interviews done and documents were collected. As a result, the study highlights how 'facts' about children's conditions are established and how they are renegotiated through the process that aims to 'protect children' (for more on the process of 'facting', see Chapter 8 in this volume). Furthermore, while doing that, the study introduces concepts such as children as social and clinical objects and the rule of optimism, just to mention a few, which have been widely influential in subsequent research in child protection. The latest reprint of the study from 2014 includes a preface written by Robert Dingwall. In that preface, the rule of optimism and organizational cultures discussed in the original study are revisited from the perspective of the early 2010s.

When describing the scale of their study, the authors (Dingwall et al, 2014) acknowledge that the implementation of their research design required a lot from the 'field'. As they write:

> Our first debt must necessarily go to the participating authorities and their staff for accepting and welcoming us into their everyday practice. This was not always convenient and was sometimes intrusive, but our presence was received not merely with tolerance and good humour but with the

confidence that a published scrutiny of the complexities of child protection would eventually benefit staff, clients and citizens. (Dingwall et al, 2014, p xii)

This acknowledgement of the input of practitioners and authorities, quite typical for ethnographies in human service organizations, is a reminder that research carried out at many sites means that the actors at the sites need to accept researchers there. In this extract, the motive for acceptance is described as the usefulness of the study. It underlines the uniformity of practitioners and agencies in their motives, as a common interest in knowledge production is emphasized. Despite the variety of agencies involved, they are said to share a consensus about their commitment to the research. I will return to this inter-agency consensus assumed by the authors later. Let me first turn to the nature of child protection sites.

Multi-sitedness nowadays

The holistic and intersectional study by Dingwall et al (2014) would nowadays be described as a multi-sited ethnography. However, the agency system, so prominent in that particular study, has evolved to be even more complex. The chain of practitioners and agencies involved in identifying, screening and making decisions about the risks for children's well-being includes not only the child protection, healthcare and legal systems but also the education and early education systems and, most importantly, different services that are being outsourced from public authorities to NGOs or for-profit service providers. This is a tendency well known in many European countries and elsewhere (Meagher et al, 2016; Kotkas, 2016). The sites to be studied have equally become more diverse, and the agencies' motives to join in research—or to withdraw from it—may have become more diversified. Although public accountability is an issue for all service providers in child protection, welcoming an ethnographer to participate in the everyday life of the agency might be a challenge for some and become an obstacle for inter-agency consensus about the research. A for-profit agency, for example, might not wish to share its treatment methods as they may consider them their own private property, an important element in competitive bidding among other similar service providers.

It is not, however, only human services that increasingly function across several sites and that thus require multi-sited research methodologies. The notions of, for example, 'global ethnography'—'ethnographically observable grounded globalisation' (Burawoy et al, 2000)—and 'anthropology of welfare'—social anthropology studying people, social institutions, networks and organizations involved in welfare services (see Edgar and Russell, 1998)—and in particular urban sociology and human geography (for example Streule, 2020) have arisen in recognition of the relevance of multiple sites for ethnography. The notion of 'mobile ethnography' has emerged as a response to the challenge of capturing the dynamics between different sites. 'Being there' is thus recognized to include moving along with people and the networks and organizations relevant to the study (for example Novoa, 2015). When people—children needing protection, parents requesting help and services as well as practitioners doing their work—move across different places, institutions and networks, it is sensible to suggest that an ethnographic researcher moves along with them.

Multi-sited and mobile ethnography is, however, influenced by the very nature of child protection. Child protection is not only about public agencies, places and networks but also about private ones. When doing their work, practitioners need to enter the private domains of families: their wishes, hopes, past experiences and fears as well as their homes, kitchens and bedrooms. Home visits can be described as threshold crossings: crossing the concrete threshold is not a big step to take, but it is a big moral step to enter someone's private home, especially if one is not welcome (Ferguson, 2011). A researcher should not do so without permission being given by the authorities, ethics review bodies and the residents of the house. If permission is given, moving around in the home may still not feel easy, as it is influenced not only by the space but also by the relations within the home. The concept of intimate child protection is helpful in highlighting these special complexities in doing research in the private spaces of child welfare. Intimate child protection is a term proposed by Ferguson (2011, pp 3–4), who writes that child protection deals exclusively with children's and families' lives in their homes and that the homes are intimate spaces. Child protection practitioners explore, support and sometimes restrict the very personal lived experiences in those intimate spaces. That makes child protection intimate and humane (Ferguson, 2011). The same holds for research: moving along with people between different places inevitably means moving into their intimate sphere too. Embodied fieldwork, typical for ethnography (Coffey, 1999), is influenced by this privacy and intimacy. This intimate and private nature characterizes research in child welfare, regardless of the concrete site—whether a public or a private space—which is something that needs to be considered.

There may be differences in the degree of intimacy and privacy across the sites. Social media sites of child welfare advocacy groups present the private and intimate nature of service-use experiences, based on the choices and intentions of the members (Stang, 2018). 'Private' then becomes very 'public' and the boundaries between the public and private become blurred. The social media sites can demonstrate the erosion of privacy, the politicization of privacy or just a new agenda for privacy in this time when personal experiences and narratives matter so much (Boddy and Dominelli, 2017; Plummer, 2001). The blurred public-private nature of these child welfare services does not make the social media sites less or more 'real' or 'interesting' for ethnographic research. Despite their richness, they may provide equally limited and narrow insights into child welfare as a single visit to a child's bedroom in his/her parental home. The methodological, social and moral obligation of the researcher is to acknowledge the fragmental nature of any site of child protection.

Navigating multi-sitedness and its gatekeepers

'Private' as a term in child welfare includes the meaning of intimacy but also that of service production: child welfare services are outsourced to service providers which are 'private' (for-profit) or non-profit. We've already suggested that this type of 'privacy' may create obstacles for a researcher due to a for-profit organization's interest in regulating and even in restricting the disclosure of its practices. For a researcher, it might not be a straightforward process to negotiate research access to a private children's home and to learn about the organization's motives for denying or granting access. As gatekeeping negotiations pose a challenge to research in countries such as Finland, where the overall majority of children's homes are run by for-profit agencies, alternative ways to get access to those services are necessary. 'Private' does not, after all, mean that everything is 'secret'.

One way is to examine what can be learnt from the public presentations of the for-profit organizations. They present their services to public authorities in procurement processes and they also market their services otherwise. Marketing is often done on 'public' internet websites or at conferences and gatherings of practitioners and policymakers, sometimes hosting more than 1000 visitors even in a small country such as Finland. They also provide (non-secret) reports on licensing processes which, as documents, provide an insight into the service rationales as presented in a formal setting (Pålsson and Shanks, 2020). The marketization of child protection could, in general, provide a number of opportunities for researchers to get access to 'private' services. In this case, the focus of interest needs, however, to be viewed from a different perspective than that of the study of Dingwall et al (2014): instead of discussing what happens in practice, the analysis should be concerned with the topic of what is promised when child protection services are provided.

However, these two focuses on 'practices in situ' and 'performances of practice' may have crossovers. In one study, we were interested in what happens just after the decision to take a child into care has been implemented. We wanted to follow up on care as it was experienced by children and young people and as it was viewed by their social workers for the first six months, and after that, for another six months. We employed a variety of methods, one of them being interviews with children in their substitute homes. The interviews focused on their experiences of entering and being in care. In one of the interviews, a young girl described how she had been taken to her new institution after the decision about her care order had been made and said that:

> 'I don't know who I came with, it was some sort of transport service thing…Some sort of men…I can't remember much about it.' (Field notes)

The remark about "some sort of transport service thing" surprised us as we could not work out what transport services could mean. We mentioned this in a workshop with social workers and they recognized the reference immediately: transport services referred to services which municipalities sometimes hire to bring children into substitute homes. Accompanying children to their placements used to be the responsibility of social workers or the carers in the substitute homes, but due to the shortage of staff and other resources, the task had been outsourced to for-profit agencies. The 'some sort of men' in the extract were most likely men working for such outsourced transport services. The transport services were employed in a transition situation which the girl later in the interview described as being emotional and mentally difficult. She was taken into public care in a state of deep anxiety, and the act of accompanying her to the substitute home was done by strangers. Her way of describing the episode reflects an analysis by Andenaes (2011), who writes critically about the ways in which child protection is represented in language, using the passive and depersonalizing vocabulary, and in which child protection placements, for example, tend to construct the child as an object to be handled as a kind of parcel. The girl indeed described her experience as if she had been a parcel delivered by transport services (Pösö, 2019). This finding led us to explore further what the transport services were about, and that is how we ended up studying the websites of these agencies.

At the time of the study, we found two transport agencies which clearly defined child welfare transport as part of their services. We looked at the written representation of these services (but excluded the visual images on the websites—although interesting—depicting staff members as friendly, smiling men in their cars or simply bright vans) in order to gain an understanding of how the transport services profile themselves in the field of child welfare and how they profile the children involved in their services (Pösö, 2019). It became obvious that on the websites the children with the most complex needs are portrayed as very 'difficult children' who needed secure and specialized transport, and the transport services are shown as providing staff who are well trained for dealing with these 'difficult children'. Their skills were described as being those of psychosocial crisis work, including skills in dealing with aggression. Transitions from the home to a substitute home were presented as separate segments which could be outsourced to people not known to the child.

As a personal experience, the girl's description of her entry into care informed us about the misrecognition of her situation: she did not require 'safe transport' but care. Instead of describing herself as 'a difficult child', she described her anxiety, sadness and how she ended up in a psychiatric hospital after a short stay in a children's home due to the emotional stress. On the other hand, the inclusion of outsourced transport services in the child protection system informed us about the readiness of the system to overlook the child's needs for holistic, relationship-based care, and how it builds on—and intensifies—the fragmentation of child protection services. I also demonstrated the ongoing shift between the responsibilities of the state and those of private service providers (Pösö, 2019). Interestingly enough, the transport services became an issue for the parliament, which changed legislation in 2019 and stated that 'transport services' may not be outsourced as they employ the use of public power. The amendment targeted runaway children in particular and their transport back to their substitute homes, but its implications became relevant for situations such as that of the girl above as well. The very mundane practice of transporting children and providing transport services had become an issue of the contract between public institutions and for-profit service providers, and an issue for the legislative bodies to guide. For a researcher, the intertextuality of the transport services websites, interview data with children in care and the new legislation provides an extremely interesting insight into human services.

Methodologically, one could ask how the study described is related to ethnography, as it did not include periods of travelling with the transport services or staying in children's homes observing how children arrived there. Being there—thereness—is, after all, an essential element of ethnography, which in this study was replaced only by some snapshots of practices in situ and practice performances. Many relevant forms of practice were excluded. For example: In what kind of circumstances did social workers employ transport services and what was the reasoning behind the use of such services? Although observation-based studies of these issues would be important (if access for research was allowed), there is some methodological potential in the snapshots as well. If the fragmented nature of current human services is acknowledged, the snapshots become useful in providing an ethnographic understanding of human services provided in little segments.

Fragmented time-in-place

Time-in-place has become a factor for human services to measure, as it is seen as indicating quality (for example the timeliness of services), efficiency (for instance the number of tasks completed according to a given timeline) and as a tool for regulating the delivery of services (prioritizing the services according to the urgency of the need, for example). In child welfare, the timelines for investigating referrals as well as for making assessments and decisions structure social work. Time-in-place is embedded also in the decision to remove a child from the parents' care into public care: the timeline for the placement may be 'permanent', 'temporary' or 'for the time being'. Children, parents, social workers and substitute carers position themselves on these different timelines, expecting either a quick return or no return of the child into his/her birth family. What time means in child protection can thus fluctuate from some hours to the full length of childhood.

Research in child protection tends to focus on the moments during which decisions or assessments are made or prepared for. The study by Dingwall et al (2014) looks at those moments, but not only at one moment, rather at sequences of them, as the research follows the process from initial referrals to final court decisions. When putting these moments together, a holistic view emerges. The time spent on each section of data collection varied, but each of them spanned several weeks, and the total length of the research was five years (Dingwall et al, 2014, p 19). Five years is a considerable period of time for an ethnographic study in child welfare.

Long-lasting research is not, however, uncommon among ethnographic studies in general, which tend to emphasize the importance of learning to know one's field well. To do that, the researcher is typically instructed to spend a good amount of time in their field. The common feature of time in ethnography is put into words by Cunliffe as follows:

> It [ethnography] differs from other approaches to research in that it requires immersion and translation. Ethnography is not a quick dip into a research site using surveys and interviews, but an extended period time in which the ethnographer immerses herself in the community she is studying: interacting with community members, observing, building relationships, and participating in community life. (Cunliffe, 2010, pp 227–228)

She continues by saying that temporality in ethnography means long-lasting relations with the field instead of snapshots, which are just 'quick dips' (Cunliffe, 2010, p 229). This categorical view could, however, be contested, as snapshots and 'quick dips' may also provide some ethnographic understanding. Cultural criminology, with its notion of 'instant ethnography', is important in this respect (Ferrell et al, 2008, pp 176–180). The reasoning behind instant ethnography is that if an act of crime can occur in an instant, studying such moments should be valued by ethnographic research. It is stated that 'perhaps conventional methods, even conventional ethnographies, have looked too long at the background and the beforehand, and not enough at the moments in which background factors explode into meaning and emotion' (Ferrell et al, 2008, p 180). In that view, it is not only the nature of crime but the speed of late modernity that requires research to approach temporality in a new way.

In child protection, if the variety of meanings of time and temporality is taken into account, ethnographic research into child protection could also include studying snapshots of moments. Such snapshots could include, for example, those previously mentioned moments when the researcher steps over the threshold of a private home to shadow a social worker during her home visit (Ferguson, 2011) or when the expressions of anger, fear and injustice by the young residents change the residential atmosphere and soundscape in a flash (Pösö, 2004). For example, I still remember a particular moment in a reform school when the young residents started shouting and banging the doors, and how dramatically and quickly that action changed the placid early evening atmosphere. That moment made me see how alert the staff became in a fraction of a second and how powerfully the tensions between the residents and staff came to the surface.

If snapshots are to be understood further in terms of performances of social life in all its variety, documents of child protection become of fresh interest for research as representing standstill moments of services. The empty templates used for recording services in child protection, for example, could provide a rich view of the institution's ways, often taken for granted, of addressing children and parents and their troubles. The templates as well as the client information systems guide the ways in which practitioners present their clients to the variety of readers of those documents (Berrick et al, 2018). In one study, we looked at the letter templates which child protection agencies use to invite children to participate in hearings in which their opinion about the care order removal is discussed (Hoikkala and Pösö, 2019). Those hearings are of particular legal and administrative importance, to say nothing of their importance to the individual(s), as the views of children over 12 years old have an impact on the decision-making protocol. Therefore, it matters that children are properly informed when invited. We were told by practitioners that the invitation letter they send is only a part of the formalities as the Finnish public administration requires that such invitations have to be validated on paper and the letter functions as a form of validation. In the practitioners' view, the 'real' invitation is given by phone or in meetings with the child in question, and these invitations allow for a more inclusive approach to explaining the purpose of the hearing and making certain that the child understands the reason for the invitation. We did not have any access to observe these interactional moments, but we had access to the empty templates used by the agencies as well as to the actual letters sent to children. Our hypothesis was that if children are perceived as bearers of rights—as they are in this hearing practice—this should also be reflected in the institutional documents of decision-making. Nevertheless, we came across letters sent to children of 12 years of age that were similar to the letter templates sent to parents. The letters included information about the legal sections, times and places for the hearing and similar issues, but one may wonder how accessible that information is for children. For us, the templates and letters demonstrated that children are not treated as the bearers of their rights in a particularized rights-based way; rather, adults are the standard for these hearings and their arrangements (Hoikkala and Pösö, 2019).

The challenge associated with snapshots of live or standstill moments in child welfare is to know how to choose the relevant moments. Is the letter template relevant or just arbitrary when it comes to understanding how child welfare, as a form of human service organization, concretely realizes children's rights in its services? Long-term involvement helps to understand the moments and their meanings. Snapshots of moments and long-term ethnography are thus not mutually exclusive. Long-term ethnography may, however, not always be feasible. Ethnographic studies including longitudinal or follow-up approaches to child welfare institutions can face changes in the field: for example, it may not be possible to revisit the child welfare institutions as they have been closed down (for example when they are abolished as 'locations'), undergone changes in terms of staff, clientele and profile, or been replaced by other types of institutions (Berridge and Brodie, 1998; Pösö, 2010). These changes demonstrate the dynamics of service provision and may be very informative as such. For long-term research design, they mean unpredictability.

Whose field?

One could think that shadowing a child (and/or the parents or the whole family) in the service system would be a core part of ethnographic studies of child protection. However, it is mainly interview studies with children (and their parents) that have explored the system from their standpoint, whereas the ethnographic view on child protection has largely been seen from the perspective of practitioners. For example, researchers have focused on shadowing practitioners in particular (Ferguson, 2010). Studies on residential child protection and after-care are an exception, as in those settings researchers have worked with children in order to understand child welfare from their point of view (for example, the institutional ethos, practices and staff as seen by young residents in Henriksen, 2019).

Textbooks highlight 'anthropological strangeness' as the mindset of ethnographic research. In child protection research, that mindset is challenged by many factors. We all know something about child protection just by virtue of being consumers of media. Media set certain parameters for our conscious or unconscious views of what child protection is about: it is about failures of recognition, malpractice or even losses of children's lives as the media tends to portray that kind of image across different countries (Warren, 2015; Biesel et al, 2020). As we all have been children and have experienced what it is like to depend on other people's care, and as many of us take care of children in one capacity or another, we may have normative views on how children should be looked after and what child protection measures should be prioritized in different organizations. Interestingly, this familiarity of child protection has moved ethnographers away from setting the field of child protection as the field of children.

Shadowing a child in the child protection system and in his/her everyday life is not ethically unproblematic. Multi-sited ethnography would require cooperation with many institutions and people therein as well as negotiations with a variety of children, parents and other people to allow the researcher to be involved, for example, in a sport club meeting. Long-term research design would cause even more concerns. Many university ethical bodies could refuse to give permission for such a study. Many researchers would claim that there is a need to protect children and young people from research input which could upset the children's position as service users (Kiili and Moilanen, 2019). Nor should one not take it for granted that children are willing to join a research project with a researcher shadowing them. In the end, the 'field' may not be extended to children. Even ethnography in its holism cannot escape the multifaceted nature of child protection in which the interests, rights and rationales of different stakeholders matter, and therefore the ethnographies are always bound to be partial.

Conclusion

As with many fields of human service, child protection, too, is a complex social institution. The societal and political views on the rights obligations of and relations between the state, professionals, parents and children constantly change what is seen as the 'protection of children' and views on how it is best done (Gilbert et al, 2011). Such change is a challenge for any type of research. In this chapter, I have highlighted how the present rationale of child protection, with its fragmented service provision, interacts with ethnographic work. I have argued that methodological issues should not be isolated from the contextual issues of human service and its logic of care. That is why I suggest that ethnography should (also) look at fragments, multiple locations and moments of human service and acknowledge that they manifest themselves in a variety of ways that as such are interesting for ethnography.

This suggestion is ultimately not very radical. Ethnography as a method and as an approach has always been dynamic and adaptable to different contexts. Even the anthropological ethnographies of yesteryear have been increasingly tied, both conceptually and methodologically, to their once silent global and colonial contexts. The kind of now classic sociological ethnographies of urban street corners and neighbourhoods are, increasingly, analytically located in broader societal contexts. As are human services. I hope that the suggestions of this chapter are taken up and encourage researchers interested in child protection to trust that child protection in its present forms is multi-sited and, equally importantly, as multi-consequential in terms of research understanding as it is in practice. In this way, even today—and especially today— ethnography can provide 'a published scrutiny of the inter-sited complexities of child protection which would eventually benefit staff, clients and citizens' (Dingwall et al, 2014).

References

Andenaes, A. (2011) 'From "placement" to "a child on the move": Methodological strategies to give children a more central position in child welfare service', *Qualitative Social Work*, 11(5): 486–502.

Andenaes, A. (2014) 'The task of taking care of children: Methodological perspectives and empirical implications', *Child and Family Social Work*, 19(3): 263–271.

Berrick, J., Dickens, J., Pösö, T. and Skivenes, M. (2018) 'Care order templates as institutional scripts in child protection: A cross-system analysis, *Children and Youth Services Review*, 84: 40–47.

Berridge, D. and Brodie, I. (1998) *Children's Home Revisited*, London: Jessica Kingsley Publishers.

Biesel, K., Masson, J., Parton, N. and Pösö, T. (eds) (2020) *Errors and Mistakes in Child Protection: International Discourses, Approaches and Strategies*, Bristol: Policy Press.

Boddy, J. and Dominelli, L. (2017) 'Social media and social work: The challenges of a new ethical space', *Australian Social Work*, 70(2): 172–184.

Burawoy, M., Blum, J.A., George, S., Gille, Z. and Thayer, M. (2000) *Global Ethnography. Forces, Connections, and Imaginations in Postmodern World*, Berkeley, CA: University of California Press.

Coffey, A. (1999) *The Ethnographic Self*, London: Sage.

Cunliffe, A. (2010) 'Retelling tales of the field', *Organizational Research Methods*, 13(2): 224–239.

Dingwall, R., Eekelar, J. and Murray, T. (2014) *The Protection of Children* (2nd edn), New Orleans, LA: Quid Pro Books.

Edgar, I. and Russell, A. (eds) (1998) *The Anthropology of Welfare*, London: Routledge.

Featherstone, B., White, S. and Morris, K. (2014) *Re-imagining Child Protection: Towards Humane Social Work with Families*, Bristol: Policy Press.

Ferguson, H. (2010) 'Walks, home visits and atmospheres: Risk and the everyday practices and mobilities of social work and child protection', *British Journal of Social Work*, 40(4): 1100–17.

Ferguson, H. (2011) *Child Protection Practice*, Basingstoke: Palgrave Macmillan.

Ferguson, H. (2016) 'Researching social work practice close up: Using ethnographic and mobile methods to understand encounters between social workers, children and families', *British Journal of Social Work*, 46(1): 153–168.

Ferrell, J., Haywads, K. and Young, J. (2008) *Cultural Criminology*, London: Sage.

Gilbert, N., Parton, N. and Skivenes, M. (eds.) (2011) *Child Protection Systems: International Trends and Orientations*, New York: Oxford University Press.

Henriksen, A. (2019) ' "So, why am I here?" Ambiguous practices of protection, treatment and punishment in Danish secure institutions for youth', *British Journal of Criminology*, 59(5): 1161–1177.

Hoikkala, S. and Pösö, T. (2019) 'The documented layer of children's rights in care order decision-making', *Child and Family Social Work*, 25(S1), DOI: 10.1111/cfs.12711

Kiili, J. and Moilanen, J. (2019) 'Participation as a methodological and ethical issue in child protection research', *Journal of Children's Services*, 14(3): 143–161.

Kotkas, T. (2016) 'From official supervision to self-monitoring: Privatizing supervision of private social care services in Finland', *Social Policy and Administration*, 50(5): 599–613.

Meagher, G., Lundström, T., Sallnäs, M. and Wiklund, S. (2016) 'Big business in a thin market', *Social Policy and Administration*, 50(7): 805–823.

Novoa, A. (2015) 'Mobile ethnography: Emergence, techniques and its importance to geography', *Human Geographies*, 9(1): 97–107.

Pålsson, D. and Shanks, E. (2020) 'Missed opportunities? State licensing on the Swedish residential care market', *European Journal of Social Work*, DOI. 10.1080/13691457.2019.1709162

Pithouse, A. (1998) *Social Work: The Social Organization of an Invisible Trade*, Aldershot: Ashgate.

Plummer, K. (2001) *Documents of Life 2: An Invitation to a Critical Humanism*, London: Sage.

Pösö, T. (2004) 'The rights and wrongs of ethnographic research in youth residential setting', in T. Eriksson and T. Tjelflaat (eds) *Residential Care*, Aldershot: Ashgate, pp 203–16.

Pösö, T. (2010) 'Revisiting residential care: Methodological considerations', *Qualitative Social Work*, 9(1): 27–42.

Pösö, T. (2019) 'The non-discrimination principle in child protection: A snapshot on a seemingly trivial practice of transitions in care', in K. Søvig and M. Skivenes (eds) *Child Rights and International Discrimination Law: Implementing Article 2 of the UN Convention on the Rights of the Child*, Milton Park: Routledge, pp 87–100.

Stang, E. (2018) 'Resistance and protest against Norwegian child welfare services on Facebook: Different perceptions of child-centring', *Nordic Social Work Research*, 8(3): 273–286.

Streule, M. (2020) 'Doing mobile ethnography: Grounded, situated and comparative', *Urban Studies*, 57(2): 421–438.

Warren, J. (2015) *The Emotional Politics of Social Work and Child Protection*, Bristol: Policy Press.

PART IV

Noticings from ethnographic distance

10

Ethnographic discovery *after* fieldwork on troubled youth

Malin Åkerström and David Wästerfors

The cultivation of ethnographic discovery is not only about being insightful in the field by paying attention to unexpected events and unforeseen social processes. We should also search for potentially surprising or disturbing findings *after* the fieldwork. This can provide additional ways to create an original and sustainable understanding of research material. In this chapter, we discuss a study of a public youth care project in Sweden to exemplify post-fieldwork ethnographic discovery. While attentively processing field notes, transcripts and documents and bracketing conventional social problems in the settings, it was possible to discover an unexpected but striking emphasis on meetings and administrative work among the service professionals, which the fieldworkers, unbeknownst to them, had inadvertently documented but not reflected upon analytically. This provided an empirical platform for post-fieldwork creativity, eventually generating a number of publications and new research ideas. The chapter ends with an attempt to turn our experiences from the youth project into proposed guidelines for how to discover unanticipated topics in ethnographic data after fieldwork has ended by way of *key readings*.

The Swedish youth care project

In an extensive evaluation of a Swedish youth care project, titled 'Fighting Violence and Gangs' (Motverka våld och gang), we ended up with a large cache of ethnographic field notes and qualitative interviews. We had interviewed young people in detention homes, parents and treatment assistants, as well as administrators, coordinators, social service staff and managers. And we had observed a range of meetings and other work-related situations. Altogether, we had collected more than 145 interviews and field observations from more than 80 occasions (Basic et al, 2009, p 13).

The project was the result of Swedish politicians' response to criticism often voiced in the media regarding the 'unruly youth problem' (that is, the collection of troubles associated with young people, violence, drugs, ethnic conflicts and urban nightlife). The government decided to commission one of the largest and most expensive projects in Sweden concerning youth care. The funds were placed with the National Board for Institutional Care who were to collaborate with a selected number of municipalities in Sweden to arrange a more efficient care chain for young people with criminal experiences.

A number of municipalities were offered a discount of 40 percent for placing the young people at issue in detention homes and to hire a new category of professionals, named 'coordinators', to oversee their constructive return to private homes. The project manager explained that for the young people in question a short stay at detention homes can be fruitful, and that the important issue was to prevent youngsters from returning to criminal gangs or progressing to even more serious infractions after having received care at detention homes. The problem was explained by politicians and social workers in terms of societal fragmentation, in which the 'social life' in question ostensibly comes apart.

After the young people were released from detention homes, the social authorities, schools, after-care agencies and others did not always cooperate, nor were even forewarned about the release, and thus not ready to take them on. This would supposedly change as part of this big project. The coordinators were trained social workers and employed to act somewhat as 'substitute parents' (Stein, 2006). Their job was to get to know the young people's experiences, the state of their schooling and their personal ambitions and wishes for the future, so as to ensure that suitable post-care plans were enacted and tailored to their needs. This could involve school placements or work training, but also other services such as helping improve relations with their parents and involvement in drug programmes. The coordinators were expected to maintain close contact with the young people and their families.

The research group

Two research groups were tasked with evaluating the project. One was ours, which followed the project and its members with an ethnographic approach, and the other was a quantitatively oriented research group that set up their investigation in a quasi-experimental design. Our group consisted of the first author as the principal investigator, a postdoc and a graduate student. The material was collected mainly by the latter two by following the coordinators' work through go-alongs (Kusenbach, 2003) and by doing qualitative interviews with coordinators, the young people, their parents, social workers and staff at detention homes. It was our detailed inspection of field notes and interviews, rather than their collection, that inspired our analyses of the human service staff as a case of *Homo administratus*, that is, actors intensely (and increasingly) occupied with meetings, documents, charts and other bureaucratic devices, with a peculiar distance from the clients and their lives.

The quantitative evaluation compared the young people in the project with an equivalent sample of youngsters that were not selected for the project and, consequently, not addressed by the new coordinators. Their conclusion was that the project did not work (Lundström et al, 2012). Our task was to qualitatively study what happened, to delve into the mechanisms within the project, whereas the quantitative study focused on the beginning and the end.

While reading the texts produced in the qualitative study, the field notes and interviews, the senior researcher (Malin Åkerström) started to discover extensive, time-consuming administrative activity among the coordinators (Basic et al, 2009, pp 225–307). Later on, this was also suggested by the quantitative research team (that referred to our work) as one of a few explanations for the failure of the project: 'Important explanations for the absence of effects, on top of the general difficulties obtaining notable positive results for this group of young people, are probably the administrative orientation of the coordinators' work' (Lundström et al, 2012, p 5, our translation).

However, it is difficult to know whether this administrative orientation had a direct bearing on the null result of the project (that is, the fact that the young people in the project did not fare better than the control group). In any case, our discovery of the prominence of everyday administration among a professional category that often complains about a lack of time to spend with their young clients created a research issue. We found a range of tangible situations in which the new coordinators were both eager and encouraged to do administration work.

Key incidents and key readings

Our discovery of the administrative orientation among the coordinators did not happen by systematically sorting the material, such as through the classic strategies for analysing qualitative data; for example, analytic induction and grounded theory. Analytic induction explicates a distinct logic for qualitative data analysis (Katz, 2001). The researcher formulates an initial hypothesis to explain a certain phenomenon and then, step by step, seeks to provide a perfectly matching explanation. If any of the studied cases do not fit the hypothesis, the hypothesis is reformulated or the type of phenomenon to be explained is redefined. 'Negative' cases are particularly useful in this context because they challenge the hypothesis and force the analyst to reformulate either what is explained or the explanation. Grounded theory offers practical procedures that advance and facilitate analysis in a more enumerative (all-encompassing) way (Charmaz, 2006). Detailed line-by-line coding is followed by 'memoing' and identifying sub-dimensions by systematically asking about conditions, interactions and other characteristics. Both strategies advocate comparisons: through negative cases in analytic induction, and through 'constant comparisons' throughout a data set in grounded theory.

But how does the researcher identify the initial hypotheses for comparison with negative cases in the first place? And how does one identify what is suitable for constant comparison? Emerson (2004) argues that, as researchers, we should allow ourselves to take our surprise or curiosity seriously, instead of following a predefined logic or technical approach. He suggests a complementary way: we may work with *key incidents* to ground ethnographic analyses, as 'theory-focused approaches leave aside entirely the actual experience of many ethnographers, the frequent sense that their eventual analyses were strongly shaped by particularly telling or revealing incidents or events that they observed and recorded' (Emerson, 2004, p 429; see also Rennstam and Wästerfors, 2018, pp 138–141).

More precisely, the type of experience that Emerson (2004, p 427) is pointing to is an intriguing observation, a key incident, that grows out of field researchers' sense that their analyses are 'touched off by and tied to particular in-the-field events or observations', and that these events or observations 'stimulate or implicate' originality. Such incidents may direct the researchers' subsequent collection of material and cause their analysis of the data to follow significant lines of inquiry and conceptual development.

Emerson relates how Howard S. Becker noticed how medical students at times used the term 'crock' (at times 'shitty crocks'). The students used this term to refer to patients with multiple complaints but no discernible physical pathology, 'which led to a sense of interest and intrigue' (Emerson, 2004, p 459). Becker's continued investigation of the meaning of 'crocks' initiated the organization of the minor classic *Boys in White* (Becker et al, 1961) in which the medical student culture was investigated. The culture emphasized actual, clinical experience rather than 'book knowledge'. In this sense, 'crocks' were worthless patients because they could not teach the students about diagnosis. They were too diffuse in their symptoms and behaviour, too multidimensional when it came to the medical language.

Another illustration is Emerson's own field study of juvenile courts. He became interested in a conversation in which a girl was categorized as a 'sociopath' in a very clear and unambiguous manner. This led him to explore how the youngster's moral character was constructed, but also the consequences of such typification. Being categorized as a 'hopeless sociopath' did not necessarily lead to incarceration; in the case that caught Emerson's interest, the court decided 'to let it go'. Practical logic of various kinds governs decisions. In other words, there was no linear logic in the categorization of youngsters and decisions on sentencing.

Similar to the idea of key incidents found during fieldwork, we will focus on *key readings* of the data after fieldwork. There are a range of circumstances that may make this analytical practice relevant. In some situations, it is not possible to continue to collect data as one may do when observing a key incident in the field, thereby pursuing and expanding one's new interest in detail. The case discussed here was a politically initiated project in social work. Such quasi-organizations dissolve quickly and depend on various rehabilitation fads and models so that the field, so to speak, changes after some time and the researchers are stuck with the material once it is collected. At other times, it is the researcher who cannot keep collecting due to deadlines, lack of finances or simply wanting or needing to leave the field for various reasons.

Even if it is possible to keep on collecting data, researchers may notice something interesting only when they read through their field notes and transcribe interviews. It may occur immediately after the fieldwork, or after some time has passed; it may occur with the help of some inspiring theory or a new analytical perspective (Atkinson, 1992) or during an interaction with friends and colleagues. A re-analysis of one's data (Wästerfors et al, 2014) may be inspired by a key reading, by being caught up in a nagging feeling about the interviews and field notes, something that keeps you alert and engaged and perhaps also a bit irritated, because you were not able to figure it out the first time you or your team members wrote it up. It is the latter case we are trying to exemplify and explain in this chapter.

Meetings, meetings, meetings

As a project leader, the first author continually browsed the textualized material but read it more thoroughly when preparing to write the final report to the Swedish National Board of Institutional Care (Basic et al, 2009). Digging into the material, she was struck by how often the word 'meeting' occurred in field notes and interviews.

One key reading concerned a day's field observation at the beginning of the project. The morning was spent at a rather large information meeting about the project with managers from the social authorities. All four regional coordinators were present, with approximately 15 social service representatives. During the meeting, the social service managers questioned the whole youth care project. After the meeting, the coordinators bought kebabs and returned to the office to eat lunch together. They decided not to discuss the morning's meeting until their regular team meeting the same afternoon. The afternoon was then spent in this team meeting at the office, discussing and evaluating the morning meeting. They all agreed that the morning meeting was unsatisfactory and that they needed to prepare and improve such meetings in the future.

This field note fuelled questions such as: Why would so many people spend a morning on an information issue? Why all four of the coordinators? And why couldn't they discuss this unsatisfactory information meeting during lunch, and get on with working directly with the young people in the afternoon? Why have a team meeting among four people? Besides, the 'team' in this context did not refer to a young boy or girl, his or her parents and a coordinator but to a group of four professionals: the coordinators. Notably, the field notes from this day did not contain anything about any specific young individual, despite the fact that the whole youth care project should revolve around individual young people in trouble.

Another day described in the first field notes involved a team meeting at the beginning of the project. The meeting was held in the apartment rented for the coordinators, which functions as their office. They each have their own room, not very cosy but functional. The rooms have standard office furniture: desks, shelves with folders, computers, office chairs and so forth. The coordinators sit in their rooms, write on their computers, email their colleagues and go through documents. The four case workers were just finishing their breakfast when the field researcher from our team arrived.

The field note from this day contains plenty of formulations that reference meetings. Some of them are very short, such as, 'We move into the meeting room, one of the rooms in the big apartment [rented for the coordinators].' Other meeting formulations contain a few sentences: 'The meeting starts, and one of the points is about structure and organisation and collaboration in the group. It's important that we don't interrupt each other, says Inez, and the others agree.'

The project members also talk about 'meeting times', such as the importance of not booking anything else at team meeting times. The team meeting should occur on Monday mornings. One of the coordinators made excuses, but pointed out that it was not possible to reschedule another meeting next time. At the end of the meeting, there was a discussion about the fact that one of the coordinators had scheduled a meeting during the upcoming week at which everybody needed to be present. The meeting would last until 12:15, and Ahmed, one of the coordinators, stated that he had to be able to have lunch at 12 if he wanted, so no one should book without asking the others if a meeting runs longer.

Again, this was a key reading, in that no comments were made about any specific young boy or girl's troublesome situation—talk that was expected by the reader. Furthermore, the first author again noticed the frequent references to meetings, and it was evident that meetings were an honoured activity; there was a special room reserved for these gatherings. There were also discussions about specific meeting times, and the members made efforts to instil their importance. Meetings were also a bit formalized. The field note states, 'Inez seems to be the one who leads the meeting.' In addition, the coordinators reminded themselves to not interrupt each other. Again, this all occurred in a work group of four people.

Now the analyst's curiosity was spurred, and a more systematic search began for wordings and interactions pointing to an administrative gaze. The subsequent field observation concerned a 'meeting-free' workday. The coordinators were busy with telephone calls and emails. We select one snippet from these notes:

> Karin makes a call. At first, I [the fieldworker] don't know who she's calling, the tone is pleasant and I think she has called a colleague. But it turns out to be a mother of a youth. The call is quite long, around 20 minutes. The purpose is primarily to inform and check on things before a meeting to be held a few weeks later. Does the mother have any questions before the meeting? Karin describes what's to be discussed. But it's also clear that in addition to this, the mother wants to talk about other things with Karin. 'Yeah, it is, of course I understand that', Karin says on the phone. The call ends, and Karin says [to the fieldworker], 'One becomes a bit of a container. They need to talk, it belongs to the job.' Now, she says, she will also call the young person, the social secretary, and the detention home, as well as write an agenda and send it out to those who will be at the meeting.

> I look into Ahmed's office. He's sitting at the computer. 'I'm doing the minutes of the meeting. I'm writing them up.'
>
> Kaj calls and gets a hold of one of the people he had been calling earlier, a young guy, A., who he wants to talk to before a 'middle meeting' at the detention home. 'Hi A., how are you?'
>
> Again, it's clear that this call contains more than checking if there's something that A. wants to raise ahead of the meeting, it is also a matter of establishing a relationship via more 'everyday' small talk. 'Do you have a gym, too, that's great!' (Field notes)

Even when engaging with the mother and the young person, the coordinators were focused on an upcoming meeting. When Karin talks with the mother on the phone, the part of the talk that does *not* touch on the meeting, what the mother communicates is not deemed to be of central importance but interpreted in terms of a function and a need ("You become a bit of container, they need to talk, that's part of the job.") After the call, Karin gets back to business; she will call the other parties for the meeting, write an agenda and send it to the participants. Ahmed is busy writing a protocol from a meeting, and when Kaj calls the young boy, A., there is amiable talk about everyday stuff, but the reason for Kaj's call is in preparation for a meeting. Again, this field note from a workday with 'no meetings' generated questions.

Why did meetings, as structured gatherings, discourse and a symbol, take the forefront? The early project description mentioned coordinators attending 'some, important meetings', but their main task was to remain in close contact with the youngsters and their social networks. And why not meet parents in a public place like a public library or café if hesitant to enter their homes? Why in a place like the social authority office, with its bureaucratic aura?

Through even more careful readings, we were able to mine the early field notes for this administrative gaze and its associated practices. We gradually discovered that the coordinators increasingly lapsed into bureaucratic language (Charrow, 1982) in both interviews and informal talk during observations, and that their practices mirrored this, with the young people themselves fading into the background.

Analytic implications

Emerson argues that, 'since key incidents are (or can be made) empirically rich and multi-stranded, the process of drawing out their analytic implications will often involve a gradual clarification and unpacking of one dimension, then another, then yet another' (Emerson, 2004, p 469). Unpacking of dimensions is similarly relevant in key readings, though they do not necessarily concern one striking event or piece of interaction. Here, it is rather a matter of complicating the reading of all data. We will exemplify this by discussing the discovery of: a) administrative struggles; and b) administrative *Eigendynamik* (that is, self-propelling process).

Administrative struggles

One dimension was the struggles resulting from the administrative orientation. Most of these struggles occurred between the professionals involved in the collaboration: the social authorities, and those working in detention homes and the project. These resulted in alliances and conflicts between various parties (for example, mothers against coordinators, coordinators against social workers, detention home staff versus coordinators) (Basic, 2012).

When reading through the material, it was obvious that conflicts often concerned administrative issues rather than immediate issues related to the young people concerned, even if these also appeared in the data (Åkerström, 2017). Such conflicts could be unpacked into new sub-dimensions. They could occur regarding ownership, as revealed in phrases such as 'their meeting' or 'our meeting' in discussions or comments by representatives of the various organizations included in the project. Such conflicts included discussions about who would be chairman, who should determine the agenda, who should write up the minutes, who should be invited to the meeting or who should be informed, included or excluded from a meeting.

We also found an administrative struggle in relation to documents. The coordinators had constructed a document, 'The Agreement', to pinpoint more concretely what various parties were expected to do and to formulate different goals and subgoals for the young people. This document competed, as it turned out, with the social authorities' 'Care plan' and the detention homes' 'Treatment plan'. This meant that the documents that appeared during the project were not used solely as a working basis and checklist for work with the young people during meetings, as plans or diagnoses or as documentation of work performed. For the coordinators, 'The Agreement' was cherished. It was the project's own working tool and perceived as essential in the work. On the other hand, representatives from social services and the detention homes claimed that 'The Agreement' overlapped with their own guidelines and would only create more bureaucracy. The document became the subject of occasional intense discussions during many meetings and formed the basis of a struggle for influence between different professional actors.

Of the textualized material concerning the young persons and their parents, the field notes were mainly from meetings in which both categories were fairly quiet; reading the transcribed interviews gave more in terms of narrated experiences and opinions. These interviews mostly described the coordinators as peripheral actors; a youngster asked a fieldworker if they were "the ones sending documents?" Some recalled their coordinators and tied them to meetings, but these experiences were sometimes retold with criticism, as with Asmee:

> 'My mom told me that she had received a brochure, she [the coordinator] didn't say anything, she had just given my mom, "if you can read"…it's strange that she comes all of a sudden and will decide, what will be decided and knows nothing [pause about 5 sec]…she came here, greeted my parents and attended the meeting, and then my mother got the same as me, one such white…' [Asmee points to a paper and writes the project name]. (Field notes)

These administrative struggles and their intensity proved to be telling in our emerging analysis of an administrative turn of the youth care project, and in our growing interest in the attractions of doing administration in today's working life in general. But we would never have discerned them in the data without allowing ourselves to take our surprise and curiosity seriously.

As the administrative struggles and conflicts were discerned in the data, we began to see this as a fruitful strand of inquiry. When youngsters represented their coordinators as people who send brochures or attend meetings, this could entail disappointment or irritation. In contrast, when the professionals argued over meetings and documents, they did this with emotional intensity. A common sociological assumption from Simmel's (1964) observation on conflict is that the more intimate a relationship is the more intense conflict will be. One promising analytic theme is thus that the intimate relationship is not only to be found in the web of relations in a human service world, but also in relation to administrative objects and events.

One nice illustration was how 'The Agreement' was cherished among coordinators but the interpretation of how it should be used occasionally caused stark conflicts during meetings: "There was a war between us", as one of them explained.

The Eigendynamik

A second and related dimension that we started to explore in our readings of the data was people's initiatives and involvement in administrative tasks. The new coordinators *had* to write certain documents and attend some meetings, but they also initiated new meetings and exhibited great involvement and commitment (Åkerström, 2019). Meetings seemed to generate new meetings, and documents and meetings fed on each other. The project's own document, 'The Agreement', took a lot of meeting time when the coordinators met with young people, their parents and the representatives for social services and the detention homes. Meetings were set up to complete the document, but it also took time because it was a contested document among other professionals who had their own documents that they claimed fulfilled the same purpose.

Even though we detected meeting-competition in the field notes and many difficulties synchronizing calendars, it was clear that the coordinators suggested new meetings themselves and wanted to attend existing scheduled meetings at the detention homes. The project manager tried to minimize these meetings but failed. He wanted to keep their focus on the young people's transition to their homes, foster parents or possibly an apartment of their own. This meeting-competition was linked to what we started to call *meeting chains* in the material, that is, sequences of internal meetings in which issues moved back and forth. Team meeting issues could be moved to a local reference group in a region, which could continue to move them to central reference group meetings, and their policies or decisions were then expected to be brought back to the different teams. The treatment of young people at the detention homes was also basically a meeting chain: acute meeting, admission meeting, meetings for planning, mid-meeting, closing meeting and hand-over meeting.

Furthermore, meetings were initiated during or after a meeting. A scheduled 'main meeting' often generated new meetings. Another type of self-enforcing quality of meetings was seen in meetings held before a main meeting to ensure that 'everybody was on board'. After such meetings, project members often discussed and reviewed each other's performances in what the social anthropologist Helen Schwartzman (1989, p 137) calls post-meetings.

Pre- and post-meetings could be integrated, as in the case when a coordinator had booked a meeting with a social worker due to the staff at a detention home feeling overrun during the 'main meeting'. The coordinator wanted things to work smoother in the future. The post-meeting, however, evolved into a pre-meeting as the two got involved in discussing what to take up at the next meeting. The coordinator noted that she had read in the central documentation system that the young person had some vision and hearing problems and believed that it was important to discuss this during the next meeting. She asked, "I'm going to raise this during the next meeting. Is that okay?" The rest of their meeting was devoted to planning for the upcoming meeting.

So, with this reading of the data as our basis, we began to try out the argument that the contemporary expansion of administrative activities in today's working life is *also* driven from below. An increasing proportion of people's working hours are devoted to administrative tasks, in which meetings and documents in particular are accentuated, and this tendency is often attributed to demands 'from above', but the key reading of the data from this qualitative evaluation of the youth care project in Sweden made us think in new directions. We started to gather the same type of data from other contexts, such as psychiatric care, academia and various social welfare contexts. We distinguished commitment and emotional involvement among meeting members and authors of documents, and we gained further inspiration from Georg Simmel (1904/1957; 1978) and his concept of *Eigendynamik*. There seemed to be self-generating forces in meeting and documentation practices.

Enhancing ethnographic creativity

Leading these discoveries was an analytic appreciation for unforeseen findings, which can be turned into some hopefully useful guidelines for enhancing ethnographic creativity.

Struck by a contrast: making it a resource

One guideline relates to what Emerson wrote in relation to key incidents: they 'are not necessarily dramatic matters, significant, or noteworthy for those involved' but a 'theoretically sensitive conviction that something intriguing has just taken place' (Emerson, 2004, p 469). Swedberg (2012), reflecting on theorizing as a skill, similarly argues that it draws on 'intuitive thinking', especially in its initial phases. An equivalent feature can be found in key readings of qualitative data, an intuitive conviction that something intriguing is apparent in the textualized material. Our field members did not seem to notice (or verbalize it), and field research workers were preoccupied with the project's formal aim, but later at our desk, with more analytical room to manoeuvre, the data seemed to make it quite clear. These new coordinators never turned into 'substitute parents', but became *Homo administrates* or administrative beings.

At the heart of the discovery, we find a contrast made into a resource. The first author had some distance from the field and the generation of the data, but she was close to the project's initiation. She clearly remembered how it was described in the beginning, when it was emphasized that the coordinators should be in close contact with the young people and their parents. The Swedish National Board of Institutional Care even used such an image in various presentations, including articles in their own magazine. One article, 'Inger makes things work out' (*Inger gör så allting flyter*), contained an interview with close-ups of a young guy, his father and Inger, a new coordinator, with the text, 'Trio that cooperates' (*Trio som samarbetar*). The following scene was depicted as they sat in the parents' home: 'There is coffee and caramel cake on the dining table. They are joking and making small talk as their dog Nova sits close to our legs, asking for attention. Yet, this afternoon coffee is a working-meeting.' (*SiS i Fokus*, 2008, p 11, our translation)

When the project manager talked about the project, he sometimes used a ready-made trope:

> 'When Andy [fictive name] gets out, we must know what he lacks, for instance, in schooling, and what he wants for his future. He needs to have a school or work placement waiting for him. We want to make sure that Andy is not forgotten when our organisation is no longer responsible for him.' (Åkerström, 2019, p 53)

Thus, an administrative orientation of the coordinators was far from given. In contrast, flexible, direct, pragmatic, personalized and goal-oriented ways were celebrated and invoked to legitimize the project. However, neither field members nor fieldworkers seemed to keep this in mind as they became more immersed in the field. The abundance of meetings did not really catch anyone's attention, or the fact that 'Andy' was eventually forgotten.

You may thus benefit from taking several steps back, by returning to the beginning, reading notes and transcriptions and by making striking contrasts into resources. This demands analytic space and liberty.

A little out of control: not turning 'resocialized'

A second guideline relates to acquiring some detachment from the field. We learned that it can be more difficult to see original (and central) themes in a social policy setting like this if you are 'there' for a long and intense period of time and excel in acquiring members' understanding of the world they take for granted. Doing ethnography in human service organizations means getting involved in fields saturated with problems-talk, solution-talk and improvement rhetoric that may absorb the fieldworker and her analyses, so detachment can be particularly important in these areas.

Those who collected most of the data in our case developed their research along other lines. Goran Basic visited detention homes and social services offices, conducting interviews with treatment staff and parents. He worked intensely, with a large amount of interviews all over the country, and was eager to find clues as to whether this project worked for the young people. He noted how some young people do not access the project even though they should, and he noted those who lacked contact with their coordinators. Being a former immigrant himself (in the 1990s), he had a keen eye for discriminatory practices and paid close attention to how few of the coordinators had an immigrant background.

Joakim Thelander, another co-worker, mainly followed the coordinators, hung around in their offices and went along during their workdays. The coordinators he met with told him about it taking a long time to acquire office computers, and how they had to go to IKEA to get desks to set up. He ate breakfast with them and heard them boasting or complaining about their localities, talking about their frustration with the lack of routines and the lack of enthusiasm from the social workers with whom they were supposed to cooperate. On their way to and from various meetings, he talked not only about the project but also about music and sports, and he saw them working hard.

Joakim Thelander's cultural immersion at the time is evident in notes in which he adopts the language of the studied members; for example, he sometimes writes about 'cases' instead of young people, and he defines meetings as the meaning of the coordinators' work. Almost all his field notes begin with a declaration such as, 'Today I will accompany the coordinators to a meeting at a detention home', or 'I didn't plan to do a "go along" today, but joined when Karin told me she was on her way to a network meeting'. It is also illustrative that he defines non-meeting times as uneventful in the notes.

> The morning is fairly 'eventless'. The coordinators check and respond to emails, make occasional calls. Karin [a coordinator] says I was a little unlucky. Due to the fact that a couple of meetings have been cancelled and moved, this week has been unusually quiet for them. We agree to try to arrange so that I can see a little more activity when I visit them again. (Field notes)

We do not want to say that these ways of generating data were wrong; both Thelander and Basic did an excellent job in accessing the field and immersing themselves not only in the members' meanings but also their ways of invoking these meanings in specific relations and interactions (Emerson et al, 1995, p 28). They were following the expectations of an ethnographer, and being somewhat captured by the internal logic of the project and the members' concerns allowed them to continue taking notes and having meaningful conversations with the people they met. They artfully sustained relationships.

What we want to point out is that the project's administrative orientation was much easier to discover when *not* in the field. Meetings and documents were very much *seen but not theorized*, not made into analytic memos or manuscript sketches, let alone ideas for future research. To make meeting struggles, meeting chains and the Eigendynamik of administration the centre of attention, a more relaxed reading of the data was required, free from the social control of Swedish youth care. An evaluation was not expected to come to a certain result, and the National Board of Institutional Care does encourage criticism, but still there were strong expectations to keep to the topic: young people, their treatment, the project. To start writing about administration, its Eigendynamik and—more specifically—the attraction of multiplying meetings and documents again and again was certainly not expected. It does not belong to the discourse about detention homes and youth care, neither in the field nor among the researchers.

But at the desk, no one was hanging over us asking for predefined evaluations (or reminding us of the parents' and the young people's pains in life), and no one invited us to meeting rooms to discuss how to manage youth care. We could see things that were not expected, and we were not 'resocialized' by the field (Emerson et al, 1995, p 2). This is what we mean by our relative freedom and detachment.

Reaching for transferrable conclusions

A third guideline is to join qualitative researchers' general efforts to work toward conclusions that can be transferred to other settings.

The first conclusion may be evident for ethnographers but necessary to point out when communicating with human service policymakers who have to succumb to contemporary quests for evidence through quantitative studies. It may be important to remind them to involve ethnographic researchers in order to understand what is happening inside the black box, that is, what people actually do and say in a programme or during the time a project lasts.

In this case, had the evaluation only consisted of a quantitative measurement, the knowledge produced would only have led to a null result. We do not know whether the administrative orientation *produced* the null results, but it likely contributed. Researchers in the field point out that personal relationships, perhaps resembling those of substitute parents, increase the chances of young people 'leaving care programmes' (Biehal et al, 1995; Stein, 2006a, 2006b; Degner and Henriksen, 2007). In the case discussed here, each individual youngster *had* a specific coordinator, but without ethnographic methods it would have been very hard to know what they actually did during their workdays.

The second transferrable conclusion we want to emphasize is that ethnographic findings from key readings can be investigated or searched for in research in other areas. In line with Simmel's formal sociology, you may find similar sociological qualities in very different contexts. A famous example is provided by Erving Goffman (1961) when he generalized his findings from an ethnographic study of a mental hospital in *Asylums* to other 'total institutions' such as boarding schools, monasteries, prisons and concentration camps.

In our case, as to human service work, the authors found both previous and contemporary Swedish studies focusing on the same administrative tendency in spite of an original 'client-perspective', such as Meeuwisse's (1996) study of a community project with neighbourhood work for which social workers had fought. She found the social welfare officers soon fled the neighbourhood and retreated to their offices. In another study of a project aiming to introduce refugees to Sweden, the authors wrote about a 'conspicuous bureaucratic involvement', with the creation of various new groups, such as steering committees and project groups, which some participants referred to as a 'meeting jungle' (Carlson and Jacobsson, 2007, p 135).

You may also venture into other settings than that of human service. In our case, the appeal of administration 'from below', found through our key readings described previously has spurred our interests in many other settings, such as medical care, schools, police and academia.

Striving for transferrable conclusions strengthens a reading of the data that highlights novel aspects. It might be wise to make room for some detachment from the setting: 'un-familiarize' yourself from your resocialized self acquired in the field, and invoke contrasts. In our case, the contrast between early descriptions of the project and the actual practices were, so to speak, given to us, but you may use other ones as well. For instance, whenever there are differences between formal goals and informal practices, or whenever people in any setting seem to set aside what they are expected to do and instead indulge in something else, there might be a space for a key reading in which the analyst allows herself to find a new track not at all expected to be investigated.

Conclusion

This chapter has focused on post-fieldwork discovery by way of 'key readings'. It is inspired by Emerson (2004), who argued that, as researchers, we should allow ourselves to take our surprise or curiosity seriously by working with key incidents that we discover whenever engaged in collecting or reviewing ethnographic field material. Predefined logics or technical approaches such as grounded theory or analytic induction leave aside how one actually finds the issues to follow up. We suggest, instead, that it is not always evident while in the field when one discovers 'research gems', the telling or revealing incidents fit for continuous research. At times one may need a bit of distance to be able to see what is sociologically significant in one's material. When reading through interviews and field notes, one may look for contrasts, or be struck by them, or discover matters that otherwise had been tangential to one's interest. These can be field relevant, as we have argued in this chapter, revealed in ethnographic discovery that transpires *after* fieldwork.

References

Åkerström, M. (2017) 'Mötesstrider och dokumentkamp i Ungdoms-vården', in B. Andersson, F. Andersson and A. Skårner (eds) *Den motspänstige akademikern*, Malmö: Egalité, pp 135–160.

Åkerström, M. (2019) 'The merry-go-round of meetings: Embracing meetings in a youth care project', *Sociological Focus*, 52(1): 50–64.

Atkinson, P. (1992) 'The ethnography of a medical setting: Reading, writing, and rhetoric', *Qualitative Health Research*, 2(4): 451–474.

Basic, G. (2012) *Samverkan blir kamp. En sociologisk analys av ett projekt i ungdomsvården. Dissertations in Sociology*, 102. Lund: Media-Tryck, available at: https://lup.lub.lu.se/search/ws/files/5378952/3129801.pdf

Basic, G., Thelander, J. and Åkerström, M. (2009) *Vårdkedja för ungdomar eller professionella?*, research report no. 5. Stockholm: Statens institutions-styrelse, available at: https://lucris.lub.lu.se/ws/files/3181567/4091880.pdf

Becker, H.S., Hughes, E.C., Geer, B. and Strauss, A.L. (1961) *Boys in White: Student Culture in Medical School*, Chicago, IL: University of Chicago Press.

Biehal, N., Clayden, J., Stein, M. and Wade, J. (1995) *Moving On: Young People and Leaving Care Schemes*, London: HMSO.

Carlson, M. and Jacobsson, B. (2007) 'Tvärsektoriell samverkan', in G. Alsmark, T. Kallehave and B. Moldenhawer (eds) *Inklusions- och exklusionsprocesser i Skandinavien*, Lund: Makadam, pp 127–159.

Charmaz, K. (2006) *Constructing Grounded Theory: A Practical Guide through Qualitative Analysis*, London: Sage.

Charrow, V.R. (1982) 'Language in the bureaucracy', in R.J. di Pietro (ed) *Linguistics and the Professions*, Norwood, NJ: Ablex.

Degner, J. and Henriksen, A. (2007) *Placerad utanför sitt sammanhang*, Örebro: Örebro universitet.

Emerson, R.M (2004) 'Working with "key incidents"', in C. Seale, C. Gobo, J. Gubrium and D. Silverman (eds) *Qualitative Research Practice*, London: Sage, pp 457–472.

Emerson, R.M., Fretz, R.I. and Shaw, L.L. (1995) *Writing Ethnographic Fieldnotes*, Chicago, IL: University of Chicago Press.

Forsell, A. and Ivarsson Westerberg, A. (2014) *Administrationssamhället*, Lund: Studentlitteratur.

Gambrill, E. (2011) 'Evidence-based practice and the ethics of discretion', *Journal of Social Work*, 11(1): 26–48.

Goffman, E. (1961) *Asylums*, New York: Vintage.

Hood, C. (1991) 'A public management for all seasons?', *Public Administration*, 69(1): 3–19.

Katz, J. (2001) 'Analytic induction', in N.J. Smelser and P.B. Baltes (eds) *International Encyclopedia of the Social and Behavioral Sciences*, Amsterdam: Elsevier, pp 480–484.

Kusenbach, M. (2003) 'Street phenomenology: The go-along as ethnographic research tool', *Ethnography*, 4(3): 455–485.

Lundström,T., Sallnäs, M. and Andersson Vogel, M. (2012) *Utvärdering av förstärkt vårdkedja*, Stockholm: Statens institutionsstyrelse.

Meeuwisse, A. (1996) 'Projektets dolda funktioner', in I. Sahlin (ed) *Projektets paradoxer*, Lund: Studentlitteratur.

Power, M. (1997) *The Audit Society: Rituals of Verification*, Oxford: Oxford University Press.

Rennstam, J. and Wästerfors, D. (2018) *Analyze! Crafting Your Data in Qualitative Research*, Lund: Studentlitteratur.

Schwartzman, H. (1989) *The Meeting: Gatherings in Organizations and Communities*, New York: Plenum Press.

Simmel, G. (1904/1957) 'Fashion', *American Journal of Sociology*, 62(6): 541–558.

Simmel, G. (1964) *Conflict and the Web of Group Affiliation*, Translated by Kurt Wolff and Reinhard Bendix, New York: The Free Press.

Simmel, G. (1978) *The Philosophy of Money*, London: Routledge.

Sis i Fokus (2008) 'Samordnaren som får saker att hända', 1: 10–14.

Stein, M. (2006) 'Research review: Young people leaving care', *Child and Family Social Work*, 11: 273–279.

Swedberg, R. (2012) 'Theorizing in sociology and social science: Turning to the context of discovery', *Theoretical Sociology*, 41(1): 1–40.

Wästerfors, D., Åkerström, M. and Jacobsson, K. (2014) 'Reanalysis of qualitative data', in U. Flick (ed) *The Sage International Handbook of Qualitative Data Analysis*, London: Sage, pp 467–480.

11

Looking beyond the
police-as-control narrative

David Sausdal

'David, let me tell you, I'm no social worker! This is also
what I told a younger colleague when he started yakking
about how it's important for us to service the community.
He was going on and on about how he liked being police
because it gave him the chance to help out. I figure he
thought I'd tell him what a good cop he was, but you
know what? I told him the same as I'm telling you now;
that it's not fucking social work we do. This is police work.
I mean, he's a sweet kid and all but he needs to understand
that this is the name of the game. Being soft doesn't get
you anywhere!'

With those words, Detective Clausen picked up his coffee cup, it
seemed, to salute what he had just told me. He, a couple of his
colleagues and I were having a short break in a Copenhagen police
station's kitchen. As always, as the ethnographer who had been allowed
to observe these Danish detectives' working day, I was listening and
taking notes. To be sure, this wasn't the first time I had heard Detective
Clausen, or colleagues of his, express opinions about how policing
shouldn't be equated with other forms of social or human service
work. Policing, they regularly made sure to point out and remind each
other, wasn't about being 'soft' but, rather, about catching criminals
and enforcing law and order.

In this chapter, I critically explore this distinction, which is drawn
not only by Danish police officers but, as research has shown, by
police across the world (for example Bittner, 1970; Loftus, 2009;
Fassin, 2013). Specifically, I will be building on recent ethnographic
studies of both Danish and Spanish detectives engaged in policing
transnational crimes. Yet, contrary to the usual conclusions drawn in

police research, which regularly confirm that many if not most police officers do indeed adhere to a strict crime-fighting and enforcement agenda (Bittner, 1970; Loftus, 2009; Fassin, 2013), I wish to nuance this 'police-as-control' narrative. In particular, I will discuss how the police, including Detective Clausen, do in fact frequently stray from this narrative and engage in work which can be seen as having less to do with control and more to do with care and community.

Because of his own caring engagements, Clausen was therefore seemingly contradicting himself when proudly telling me how he had berated his younger colleague for not being tough enough. However, this may not have been a conscious contradiction on his part. For Detective Clausen as well as for other police officers across the world, telling themselves that 'real police work' (Manning, 1977) is essentially about law and order is often a truly heartfelt expression. Their practice may negate their perception (it often does!), nevertheless, to a large extent they remain convinced in their belief about what policing is or, at least, should be—a belief that is in line not only with the conclusions of much police research (for example Bittner, 1970; Loftus, 2009; Fassin, 2013) but also with the popularized representations of a Dirty Harry–style cop (Klockars, 1980). As Reiner has argued (2010), we live in an age when the government's need for the police to exist as law enforcers is beyond question. This police fetishization, Reiner reasons, has seeped into society and established itself as a fact of life. Yet, I would argue that it has not only persuaded the public of its necessity but also the police themselves.

Herein lies the paradox discussed in the following pages: How can one, as an ethnographer, resist uniform depictions of police as a controlling force when this is the perception not only of the public and of academics but of the police themselves? How, in other words, may one go beyond the police-as-control narrative when much of what the police do and say seems to confirm it? In answering this question, I contemplate how doing police ethnography often demands more than being granted access and establishing rapport. It also demands that ethnographers find ways to penetrate the police's insistence, if not self-deception, that they are most of all ruthless enforcers of the law. Later, I will offer additional examples of how police officers insist on their being ruthless, as well as a discussion of how to look beyond that assertion.

Difficulties of police ethnography

By way of a contextualizing background, I will first give a condensed description of how the difficulties of doing police ethnography are usually considered. A good place to start is Reiner and Newburn's 'Police research' (2007). In their essay, Reiner and Newburn outline the key challenges and potentials of doing ethnographic research on policing. As police research itself, like few other sociological-cum-criminological subdisciplines, is founded on ethnographic methods, the challenges and potentials have long been recognized. Pinpointing the benefits of researching the police ethnographically, Van Maanen, for example, has argued that it is necessary 'to penetrate the official smokescreen and observe directly the social action in social situations which, in the final analysis, represents the reality of police work'(Van Maanen, 1973, p 5). Because the police, in a Goffmanian sense, so meticulously curate their public, front stage appearance, there is a need, the argument goes, for researchers to be allowed backstage to get a better grasp of what the police actually do and think.

Here we have the first methodological problem, namely the question of how to gain access to the police's working day. Though 'access' is a problem known to all ethnographers, gaining access to an organization and societal institution like the police is particularly difficult. As Nader famously discussed in her essay on the problems of 'studying up' (1972), a powerful organization like the police won't easily allow outsiders inside without the outsider providing a good reason—one that should not only point to scholarly benefits but be of relevance to the police as well.

Having successfully negotiated access to the backstage of policing, a new and well-known challenge meets the ethnographer. It is one thing to be permitted to observe the working day of a given police unit, but another to be accepted and trusted by the personnel working in that unit. Put in methodological terms, the ethnographer needs to 'establish rapport'. As many studies have shown (see Reiner and Newburn, 2007), this is not an easy task, as police officers are known for being sceptical of all newcomers, outsiders and strangers. The police, in other words, tend to be suspicious of people with whom they don't already have a working relationship, including other, more distant policing colleagues. This culture of scepticism gains added momentum when it comes to academics—a group of people whom the police believe to be not only outsiders to but opponents *of* policing (Reiner and Newburn, 2007). Therefore, the ethnographer often has to overcome two layers of police scepticism before being able to establish trusting relationships. To be honest, establishing a full rapport is almost an impossibility in a professional field fraught with political tensions. Indeed, as Reiner and Newburn point out, the ethnographer, no matter how successful s/he is, is bound to be met with recurring comments about whether what the police say and do will 'end up in the tabloids' (Reiner and Newburn, 2007), something I myself have been asked many times during my police research.

This underlines the fact that gaining access and establishing rapport is not an easy task when undertaking an ethnography of the police. It takes time and perseverance and even when you feel that you are truly on the inside, there are often further layers to penetrate. One of these added layers has to do with the position and role you are assigned as an ethnographer. First of all, as most of us are not trained police officers, we cannot fully commit to 'participant observation'. We have to make do with a more observational role. Who and what we are also add to the problem. As Hunt (1984) has observed, being a woman ethnographer studying a very masculine world affects your role, limiting you in some ways and granting you access in others. The same can be said for ethnic or sexual minority ethnographers who are likely, at least initially, to be pigeon-holed by the police they are observing (Hunt, 1984).

Lastly, a problem often touched upon in the literature relates to what Westmarland has discussed in her article 'Blowing the whistle on police violence' (2001). Westmarland zeroes in on the problem of how to research a violent profession and the question of when/if to report the use of excessive force by the police. Although she doesn't provide any clear-cut answers to these problems, she aptly outlines the methodological issues. For example, while often presented in binary terms, the question of police violence is complex. It is not unusual for the police to use force in a way that, even to themselves, is difficult to assess in terms of its legitimacy. Though regulations specify what is right and wrong, workaday life is less straightforward. As a result, the police often find themselves reflecting on whether their use of force in a specific situation was in fact reasonable in relation to what the situation demanded—though, to be sure, they often conclude that they were in the right (Westmarland, 2001).

The same ambiguity can be found in relation to the use of discretion by the police. Here, as many studies have revealed (Lipsky, 2010), there is also a fine line to walk between appropriate use of discretion and acts of discrimination. Obviously, this makes it difficult for the ethnographer to decide if and when to blow the whistle. Policing is often done in murky waters, necessitating a certain hesitance in the ethnographer's judgments. Adding to the problem, as ethnographers we are constantly aware of what would happen if we did decide to report our police interlocutors—a 'ratting out' that might cut us off from any further studies of the police.

Caring less

A thread that runs through all this is that it is difficult to do ethnographic studies of the police. Yet, for all its complications, it is still seen as the best scholarly way of providing insights into an otherwise closed and self-protective world.

Having once gained access to the backstage of policing and established a rapport, one of the principal ethnographic findings is the discovery of a particular 'police culture' (Cockcroft, 2020). As Loftus has described in one of the more recent ethnographic studies specifically centred on the exploration of police culture, this is a culture of conservatism, scepticism and machismo that favours the action-based and crime-fighting aspects of the job (Loftus, 2009). This is the police-as-control narrative; that is, that policing is, essentially, believed to be about enforcing law and order more than supporting the community. Indeed, this observation and portrayal of policing has been with us since some of the discipline's foundational studies, which highlighted how 'real police work' wasn't believed to be about 'paperwork' or 'social work' but, indeed, about 'crime-fighting' (see for example Manning, 1978).

With this police-as-control narrative in mind, let us now return to the empirical world of Danish and Spanish transnational policing. Doing so, we will see that much of what has been described rings true. In my ethnographic studies, I have encountered many police officers and many situations that mirror this tale about the existence of, if not need for, police callousness. Many examples come to mind, but I will restrict myself to providing two particularly telling ones; the first concerning how Danish detectives apparently looked up to one of their colleagues who was hailed as being a no-nonsense cop; the second concerning the Spanish immigration police's seeming disregard for human smugglers and for the welfare of migrants trying to make their way across the Mediterranean into Spain.

'He's hardcore!'

'He's hardcore!' These or similar words were often uttered in relation to one of the Danish detectives' colleagues—words of admiration rather than disapproval. Instinctively, I understood what they meant. Not that I also admired him, but in a police culture that spoke highly of the 'hardcore' and badly of the 'soft', he was emblematic of what policing was supposedly all about. Around fifty years old with a buzz cut, piercing eyes, a wide frame and a purposeful stride, the 'hardcore' detective left few people unaware of the fact that he would be unyielding, and perhaps more than that, in his work. When he greeted you, he did so with a crushing handshake. When he talked, he only said what needed to be said. His opinions about ethnic and sexual minorities weren't positive. And his appreciation of criminal suspects ended with them in handcuffs. He didn't "give a fuck!", he said. "I couldn't care less", he also once told us after returning from a sting operation and a violent tussle with a suspect who "deserved what he got".

In this way, the stories that spread at the police station and among his colleagues seemed to confirm that this particular detective was a policing icon, a symbol of how it is to be a 'real cop' and of the policing-as-control narrative. Yet, after hundreds of hours spent at the station and with the detectives, I started to notice a different pattern. The 'hardcore' detective was still highly praised and seemingly remained 'hardcore', both on the streets and inside the police station. However, I also noticed how some of the other detectives sometimes seemed to look away from him when he spoke; only a very little, but enough to notice as the pattern repeated itself. It was also noticeable that, while speaking highly of him, few of his colleagues actually called by his office for a coffee and a chat, nor did it really seem that they wanted to partner up with him. Moreover, when speaking in more general terms about 'the old days' and how "the old days were more 'real', with no bullshit and more consequence!", as a fellow detective put it, the detectives in general, though rather reluctantly, agreed that the old ways were perhaps outdated, too harsh and, most of all, ineffectual. While reminiscing about the past, they almost always, though often in passing, ended up mumbling that "things are probably better today".

Moreover, while the 'hardcore' detective surely was tougher than your average Danish officer, in reality his actions were not that fierce. I'm not claiming that he was putting on a show, but the time I spent with him, both in and out of work, afforded me another view. For example, in the aforementioned tussle with the criminal suspect, the detective was definitely lying on the ground, fighting the suspect who was trying to escape. Yet, the detective's own story about how he "couldn't care less" seemed only to be a half-truth. In the minutes following the arrest, he actually expressed how he was annoyed that the situation had developed as it did, and he openly wondered "whether I could have done something different?" This is not to say that he felt sorry for the suspect. He didn't. But his concern did reveal that that he wasn't unswervingly committed to his own apparent callousness.

As Westmarland has also shown (2001), such a reflection or even hesitation is indeed common among police officers in relation to their use of violence, yet, unfortunately, these reflections quickly pass by and are hard for the ethnographer and maybe also the detectives themselves to catch. Nevertheless, such reflection, such uncertainty, even with this 'hardcore' detective, coupled with the hard-to-notice but frequent hesitation towards him among his colleagues, neatly illustrates the point that I'm making here: namely that beyond the widespread and thus very captivating displays of police toughness there are alternative sentiments and sensitivities—not contradicting sentiments as such, but offering different nuances to the 'hardcore' detective image—that ethnography, unlike more experience-distant methods, makes available to us.

Much the same can be said of this next example drawn from my study of the Spanish national police and their policing of transnational crimes, including the smuggling and trafficking of migrants. During the study, I was invited to visit the police central office in Madrid from where they ran their operations against migrant smuggling and trafficking. I interviewed the senior management, one of their investigators and was given a thorough introduction to their 'trafficking hotline'—a hotline that victims of trafficking or the public can phone anonymously and tip off the police. The police allowed me to listen to some of the phone calls and read some of the investigation reports that the calls had generated. While listening and reading through these, one of the detectives left my side to, as he said, "get you something, which shows what we're trying to do here". He came back with a bunch of big posters. Each of the posters warned, either in Spanish, Arabic or English, would-be migrants against the inherent evilness of human smugglers and traffickers. In the posters, whether travelling by sea, land or air, migrants were depicted as being preyed upon by ravenous criminals, graphically represented as petrifying carnivores. An aeroplane wasn't an aeroplane but a scary eagle, a jeep not a jeep but a scorpion and boats not boats but bloodthirsty sharks. "You see, David, we're trying to help the migrants understand that they're being taken advantage of by no-good villains. It's as easy as that. These people don't care about them. And, let me tell you, I don't care about *these people!*" he said with particular emphasis.

Besides visiting their central office, I also spent time at one of the Spanish National Police facilities from where they patrolled the Mediterranean Sea for smugglers and incoming undocumented migrants and processed any migrants they detained while they were trying to cross by sea from North Africa to Spain. I was shown the old industrial complex that the migrants are taken to, the bunk beds they are given to sleep in, the communal bathrooms and the makeshift desks set up where personnel from the Spanish police and Frontex interview the apprehended migrants. The interviews are meant to clarify who each migrant is, where they are from, why they have attempted to cross the border into Spain, and how they have managed to travel all the way from their supposed place of origin to the Strait of Gibraltar. While trying to establish whether the migrant is telling the truth and is entitled to be treated, under the ruling convention, as a refugee and not an illegal immigrant, the interviewers are also much interested in finding out whether the interviewee knows who the smugglers are—and even whether the interviewee is one of these "evil smugglers". As Detective Diaz told me, "This is what it's about, really. Us trying to find these idiots and bring them to justice. They show no mercy, and neither will we!" His ruthless sentiment was certainly one shared by the other officers who worked at this facility, trying to "plug the hole", as they also put it, at the Strait of Gibraltar—a sentiment obviously echoed at the National Police central office and by the aforementioned posters and the graphic campaign against predatory human smuggling.

Ostensibly, again, we here have a case of self-confessed police ruthlessness. As illustrated, the perpetrator, the human smuggler, was repeatedly presented in a truly malevolent light. This uniform and evil rendering of human smugglers is also something discussed more widely in research on the political and policing discourse on human smugglers (compare Sanchez, 2014). But, while the police surely have a low opinion of human smugglers, my study yielded a somewhat more nuanced narrative. During ethnographic field visits, observations and interviews, I was indeed given the initial impression that the officers of the Spanish National Police only wished ill upon human smugglers—and also, for that matter, upon the people they were supposedly smuggling. This disregard was written into their reports, resounded in their talk and was literally drawn onto posters. In this way, it's easy to understand how this disregard has caught the attention of fellow scholars who have been studying similar issues of migration policing (compare Weber, 2013; Franko, 2019).

Nevertheless, a couple of different situations led me to question this all-out negative narrative. For example, as I was about to return to Denmark at the end of my fieldwork, I met up with the aforementioned Detective Diaz for a farewell breakfast. We sat in one of the main squares in the coastal town of Algeciras, ordered a croissant and a coffee and had a chat about what I had found out during my stay. I told him, among other things, how it seemed that they had "very little compassion for the migrants, and even less for the smugglers". At first, Detective Diaz agreed. "That's right", he said. "I mean, most migrants lie. They don't want to cooperate and, therefore, neither do we. And the smugglers profit from other people's misery. So, yeah, to hell with them!" Having said that, he paused for a bit, and resumed:

> 'Then again, you've seen how it works. Of course, it's hard not to feel a bit compassionate about these people. Even if they lie, they often come here with nothing. There are sometimes women with tiny babies in their arms. And, yes, we also know that it's hard to make a strong distinction between the smugglers and the smuggled. Some smugglers don't just do it to make money but to survive. Many are also migrants themselves, having just taken the smuggler role upon themselves, enabling them to help others but also themselves travel into Spain. It's a complex thing this. But you know how we police are, we like speaking in extremes.' (Field notes)

Caring more

What can we take from this chapter? First, that there are plenty of examples of how the police present themselves as knowingly careless and sometimes even as callous. Hence, it is both understandable and quite accurate for research to point to the existence of such a tough 'police culture' and for 'real police work' to be understood as enforcement oriented more than empathetic. Secondly, the examples also point to some of the cracks that can be found in this otherwise seemingly impenetrable, rugged exterior. To these we will now turn. In particular, I will consider how these 'cracks' have been, albeit rarely, discussed in the literature, and I will then offer some simple methodological recommendations as to how we as police ethnographers may, staying with the metaphor, notice both the existence of the rugged exterior and its cracks.

To be sure, quite a lot of research has pointed to the fact that policing includes many aspects that don't fit the police-as-control narrative. It has been shown that both police investigations and patrols consist of relatively few moments of action and many more moments of waiting and even boredom (compare Fassin, 2017). It has also been noted that, even though the enforcement of law and order might be the ideal, the police nonetheless spend more time doing paperwork and simply mediating street-level and domestic conflicts and risks (Ericson and Haggerty, 1997). However, despite these insights, few researchers have gone on to engage thoroughly with the reality of policing, which does not so easily fit the enforcement narrative. It has, as Fassin also argues

(2013, 2017), been empirically described, but only sparsely analysed (see also Sausdal, 2020a).

As a head-on discussion of how policing includes more than matters of control, Muir's old book *Police: Streetcorner Politicians* (Muir, 1979) is particularly edifying. In it, Muir attempts to answer the difficult question: 'What makes a good police officer?' Answering this question, he, in short, argues that a good policeman is one who is able to use violence on the job while remaining conscious of why s/he has been afforded such violent powers and, not least, of the wider human condition they play themselves out in (Muir, 1979). Elaborating on this distinction, Muir helps us see that the popular idea that action-oriented and violence-prone officers dominate and dwarf the more thoughtful ones is somewhat false; instead he helps us to understand how the two may go hand in hand.

That policing does include an awareness beyond the rhetoric of law and order has equally been the focus of some older and more recent ethnographic studies. Björk's (2008) study of police cynicism comes to mind. In it, contrary to the popular belief that police officers almost enjoy a cynical view of the world (compare Loftus et al, 2015), Björk demonstrates how police officers invest much time in 'fighting cynicism' (2008)—that is, in trying not to let themselves and their world completely darken due to the strains of their job. As Björk explains it, the officers keep cynicism at bay by, for example, openly discussing their frustrations. In the literature, this is a form of therapeutic venting also discussed in specific studies on the genesis and use of police banter (see Waddington, 1999). Cynicism, Björk continues, is also fought by the officers, as Muir advocated, as they make conscious efforts to see the bigger picture—understanding how crime comes about not just because people are 'evil' but because of wider personal or societal issues. These thoughts are also mirrored and developed in Feldman's (2019) ethnography of transnational policing. And they are part and parcel of some prior publications of mine wherein I discuss how the Danish police feel professionally dissatisfied in a policing world that is becoming increasingly delocalized and technological, making them feel more and more distanced from and (both literally and conceptually) out of touch with the people they police (Sausdal, 2018a; 2018b; 2019a; 2019b; 2020b).

Four recommendations

While too often undermining themselves through their practices and their combative declarations, the police do in fact think and care about their work as being more than just the menacing mechanics of law enforcement. Of course, one may rightly claim that no profession is so monofaceted—even though the police themselves may lead us to believe that this is the case, recalling for example Detective Clausen's simplifying maxim "*This* is police work!"

Now, if we accept that the police do care more than they want/are able to admit, the important question is how we as ethnographers can become better at noticing this. As already discussed, this is not an easy task because one often faces a wall of seemingly contradictory evidence. Yet, there are some methodological 'tricks' which may allow us to look beyond the police-as-control narrative. While others surely exist, I will here home in on four recommendations that I believe to be especially expedient.

Duration

The first recommendation is well-known to ethnographers. As our experiences show, the period you spend in the field matters. While initial impressions and wonderings are of great worth, there are also many insights to be garnered as time goes by. This has to do with analytical depth and the ability to evaluate preliminary findings. Our interlocutors rarely tell us about their deeper and darker secrets from the get-go. The police, for example, keep professional and personal secrets close to the chest. Moreover, duration allows the ethnographer to return and correct his/her initial impression (Emerson et al, 1995). In this way, in wanting to study the actual practices and perceptions of any given world, allowing ourselves a good amount of time in the field is methodologically meaningful. Duration, in relation to this chapter's focus, matters very much when it comes to seeing beyond the police's self-professed ruthlessness. Though time spent building rapport with the police won't necessarily make them stray from their grand narrative, it does allow us to better see when their grammar falters. Put differently, as shown in the aforementioned examples, it was the extended amount of time I spent with the detectives that allowed me to notice how the acclaimed 'hardcore' detective wasn't actually that revered after all. Ostensibly, through his colleagues' words and grand gestures, he was pronounced a police officer par excellence, but as I amassed many hours of minute yet significant observations, like an eye fleetingly turned or others' general disinclination to work with him, I was able to notice how officers actually were not completely swayed by their colleague's brashness.

Resisting uniformity

Another recommendation known to ethnography is to be found in the importance of resisting uniform and simplistic representations of our field and interlocutors (DeWalt and DeWalt, 2011). From the 1960s onwards, for example, this has been central to anthropological critique of its own past. Starting with the Manchester school and culminating in the postmodern critiques of the 1980s, including postcolonial, literary and feminist critiques, we anthropologists and ethnographers reflected on our ways of representing our interlocutors and their lifeworlds. Concerned with power relations and prejudices, these critiques have been centred on the need to avoid describing, whether consciously or not, the people we study as mere representations of a given structure but, instead, to describe people's various (counter)practices, differing thoughts and the many significant differences that also exist between them. In short, a call has been made to avoid describing people, cultures, societies, organizations and so forth as complete and uniform sociological entities, and to foster a greater ethnographical attentiveness toward in-group complexities and their meaning. Unfortunately, this is an attentiveness not always found in police research. As Fassin has recently argued (2017), police research (too) often uses ethnographic observations to further sociological generalizations rather than to discuss internal differences and distinctions. I agree. While such generalizations are valuable, as they teach us something about what lies at the heart of policing as well as its wider societal effects, the risk is that they miss important nuances. In the case of this chapter, a too unconscious generalizing—describing, for example, 'police culture', 'real police work' or the norms and values of police officers in one-dimensional terms—runs the risk of missing some of the practices and perceptions that don't necessarily fit the narrative. As here described, these alternatives may indeed be limited and hard to notice, but may nevertheless be of some importance. One initial step towards actually starting to notice them is to remain vigilant and self-critical if one ends up with a too singular and uniform representation of who and what the police are.

Go beyond the backstage

Another useful thing is for the ethnographer to, so to speak, 'go beyond the backstage'. It is, as mentioned previously, not enough to gain access and establish rapport when doing an ethnographic police study. You might have gotten behind the police front stage and been able to observe their backstage work. Officers may even talk to you freely about what they 'really' do and think. The problem, however, is that the specific vocational setting has strongly shaped what they believe to be true representations of what they do and who they are. Policing comes as a packaged good, as Rabinow (1977) has termed such pre-conscious epistemes. This is why an added level of penetration is needed—that is, why there is a need to dig deeper and go beyond or beneath the backstage to gain a better view of the occupational setting that is conditioning them. In my experience, for example, going for a drink, visiting their families or in other ways stepping outside the confines of police officers' jobs has the potential to allow for such unpacking. As the police-as-control narrative has such a strong hold on officers, this won't necessarily be enough, but sometimes it might be. As illustrated, it was through having breakfast, and perhaps also through his knowing that my fieldwork had come to an end, that Detective Ruiz suddenly nuanced his narrative.

Talking the talk

As I regularly experienced, my attempts to depict the officers as having considerations beyond crime-fighting often ended up in them denying this altogether (see also Jacobsson and Åkerström, 2012). Many times when I tried to point to how they had been compassionate towards, or more deeply interested in, the suspects they encountered in their work, I was met with the detectives schooling me in how they, for example, were "no damn humanist like you. This is police work". Yet, they sometimes themselves, almost as a side note, mentioned how they did indeed have such 'humanist' interests. Often this happened when I, instead of trying to call them out, 'lured' them into saying a bit more about what they thought about it all. Following sound advice to ask active, explorative questions (Holstein and Gubrium, 1995), yet doing so while acknowledging the police-as-control narrative, I asked the detectives questions along the lines of: 'I know it's not social work, that your job is not about saving their souls but about enforcing the law, but, correct me if I'm wrong, there still seem to be other aspects of the job you appreciate, no?' Asking such a veiled question, which allowed them to maintain the narrative of themselves as agents of crime-fighting and control while probing beyond it, at times proved productive (for a similar approach see Jacobsson, 2008). It was a way for me to show that I could 'talk the talk', to perform an appreciation of hard-heartedness as their governing story while searching for other views and ideas that they might have about policing.

Conclusion

As I write this in the early summer of 2020, people all over the world have taken to the streets to demonstrate against police brutality. Following the killing of George Floyd, and many other tragic examples of police violence and racism in the US and elsewhere, a stark and more than understandable discontent with the police (and the societies they work in) has emerged. People demand change. And so they should. The million-dollar question, of course, is what such change should include? Many suggestions are being thrown around, some more radical than others. Essentially, they range from proposals to reform the police, via defunding them, all the way to the complete abolition of policing as we know it. I'm not going to weigh in on the specifics of this debate here. One point I can repeat is that the current situation clearly shows that there are many problems with the police—problems tied to the fact that the police, in some places more than others, act in overly assertive and prejudiced ways. In this way, there is no apparent need to deny the realness of the police-as-control narrative. Rather, one may well reiterate it.

That said, I'll end this chapter with a qualification. While I agree with the reading of the police as, by and large, a hard-nosed bunch, I also believe that my own and others' research has revealed that there are important nuances to be added. Police officers do certainly adhere to a police-as-control narrative, but when we look more closely, other stories also appear. As explored in this chapter, these nuances are, however, too frequently overlooked in the literature. A reason for this is, without much doubt, the existence of certain wider sociocultural as well as academic concepts about policing alongside the police's own resolve that they are truly tough—something they not only perform but actually wholeheartedly believe. Hence, it is hard for the ethnographer's thoughts and findings not to be swayed by the extremely evocative nature of these rougher aspects of police work.

Nevertheless, I have in these pages offered examples of police officers being not so uniformly committed to crude enforcement (as well as ways to locate such variances). Enforcement is certainly a central part of their vocational DNA, but it doesn't make up the entire story in terms of what they find to be meaningful and interesting about their work. I, in other words, maintain that most police do somewhat care about those they encounter in their work beyond their criminality. This is not a care as profound as that found in other human service jobs. But it is a consideration that extends beyond simple ideas about law and order, and qualifies our considering their work as an example of human service provision. Unfortunately, this aspect of policing is too often trumped by (scholarly, popular and policing) stories of the police as unsophisticated brutes.

Now, while admitting that my view is perhaps utopian, I have a hunch that one way to transform the police is by fostering this supplementary tale of their more caring and considerate characteristics. This is, essentially, why I have written this chapter. I believe that one way forward, among others surely, may be to promote a policing narrative that allows for other ways of understanding what the police do and are to become 'the metaphors we live by' (Lakoff and Johnson, 2008). Sadly, these days, many among the public, politicians and pundits, as well as the police themselves (regardless of whether they think it's right or wrong), find themselves in a catch-22, whereby they keep telling themselves the same story. Yet, ask yourself: What might happen if we change the narrative? What would happen if we, as scholars, help not only the scholarly community but, more importantly, the police themselves to truly appreciate that there is more to their job than being hard-hitting crime-fighters? Certainly, such a narrative already exists out there, but mostly among police management or police specialists and less so among the frontline officers. Maybe the grip that the narrative currently has can be slowly but surely loosened if different stories are told and circulated, ones that recall the classic narrative of 'protect and serve' rather than strictly being about law and order.

This chapter is a methodological precursor of such a story. While it might be guileless of me, I hope that more studies will join in and help nuance the policing narrative for the sake of the police and those they work among. Recalling Reiner's description of the existence of 'police fetishism' (2010), this may indeed be one way of defetishizing what the police have come to represent. Seen in a more general light, and in the scope of this anthology, one may even argue that what this text has been devoted to is an emphasis of the importance of ethnographers not letting ourselves be easily subjugated to the 'packaged goods' of our fields, be they etic or emic. In ethnographies of human service work there is unquestionably a risk of being swayed by ruling occupational understandings. Having here used the police as a peculiar yet telling example, we however risk endangering not only our analyses but also the possibilities for change if we don't stay alert. At least, this is true if we believe that the stories we tell matter.

References

Bittner, E. (1970) *The Functions of the Police in Modern Society: A Review of Background Factors, Current Practices, and Possible Role Models*, Bethesda, MD: National Institute of Mental Health, Center for Studies of Crime and Delinquency.

Björk, M. (2008) 'Fighting cynicism: Some reflections on self-motivation in police work', *Police Quarterly*, 11(1): 88–101.

Cockcroft, T. (2020) *Police Culture: Research and Practice*, Bristol: Policy Press.

DeWalt, K.M. and DeWalt, B.R. (2011) *Participant Observation: A Guide for Fieldworkers*, Lanham, MD: Rowman Altamira.

Emerson, R.M., Fretz, R.I. and Shaw, L.L. (1995) *Writing Ethnographic Fieldnotes*, Chicago, IL: Chicago University Press.

Ericson, R.V. and Haggerty, K.D. (1997) *Policing the Risk Society*, Oxford: Oxford University Press.

Fassin, D. (2013) *Enforcing Order: An Ethnography of Urban Policing*, Cambridge: Polity Press.

Fassin, D. (2017) 'Boredom: Accounting for the ordinary in the work of policing (France)', in D. Fassin (ed) *Writing the World of Policing: The Difference Ethnography Makes*, Chicago, IL: University of Chicago Press, pp 269–292.

Feldman, G. (2019) *The Gray Zone: Sovereignty, Human Smuggling, and Undercover Police Investigation in Europe*, Palo Alto, CA: Stanford University Press.

Franko, K. (2019) *The Crimmigrant Other: Migration and Penal Power*, Abingdon: Routledge.

Holstein, J.A. and Gubrium, J.F. (1995) *The Active Interview*, London: Sage.

Hunt, J. (1984) 'The development of rapport through the negotiation of gender in field work among police', *Human Organization*, 43(4): 283–296.

Jacobsson, K. (2008) ' "We can't just do it any which way": Objectivity work among Swedish prosecutors', *Qualitative Sociology Review*, 4(1).

Jacobsson, K. and Åkerström, M. (2012) 'Interviewees with an agenda: Learning from a "failed" interview', *Qualitative Research*, 13(6): 717–734.

Klockars, C.B. (1980) 'The Dirty Harry problem', *Annals of the American Academy of Political and Social Science*, 452(1): 33–47.

Lakoff, G. and Johnson, M. (2008) *Metaphors We Live By*, Chicago, IL: University of Chicago Press.

Lipsky, M. (2010) *Street-Level Bureaucracy: Dilemmas of the Individual in Public Service*, New York: Russell Sage Foundation.

Loftus, B. (2009) *Police Culture in a Changing World*, Oxford: Oxford University Press.

Loftus, B., Goold, B. and Mac Giollabhuí, S. (2015) 'From a visible spectacle to an invisible presence: The working culture of covert policing', *British Journal of Criminology*, 56(4): 629–645.

Manning, P.K. (1977) *Police Work: The Social Organization of Policing*, Cambridge, MA: MIT Press.

Manning, P.K. (1978). 'The police and crime: Crime and the police', *Sociologische Gids*, 25(6): 487–501.

Muir, W.K. (1979) *Police: Streetcorner Politicians*, Chicago, IL: University of Chicago Press.

Nader, L. (1972) 'Up the anthropologist: Perspectives gained from studying up', in D. Hymes (ed) *Reinventing Anthropology*, New York: Pantheon Books.

Rabinow, P. (1977) *Reflections on Fieldwork in Morocco*, Berkeley, CA: University of California Press.

Reiner, R. (2010) *The Politics of the Police*, Oxford: Oxford University Press.

Reiner, R. and Newburn, T. (2007) 'Police research', in R. King and E. Wincup (eds) *Doing Research on Crime and Justice*, Oxford: Oxford University Press.

Sanchez, G. (2014) *Human Smuggling and Border Crossings*, Abingdon: Routledge.

Sausdal, D. (2018a) 'Everyday deficiencies of police surveillance: A quotidian approach to surveillance studies', *Policing and Society*, 30(2): 1–17.

Sausdal, D. (2018b) 'Pleasures of policing: An additional analysis of xenophobia', *Theoretical Criminology*, 22(2): 226–242.

Sausdal, D. (2019a) 'Policing at a distance and that human thing: An appreciative critique of police surveillance', *Focaal*, 2019(85): 51–64.

Sausdal, D. (2019b) 'Terrorizing police: Revisiting "the policing of terrorism" from the perspective of Danish police detectives', *European Journal of Criminology*, DOI: 1477370819874449

Sausdal, D. (2020a) 'Everyday policing: Toward a greater analytical appreciation of the ordinary in police research', *Policing and Society*, DOI: 10.1080/10439463.2020.1798955

Sausdal, D. (2020b) 'Police bullshit', *Journal of Extreme Anthropology*, 4(1): 94–115.

Van Maanen, J. (1973) 'Working the street: A developmental view of police behavior', MIT Working paper no 681-73, available at: https://dspace.mit.edu/bitstream/handle/1721.1/1873/SWP-0681-14451100.pdf?sequence=1&isAllowed=y

Waddington, P.A. (1999) 'Police (canteen) sub-culture: An appreciation', *British Journal of Criminology*, 39(2): 287–309.

Weber, L. (2013) *Policing Non-Citizens*, Abingdon: Routledge.

Westmarland, L. (2001) 'Blowing the whistle on police violence. Gender, ethnography and ethics', *British Journal of Criminology*, 41(3): 523–535.

12

Embracing lessons from ethnography in non-Western prisons

Andrew M. Jefferson

Is prison life mundane, dreary, monotonous and exhausting? Or is prison life dangerous, dramatic and unpredictable? The brief answer to both these questions is yes. Prison life, like life in general, can be both under- and over-stimulating. It can be deathly tedious and deadly dangerous. In this respect, the experience of prison life differs to non-prison life in degree and intensity rather than substance, notwithstanding its involuntariness and punitiveness. But the differences in degree and the amplification of intensity do matter and they matter also for the researcher.

This chapter illustrates the value of applying an ethnographic sensibility to sites of confinement and control. With reference to experiences of fieldwork in prisons in Nigeria and ongoing research projects in Myanmar and Tunisia, the chapter explores the dilemma-filled practice of conducting ethnographic research on and in prisons and calls for increased interaction between researchers and practitioners in the quest to put knowledge to work. The chapter takes its point of departure from three examples from different times in my research career. The first is a description of the mistakes of a novice in the field; the second a discussion of the lessons learned from boundary negotiations with prison officials; the third an account of doing fieldwork from a distance as part of a team. In each case, the 'how to' of ethnographically inspired research practice is implicit, if not explicit. Following the three examples, I present some reflections on the status of the knowledge such research generates and the possibilities that collaborative work might engender. By way of a conclusion, I present, for inspiration rather than mechanical replication, a series of nine paired pieces of advice on what to do and not do in the field. I begin with some reflections on prisons and prison research.

Prisons and prison research

At first glance prisons might not be obvious candidates for inclusion in a collection such as this focused on human service provision. And yet when I was invited to contribute to this volume, I jumped at the chance for two reasons. Firstly because I am sympathetic to the agenda of promoting the value of applying an ethnographic sensibility and practice to bounded institutions, and secondly because, while I was initially puzzled by the idea of prisons as sites of human service provision, in fact this somewhat unusual framing gels nicely with arguments I have made about the best way to understand prisons being through a relational rather than a functional lens (see Weegels et al, 2020).

Some prison scholars have made a strong case for the uniqueness of prisons as institutions and as research sites. Yvonne Jewkes writes, for example, that 'the prison is different to even ostensibly similar institutions and social worlds.' (Jewkes, 2014, p 388). And further: 'There is something about prisons being so spatially and temporally defined—and in the most limiting, constraining ways imaginable—that makes prison ethnography unlike any other qualitative enterprise' (Jewkes, 2014, p 389). Similarly, Alison Liebling has noted how 'prisons are raw, and sometimes desperate, *special* places' (Liebling, 1999, p 152, my emphasis). Others (for example, Turner et al, 2019; Weegels et al, 2020), however, have considered prisons as one type of containment site among many, developing Wacquant's idea that there are 'striking similarities and intriguing parallels' between prisons and ghettos (Wacquant, 2001). As I concluded on the basis of encounters with occupants of prisons and poor urban neighbourhoods in Sierra Leone (Jefferson, 2012), there is ample evidence to support Wacquant's claim and Bauman's hunch (2000) that there are important resemblances between different types of confining sites and practices, not least at the level of personal experience.

While at first glance prisons and care homes for the elderly might have little in common (or prisons and homeless shelters, see Umamaheswar, 2018; or prisons and home-based dementia care, see chapter 6 in this volume) a basic premise of this chapter is that, methodologically speaking, there is potential in juxtaposing lessons learned in one site with lessons learned from another as the editors of this volume strive to do. We might, with good reason, not spend too much time comparing apples and pears, but there is no reason why we should not compare ways of working in an orchard.

How might we accurately characterize prisons? Notwithstanding claims made for the rehabilitative or reformative potential of prisons, they are at heart places that are designed to deliver punishment through the deprivation of liberty. Such deprivation is meant to be painful; it is meant to teach the offender a lesson. Prisons are anxiety-inducing sites of surveillance and control. They call for adaptation; they are mortifying (to use Goffman's famous expression). They feature disconnection and connection, lack of autonomy and varying degrees of isolation and overcrowdedness, the intrusiveness of other prisoners and staff, arbitrary power and often violence. They are tension-filled institutions that embody specific paradoxes, most notably perhaps the twin imperatives of care and control. They are not the easiest places to live, work or conduct research in. They should carry a public health warning. Studying them is not for everyone.[1]

Prison research involves the generation of knowledge under constrained conditions of surveillance and control often featuring suspicion and sometimes explicit resistance to scrutiny. The field calls for innovation and experimentation and sometimes simply 'making it up as you go along' (Jefferson and Schmidt, 2019). Ethnography is most well known for its attunement to everyday realities and the meanings people attribute to their experience, achieved by immersion in the field. Ethnographic research is relatively rare in prisons. This is particularly the case in non-Western countries where the ethnographic gaze is mostly absent and the value of research is underappreciated and ill understood.[2] Work by Martin et al on the concept of prison climate (emerging from and applied to the Global South) highlights the desirability of analyses that bridge local institutional and relational practices and the concrete situatedness of prisons in society and history. The nurturing of an ethnographic sensibility (Schatz, 2009; Shore et al, 2011), attuned to practices and ascribed meanings at the level of the everyday, is an important path towards generating this kind of knowledge in places where access can be difficult to attain and indirect routes to knowledge through the adoption of what Schatz (2009, p 307) has termed 'the nearest possible vantage point' are necessary.[3]

I turn now to the first of my three examples which is about the necessity of investing enough time and energy to enable one to 'get to know'.[4]

Getting to know

In the first published piece based on my fieldwork in Nigeria (Jefferson, 2002), I included a verbatim account from my field notes describing my first ever entry into a Nigerian prison. Included in this account was a description of a prison officer as aggressive and hostile. As I later got to know the officer—let's call him Joseph—I came to realize that my attributions had been unfair. I had failed to take the necessary time to get to know him. Join me at the prison:

On a return visit to the prison I was led into the same office that I had previously visited to meet 'the same old intimidating, resistant second-in-command (2iC)' (field note). I presented my letter of authorization from the controller general. Joseph studied it carefully and quietly before he instructed someone to put it in a file. A folder was found where my authorization was filed with a couple of scribbled endorsements made on it. Everything was being done fastidiously, according to the rules, and it struck me that the 2iC took his responsibilities very seriously. But I felt nervous and as we waited; I tried to make conversation describing my work in Kaduna—a strategy to give my current attempt extra legitimacy—but Joseph admonished me, advising me not to be in such a hurry to do my work. I felt put in my place yet again. I sat back and decided to wait him out. As 2iC, it was he who had the authority over the prison. It was I who was imposing on his time and his institution. This sitting back marked the beginning of a shift in attitude whereby I adopted a less pressing style, choosing rather to subjugate myself explicitly to his authority. We talked about the people I wanted to interview, former graduates of the staff training college, and I wrote in my notes that 'the 2ic is very cautious, very wary, very suspicious'. I later came to believe that he was not so much attempting to conceal anything as being extremely security conscious and basically just doing his job.

Our third meeting was embarrassing. At the prison, I walked authoritatively (this time) to the gate. Peering through the grill, I asked for the head of operations. I was demanding to be let in but on turning I saw a man staring beckoningly at me. I stared back, puzzled, before asking the dumbest question in the world, mistakenly believing him to be an officer from Kaduna: "What are you doing here?" In fact, it was Joseph. I hoped he had not heard my mumbled question, but feeling foolish and embarrassed, I uttered a clumsy explanation about not expecting to see him outside. To be honest, I had not been paying much attention to the people outside, intent as I was on getting through the gate, though I had spotted quite a degree of activity—armed squad members standing around, prisoners being escorted out. Perhaps it was this activity that distracted me from the solitary man seated on the low wall that rims the ramp up to the main gate? He was there, he told me, to supervise the escort of some serious prisoners to court. As we sat together watching proceedings his tone lightened somewhat and I sensed myself relaxing and becoming more patient. We discussed the pros and cons of having a prison truck, as we observed the loading of a prison ambulance to transport the prisoners to court.

When Joseph asked whether I would rather see the yard first or interview the warder, I decided to take the yard first. He escorted me up to some staff members and, as he indicated that a welfare officer I knew would escort me, stated "better a snake you know than an antelope you don't", demonstrating a sense of humour I had certainly not anticipated during either of our previous encounters. Some days later, after conducting an interview, I checked in with Joseph again and, deliberately drawing on my previous experience, said to him "With your permission I will return tomorrow". "You will be welcome", he declared "on your own permission". I was struck by this shift in tone, a turnaround clearly prompted by my own repositioning of myself in relation to him. It was at this point that I began to realize the importance of the ongoing relationship for my perceptions of the officer and his perceptions of me. It was not that we were to become the best of friends, but I did slowly learn to take him and his world seriously.

The crucial, though basic, take-away here is that we cannot assume we know much about persons or their practices unless time is invested in getting to know them. Here I understand getting to know not as a meeting of minds but a meeting of persons occupying a partially shared universe. This universe only becomes shared over time. What happened between Joseph and I was that via repeated encounters our relationship matured and understandings unfolded, not least about how to be together. Such encounters are of a personal and institutional nature. A core element of them is the negotiation of boundaries, which is the subject of my second example.

Negotiating boundaries

Since 2015, I have been working (with Bethany Schmidt from Cambridge University's Prisons Research Centre and three local research assistants: Yasmin Haloui, Souhir Châari and Nissaf Brahim) to build trust with prison authorities in Tunisia as preparation for a study of the quality of prison life there. Our initial trust-building exercise involved four periods of brief but intense fieldwork in four different prisons over two years. The need to experiment with trust was recognized as a necessary precursor from a very early stage of our interaction with the authorities. Surprisingly, an open acknowledgement of the likelihood of mutual suspicion early in the negotiations seemed to pave the way to our getting access. But access was never guaranteed, and often we would land by plane in Tunisia not knowing whether we would get to set foot in a prison. We came to characterize our interactions with the authorities as a dance of concealment and revelation.

Over time, we slowly learned that researchers like us did not necessarily meet the expectations of our interlocutors, not necessarily through any fault of theirs or ours but because we were an unfamiliar and unknown quantity. As we have written about elsewhere, our role as researchers was often misunderstood. Our methodology of hanging out and waiting for prison life to unfold puzzled the staff and was likely an irritation to those who were tasked with accompanying and keeping an eye on us. Our presence was a subject of consternation. It was as though prison staff really could not make sense of why we would congregate in the strangest of places, or why we would roam up and down corridors or spend time sitting in the visitors' hall or in a corridor opposite the prison store. They didn't understand our preoccupation with history and old, disused buildings, the effects of the revolution on the prison, or our desire to look at blueprints and go up in control towers. And we didn't always understand why certain (ostensibly not very sensitive) places were off limits while other practices were openly revealed.

Our methodology was also sometimes questioned more explicitly and more aggressively in a fashion such that our credibility and legitimacy as researchers was challenged. "Where is your questionnaire?" was the question in one prison. Our encounter with one senior officer is instructive. When we first met him, he emphasized objectivity in research, stating that he was sure we could contribute given that we were not subjective. The following day, however, the same officer under more informal circumstance lectured us on our faulty methodology. How could we evaluate services if we did not have a grid where we could check boxes, he asked. I defended our methodology quite robustly as we walked through the prison compound and later recorded that I think he understood: 'At least he acknowledged he was not going to tell us how to do our work' (field note).

What seemed to make him nervous was the possibility that we might criticize the prison. He shared with Bethany that we could not possibly evaluate accurately before all the new systems were in place. However much we insisted that we were there to understand and not to judge, this message failed to gain traction. What this officer embodied was a general sense of institutional nervousness that the researcher can always expect to encounter and must take steps to ameliorate—however impossible that might in the end be.

Clearly, we would have been more highly valued had we come in and looked more 'positivist', if we had done inventories or if we had a measuring instrument to apply, perhaps if we had worn white coats. In another prison I had a long conversation with a prison officer about objectivity contra subjectivity. Despite what I see as the shared experience of using one's self as a tool in an embodied, semi-participatory fashion (common to the researcher and the prison officer), this prison officer at least had a more traditional view of what would count as an appropriate scientific method. He said it was going to be unreliable to base analysis on what people said because they lie. I wondered afterwards whether this was some kind of confession. Whatever the case, potential prison scholars need to remember that there is always a politics around knowledge production and the idea of the participating, observing researcher often carries little weight. The researcher must constantly fight for legitimacy. A first step towards this is consistently acting credibly and honourably in interpersonal relations.

Creating a list of dos and don'ts is not an easy task when it comes to prison ethnography since so much of what we do now is instinctual, even when highly deliberate. It is about occupying the field in a manner which is respectful but not (usually) subservient, and dialogical rather than argumentative. It is about being decent, and fair and acting with integrity, not honestly necessarily but honourably.[5] It is not without frustration. Reviewing some field notes, I was surprised by the relatively high levels of irritation recorded, especially with people I perceived as either blocking or not fully understanding our purpose.

Becoming a prison ethnographer can be learned but it is difficult to teach. Mentoring two novice researchers in the form of our research assistants taught us this. Their questions about why we did this and why we did that taught us how much we took for granted our own ways of moving, speaking and making choices in the prisons. Bethany and I are not alike in our styles, and this is important. The novice fieldworker in prison must find their own style, learn how to manage their own self and project an image (and substance) that works for them. Doing this within a relatively safe team environment with regular briefings and debriefings is desirable.

Research seems to be increasingly becoming a team effort. It is harder and harder, for example, to find grants that are for solo research projects. For better or for worse there is a drift towards larger-scale collaborations. My third example concerns a team effort.

Doing ethnography from a distance

The overarching study from which this example is drawn is called *Legacies of Detention in Myanmar* and aims to illuminate past and present processes of state formation and transition in Myanmar through what we call the 'prism of prison'.[6] It is a multi-stranded study featuring a range of actors situated in different locations and positioned differently from one another in significant ways, most significantly, as we shall see, as 'locals' and 'foreigners'.

As this work is ongoing, it is less easy to make strong claims about lessons learned. In many respects we are still feeling our way. Nevertheless, there are lessons to be learned about a different kind of ethnography, one that is designed to operate under the compromised conditions that faced us in Myanmar. The project began just after elections that saw a landslide victory for the National League of Democracy headed by Aung San Suu Kyi, signalling a civilianizing of rule and a (partial) end of decades of authoritarianism by the military and, more recently, by former generals in civilian clothes. Decades of repression, censorship, surveillance and social control, as well as shut-down universities, presented a rather peculiar situation wherein we anticipated that the kind of actions associated with ethnography (conversation, participant observation, interviews, critical thinking, privileging of personal perspectives rather than the 'party line' and so forth) might be met with suspicion or puzzlement, and where prison gates were likely to be fiercely protected.

Anticipating this, and aware of the limitations posed by our lack of cultural and linguistic competence and our status as foreigners (attached to a human rights organization), we sought out ways of establishing the closest possible vantage point. This section is therefore about conducting qualitative research at a distance, indirectly and by proxy. Before coming to some of the challenges associated with working in this fashion let me first share an example from the field that vividly confirmed our suspicion that being present in the field as foreigners might be difficult.

This example is based on the field notes of my colleague Tomas Martin[7] wherein he describes his visit, along with the local team (members of Justice for All (JFA)), to court holding cells and police lock-ups. It was the team's first fieldwork experience and Tomas accompanied them in a supervisory capacity. His notes are infused with tension and doubt.

They began by negotiating the necessary permissions to take a look at the police holding cells, but as they walked in that direction a 'stern-looking guy' shouted out telling them to stop and 'another officer pulls up on a bike' insisting that they go into a nearby office. There they were 'stared down' by the stern officer and accommodated in a friendly fashion by another. Phone calls were made to superiors to check up on them. The notes continue: 'Apparently, he says that we cannot go because we bring a foreigner. ...What has happened is not clear. Maybe they got cold feet' (field notes). It is unclear whether the doubt and tension expressed here belongs to the researcher or to the situation. Probably both as the two are so closely entwined.

Before this description there are repeated references to members of security forces: 'an entourage of police officers'; a 'mass of uniforms'; a 'posse of armed officers'. Tomas has a jokey exchange with a police officer who teases him about his long nose, and Tomas teases back with reference to the weapon he is carrying ('small man, big gun'), immediately regretting his choice of words. As he reflects later about the (un)smartness of this remark he registers 'a sense of how this tone can be joking, mocking, degrading and menacing in a matter of split seconds' (field notes). Ostensibly referencing the tone of the jokey exchange, this can equally be read as referencing the tone of the situation more generally, a reference to the unpredictable atmosphere, a sense of imminent danger and Tomas' (and the team's) sense of vulnerability in it.

The notes exude a sense of vulnerability and lack of control rooted in a toxic mix of anxiety about being an outsider (in the field for the first time without much capacity to make sense of what is going on) and knowledge that outsiders have for decades been considered highly suspect by the martial authorities. 'This is not our place' Tomas writes drily at one point, almost incidentally, yet this articulation of not belonging is perhaps the phrase that captures most clearly the lesson of these encounters.

It was this incident—and another similar one at another court—that taught us that in some ways our presence in the field might be a liability. I am in little doubt that with the right amount of time available we could have 'gotten to know' sites like this in a similar way to that in which I got to know prisons in Nigeria. But given our project design, it was much more attractive to let the local team do the work, recognizing their ability to negotiate access qua their status as local lawyers. The closest possible vantage point turned out to be quite far away—for us foreigners at least.

So, what have we learned subsequently about conducting research from a distance under such constrained and constraining circumstances? Working in partnership with JFA is an integral part of the design of our project. There are many advantages: The team have access through their networks to former prisoners and professionals with a stake in the field; they have linguistic and cultural competences that we lack; and they are ever present in the country (if not in the field).[8] But researching by proxy also brings with it some challenges that we are still learning about and that I will present here as four questions:

- How can we avoid different strands of our project activities compromising or undermining each other?
- What are the relative risks of being present or distant given local histories of surveillance and control? (Or: When, where and for whom is it safe to write and speak about what?)
- How can we carry out research, education and mentoring towards the development of an ethnographic sensibility given the authoritarian histories of our research context (for example, its discouragement of critical thinking, emphasis on hierarchies and silencing of the people) and our own constraints (for instance, our linguistic and cultural limitations)?
- What power dynamics and dependencies are brought into play by such arrangements?

Variations on these questions, we suggest, might be of value for consideration beyond our own project, as may be the issue of the take-up and status of the kind of knowledge generated by qualitative, ethnographic research as I consider here.

Curating the gift of imponderable knowledge

In this penultimate section I consider the status of the kind of knowledge produced through research with an ethnographic sensibility and reflect on the challenges of take-up. Michel Foucault was once asked whether he was an optimist or a pessimist. He responded: 'My point is not that everything is bad, but that everything is dangerous, which is not exactly the same as bad. If everything is dangerous, then we always have something to do' (Foucault, 1983). The question is: On what should we base our practice? Legal precepts might offer some guidance. Or morality. Or numbers (gift-wrapped as big data). Or even so-called best practice (though I have my reservations). An alternative basis for action could be knowledge developed at the nexus of theory and practice, emergent knowledge, imponderable knowledge. This latter term is appropriated from philosopher Stanley Cavell to refer to knowledge that is 'grounded, everyday, close, suggested, endlessly open, innovative and experimental, shimmering and hesitant. Not doubtful but expressive of doubt' (Buch and Jefferson 2012). This formulation has grown out of some joint thinking with anthropologist Lotte Buch about the importance of doubt, or more specifically 'the doubt that is revealed in ethnographic human encounters and the doubt equally endemic to the process of translating ethnographically gathered material into uncertain, tentative knowledge' (Buch and Jefferson, 2012). This has some specific kind of implications.

Ethnographic research of the type discussed in this chapter, typically produces knowledge about the everyday not the dramatic, about people and their perceptions, and about the world as it is, untrammelled by the baggage of how it ought to be. This kind of knowledge is crucial in exposing hidden and faulty assumptions, debunking myths and providing grounds for critique. But, at the same time it might helpfully be considered as a kind of wager, a more or less safe bet. Offering no guarantee, the knowledge produced through ethnography is open to contestation. It comes with few conditions. It does not impose itself except as a gift might. What is done with it, and the degree to which it is taken up by others, is often beyond the control of the ethnographer. Just as seeking access is an iterative process of (boundary) negotiation, the sharing of ethnographic knowledge implies gentle persuasion rather than arrogant insistence. It typically involves multiple stakeholders positioned differently with a range of political views about fundamental matters. In torture prevention work, for example, these differing views might concern the nature of good and evil, the role of punishment in society, notions of suffering and humanity and even the meaning of life itself.[9]

Over some years of engaging closely with practitioners caught up in the important work of trying to reduce levels of torture and human rights violations in the world, I have come to think of the kind of qualitative research I conduct in three distinct ways. These are: research as investigation, research as intervention and research as innovation. Research as investigation refers simply to data collection, that is, the methodological and systematic gathering of empirical material to address a question of concern, for example, under what conditions does torture thrive.[10] Research as intervention speaks to the idea that when one is in the field conducting investigations and explorations, especially in sensitive sites such as prisons, one has the opportunity to model positive forms of behaviour, for example listening and speaking respectfully to prisoners or prison staff, recognizing their inherent worth, rather than judging or patronizing them.[11] Finally, research as innovation is about the way qualitative research can have a significant impact on changing the ways problems and issues are framed, thought and talked about. Through the generation of fresh perspectives and new concepts, ethnographic research can help us challenge existing assumptions by creating (albeit doubt-filled) new languages through which we are enabled to renew our thinking about the issues that concern us in practice.

Those who work to bring about change or provide the most effective service provision under circumstances of low resources and pressured daily schedules might not care too much to rethink their assumptions or learn new ways of thinking about their work. Having one's attention drawn to the indeterminacy of the world is not always that attractive. The issue of why we need this kind of knowledge is a pertinent one. A 'legally-minded' colleague[12] (as designated by our partners in Sierra Leone) recently asked me why anti-torture practitioners don't take social science more seriously. I responded a little hesitantly that I am probably not the one to answer that question given the stake I have in the issue. But one reason is the issue of the urgency of responding to human suffering and the time that it is perceived to take to think anew and differently. Also, where qualitative social science sees positive value in generating new questions, normatively driven practitioners are often understandably calling for answers. To embrace a more ethnographically oriented research agenda more fully would likely require a partial shift in mindset and the asking of different questions; for example: not 'Does torture prevention work?' but how does it work and not work, what are the drivers and sustainers of torture and how can we address them. This shift in mindset is necessary if practitioners are to benefit from the full potential of research. Thankfully, these questions are beginning to be asked and answered (for example, Celermajer, 2018; Kelly, 2019; Kelly et al, 2020). It may also imply a different way of thinking about utility, that is, about how knowledge can be used, a shift from thinking about the producers of knowledge and the users of knowledge as separate entities and a move to more collaborative practices.

Ethnographic research can helpfully be conceived of as a craft, as a form of hands-on engagement that reaches beyond immersion in the field during data collection, into the world of practice. Closer connections between researchers and practitioners can help this endeavour, especially if knowledge and intervention projects are better integrated. This would involve researchers embodying the knowledge they produce; joining in the production of new forms of intervention and new projects; putting their skills, experience and ways of thinking at the disposal of others. Saying to others, 'Come use me, let me help you', is likely more effective than insisting people read peer-reviewed articles drafted ostensibly with a different kind of audience in mind. One final remark: Knowledge that is persuasive confers authority on its producers that requires wisdom and discernment to carry appropriately. But the onus is also on recipients to pursue the opportunities that new knowledge opens up. The sharing of gifts of knowledge is an invitation that creates an imperative to imagine and think afresh about practices of intervention (for example, torture prevention, prison practice or service provision more generally).

Conclusion

By way of a conclusion I would like to reiterate some of the lessons I have learned across a range of fieldwork experiences over a twenty-year period, some of which I am first beginning to articulate as I draft this chapter. Encouraged by the remit proposed by the editors of this volume I offer a series of nine pairs of advice each containing a 'do' and a 'don't'. One caveat seems necessary. This is an experience-based list that likely matches well my way of being in the field, indeed my way of being in general. It is not a guaranteed recipe for success nor is it a set of rules to follow.

First of all, hesitation is a virtue worth nurturing, standing in sharp contrast to any desire to dive straight in with eyes closed. Second, it is important to be flexible and opportunistic rather than afraid or risk averse. Indeed, following a recent, powerful article by Schneider (2020), I am inclined to lobby for what she terms the 'right to risk' as a counterpoint to increasingly risk-conscious universities and funding agencies. Third, the 'doing' of trust (that is, trusting, even when the grounds for trust are absent) is vital and can usefully be combined with trusting processes too. This involves refusing (mostly) to take no for an answer. Fourth, be humble, swallow any pride you may feel entitled to and avoid acting superior or undervaluing the people and institutions you are engaging with. Fifth, be patient and persistent; don't claim authority, work for it. Sixth, always expect and seek out the unexpected. Don't ever presume to know and don't take anything for granted. Seventh, and this might seem obvious, always be courteous and demonstrate humility; don't impose and don't interrogate—as my key informant from a Nigerian prison taught me: "Ask too many questions, get told too many lies". Eighth, try to appreciate rather than judge, whereby I mean appreciate not in the sense of being thankful but in the sense often used, say, in literary criticism to mean engaging meaningfully with and seeking to decipher, interpret and understand the field in its own terms. Ninth, and borrowing from my colleague once again, embrace your qualms and seek edification (Martin, 2019), or put differently, do not deny the dilemmas and moral quandaries that can and will appear at any moment in the course of a study.

Earlier in this chapter I pointed to how some scholars have highlighted the uniqueness of prisons while others (myself included) have emphasized their resemblance to other institutions and sites of confinement both because of obvious similarities and parallels but also because of the way they are experienced similarly. In a special issue of a journal on bureaucracies, Bethany Schmidt and I referred to prisons as *amplified* bureaucracies (Jefferson and Schmidt, 2019). While they share characteristics with other bureaucratic institutions, they are bureaucratic in an amplified fashion. They resemble other institutions but are also somehow *more* than other institutions. This is a question of degree rather than essence. So, while we should recognize the intensity of prisons and the prison experience, we should avoid fetishizing it. Prison ethnography is nothing special in a value-laden sense, though it is quite peculiar. The amplified and amplifying prison brings the quandaries of research, the skills it is necessary to acquire and the pitfalls to avoid into sharp focus, as I have shown in this chapter. Therefore, it makes sense to look to prison ethnography as a source of inspiration for how to conduct human service ethnography in other sites.

Ethnographic research of the kind that I have described in this chapter offers new understandings that aim to 'qualify' the world and help make it more fathomable and easier to manoeuvre in. It is valuable not only for the knowledge that is co-produced but also for what that knowledge does to those who produce it (that is, who it forms as a result) and the relationships it enables. Mirroring my three examples, we might be well advised to recognize that the generation of such knowledge requires processes that: a) enable the possibility of getting to know (relationships) and learning from mistakes; b) create opportunities for the (re)negotiation of boundaries; and c) facilitate complex, multi-stranded research projects with a range of possible outputs. The facilitation of such processes while cognizant of the vulnerabilities of the field, the researcher and the knowledge produced promises to help us significantly in our quest to understand sites of human service provision.

Notes

[1] For a personal account of the simultaneous feeling of fascination and repulsion evoked by prisons see Jefferson (2014).

[2] One important resource available to the aspiring prison researcher is the *Handbook of Prison Ethnography* (Drake et al, 2015), a volume that registered a resurgence of interest in qualitative studies of prisons, not only in the West but also in other parts of the world. Other references worth following up include Piacentini's (2004) study of Russian prisons; the Special Issue edited by Jewkes *Doing Prison Research Differently*; and Drake and Harvey's (2014) reflections on the importance of performance and impression management.

3   See Gaborit (2019) for an important discussion of studying imprisonment mostly from the outside based on fieldwork in Myanmar.

4   The reader should be forewarned that the examples I have chosen are mostly about the negotiation of boundaries with the institution through its staff. I do not have much to say here about ethnographic research with prisoners, which, while not impossible, brings further challenges.

5   Note: honesty and honourability are not identical but have a common Latin root.

6   https://legacies-of-detention.org/ The project has also developed a good collaborative relationship with UNODC (United Nations Office on Drugs and Crime) and through this had interactions with the Myanmar Prisons Department, who granted cursory access to prisons to two of the Danish researchers.

7   There is also vulnerability demonstrated in the sharing of such a personal product as a set of ethnographic field notes.

8   This is not to downplay the significance of their own positionality: as Yangon-based; as predominantly Bamar; as predominantly male; as predominantly lawyers by background.

9   See Stevenson (2014) and Singh (2015) for insightful, empirically driven analyses of this question.

10 I find it useful to distinguish between information (as what research subjects think you want to know and often share in a pre-packaged form), material (as what you can observe, hear, experience and sense in the field) and data (as what material can become when systematically collated and ready for analysis).

11 Research as intervention can also refer to more commonly recognized forms of collaborative research such as action research or practice research that involve the design and implementation of research projects together with practitioners (see Chapter 3 of Jefferson and Gaborit).

12 Thanks to Ergun Cakal for limitless curiosity and unceasing questions.

Acknowledgements

Parts of this chapter draw on research funded by the Danish Ministry of Foreign Affairs. The chapter has benefited enormously from the engaged participation of Hannah Russell, Eva Zahia Nassar and Ergun Cakal who have 'shadowed' its development from start to submission, and as always from the perceptive insights of my collaborator and comrade Tomas Max Martin. My thanks go also to Morten Olesen for encouraging and facilitating the development of this kind of research output and to the editors for inviting me on board.

References

Bauman, Z. (2000) 'Social uses of law and order', in D. Garland and R. Sparks (eds) *Criminology and Social Theory*, Oxford: Oxford University Press.

Buch, L. and Jefferson, A.M. (2012) 'Knowledge, doubt and obligation: Interrogating imponderability', Unpublished manuscript.

Celermajer, D. (2018) *The Prevention of Torture: An Ecological Approach*, Cambridge: Cambridge University Press.

Drake, D.H. and Harvey, J. (2014) 'Performing the role of ethnographer: Processing and managing the emotional dimensions of prison research', *International Journal of Social Research Methodology*, 17(5): 489–501.

Drake, D.H., Earle, R. and Sloan, J. (eds) (2015) *The Palgrave Handbook of Prison Ethnography*, New York: Palgrave Macmillan.

Foucault, M. (1983) 'On the genealogy of ethics: An overview of work in progress', in H. Dreyfus and P. Rabinow (eds), *Michel Foucault: Beyond Structuralism and Hermeneutics* (2nd edn), Chicago, IL: University of Chicago Press.

Gaborit, L.S. (2019) 'Looking through the prison gate: Access in the field of ethnography', *Cadernos Pagu*, 55.

Kelly, T. (2019) 'The struggle against torture: Challenges, assumptions and new directions', *Journal of Human Rights Practice*, 11(2): 324–333.

Kelly, T., Jensen, S. and Andersen, M.K. (2020) 'Fragility, states and torture', in M.D. Evans and H. Modvig (eds) *Research Handbook on Torture: Legal and Medical Perspectives on Prohibition and Prevention*, Cheltenham: Edward Elgar Publishing.

Jefferson, A.M. (2002) 'Forskning om det nigerianske fængselsvæsen: De første indtryk', *Psykologisk Set*, 19(45): 26–35.

Jefferson, A.M. (2012) 'Conceptualising confinement: Prisons and poverty in Sierra Leone', *Criminology and Criminal Justice*, 14(1): 44–60.

Jefferson, A.M. (2014) '"Lines of flight": On the desire to know but not know prisons', Newsletter of European Group for the Study of Deviance and Social Control.

Jefferson, A.M. (2015) 'Performing ethnography: Infiltrating prison spaces', in D.H. Drake, R. Earle and J. Sloan (eds) *Palgrave Handbook of Prison Ethnography*, New York: Palgrave Macmillan.

Jefferson, A.M. and Gaborit, L.S (2015) *Human Rights in Prisons: Comparing Institutional Encounters in Kosovo, Sierra Leone and the Philippines*, Basingstoke: Palgrave Macmillan.

Jefferson, A.M. and Schmidt, B.S. (2019) 'Concealment and revelation as bureaucratic and ethnographic practice: Lessons from Tunisian prisons', *Critique of Anthropology*, 39(2): 155–171.

Jewkes, Y. (2014) 'An introduction to "doing prison research differently"', *Qualitative Inquiry*, 20(4): 387–391.

Liebling, A. (1999) 'Doing research in prisons: Breaking the silence', *Theoretical Criminology*, 3(2): 147–173.

Martin, T.M. (2019) 'The ethnographer as accomplice: Edifying qualms of bureaucratic fieldwork in Kafka's penal colony', *Critique of Anthropology*, 39(2): 139–154.

Martin, T.M., M. Bandyopadhyay and Jefferson, A.M. (2014) 'Sensing prison climates: Governance, survival, and transition', *Focaal: Journal of Global and Historical Anthropology*, 68.

Piacentini, L. (2004) *Surviving Russian Prisons: Politics, Punishment and Economy in Transition*, Cullompton: Willan.

Schatz, E. (ed) (2009) *Political Ethnography: What Immersion Contributes to the Study of Power* (1 edn), Chicago, IL: University of Chicago Press.

Schneider, L. (2020) 'Sexual violence during research: How the unpredictability of fieldwork and the right to risk collide with academic bureaucracy and expectations', *Critique of Anthropology*, 40(3) DOI: 10.1177/0308275X20917272

Shore, C., Wright, S. and Per, D. (eds) (2011) *Policy Worlds: Anthropology and Analysis of Contemporary Power*, New York: Berghahn Books.

Singh, B. (2015) *Poverty and the Quest for Life. Spiritual and Material Striving in Rural India*, Chicago, IL: University of Chicago Press.

Stevenson, L. (2014) *Life Beside Itself: Imagining Care in the Canadian Arctic*, Berkeley, CA: University of California Press.

Turner, S. and Jensen, S. (2019) *Reflections on Life in Ghettos, Camps and Prisons: Stuckness and Confinement*, London: Routledge.

Umamaheswar, J. (2018) 'Studying homeless and incarcerated persons: A comparative account of doing field research with hard-to-reach populations', *Forum Qualitative Social Research*, 19(3), art. 24.

Wacquant, L. (2001) 'Deadly symbiosis: When ghetto and prison meet and mesh', *Punishment and Society*, 3(1): 95–133.

Weegels, J., Jefferson, A.M. and Martin, T. (2020) (eds) 'Confinement beyond site: Connecting urban and prison ethnographies', *Cambridge Journal of Anthropology*, 38(1), special issue: 1–14.

Index

Note: References to figures appear in *italic* type.

A

ableism 78
Abramson, C.M. 6
Abu-Lughod, Lila 4
addiction treatment, Norway 10,
    119–120
  artefacts, times and spaces 126–128
  configurations of worlds and
    organizations 123–126, *125*
  context of 120
  dissemination challenges 128–129
administrative conflict 180
affect theory and 'affective practice' 71
analytic induction 173–174
analytical ethnography 69–71
Andenaes, A. 159
Anderson, Elijah 7, 72
anonymity 128
'anthropological strangeness' 164
'anthropology of welfare' 157
'assertive community treatment' 23
'atrocity stories' 40
Aung San Suu Kyi 216
auto-ethnography 52

B

Barbalet, J. 51
Bauman, Z. 210
Becker, Howard S. 174–175
being 4
belief, suspension of 5, 6
Bensing, J. 20
Berg, M. 20
Björk, M. 200
Blee, Kathleen 70–71
Blumer, Herbert 68–69, 70, 72, 79
'border work' 10
Bourdieu, Pierre 4–5
bracketing 5
Brazil, dementia care logics 101–113
Buch, Lotte 218–219

C

care ecology 102
care logics *see* dementia care
    logics, Brazil
care workers
  definition 21, 31

everyday practices of 21–23
shadowing of 8, 21–33
carers
  'burdened by care' 105
  see also dementia care logics; Brazil
case sense 90
category sense 90
Cavell, Stanley 218
Ceci, A. 21, 31
ceremony, Goffman's theory of 70
child protection
  'affective practice' in 71
  emotions, in child welfare decision-
    making 8–9, 49–62
  facting, and concealed pregnancy 5,
    10, 133–150
  fragmented human services in 10,
    153–166
  intimacy and privacy in 157–158
  intimate child protection 157–158
  letter templates in 163–164
  and media 164
  non-accidental injuries 135,
    136–137, 138–139, 142, 148
  transport agencies 159–161
children
  institutionalization of childhood 36
  non-accidental injuries to 135, 136–
    137, 138–139, 142, 148
client centredness 76
'client-perspective' 186
concealed pregnancy, and facting 5, 10,
    133–135
  Baby Parker case 133–134, 135–150
Connelly, Peter 137
court proceedings *see* facting, and
    concealed pregnancy
critical consciousness in ethnography 6
cultural criminology 162
culture
  as a concept 4
  medical students' 174–175
  police culture 195, 199, 202
Cunliffe, A. 162
Czarniawska, B. 22

D

Das, R. 102, 111
Das, V. 102, 106, 111

Deener, Andrew 69
Delgado, R. 46
dementia care logics, Brazil 9–10, 21,
    101–103
  'ensemble logic' in public geriatric
    unit care 101–102, 103–107,
    111–113
  'routine logic' in care within
    households 103, 107–110, 111–113
Denmark
  emotions in child protection
    services 8–9, 49–62
  police service 191–192, 195–197
  sensitizing concepts in homelessness
    and disability 9, 67–79
Denzin, N.K. 50
difference, and 'othering' 78
Dingwall, Robert 7–8, 40, 155–156,
    159, 161–162, 166
disability
  disabled children and families
    study 84–96
  and 'othering' 9, 67, 68, 77–79
discretion, in policing 194
discrimination, in policing 194
display rules 60–61
documentation 5, 6
  letter templates in child protection
    services 163–164
  social life of documents 9, 83–94,
    94–96
    assessing need 85–87
    contesting need 91–94
    ethnographic field of study 84–85
    inscribing need 87–90
    mobility of documents 90–91
doubt, importance of 218–219
Duneier, Mitchell 72

E

EBM (evidence-based medicine) 19–
    20, 32, 33
  hospital-based person-centred
    care 19, 22, 29–32
EBP (evidence-based practice) 19–
    20, 33
Eekelaar, John 7–8, 155–156, 159,
    161–162, 166
Eigendynamik 181–182
Emerson, Robert M. 7, 174, 175,
    178–179, 182, 187
'emotionally-sensed knowledge' 53
emotions, in child welfare decision-
    making 8–9, 49–51, 61–62
  case example 54–57
  control of 58–61, 59
  everyday practices of 52–54
empirical complexity 71–73, 79

disability and 'othering' 9, 67, 68,
    77–79
  homelessness 9, 67, 68, 73–77
ethnographic creativity 182–187
ethnographic distance 10–11
'ethnographically observable grounded
    globalisation' 156–157
ethnography 1, 2, 3
  analytical ethnography 69–71
  auto-ethnography 52
  critical consciousness in 6
  field-specific 2, 3, 7–8
  'global ethnography' 156
  'instant ethnography' 162
  location for research 153, 154
  long-term research 162, 164, 201
  mobile ethnography 157
  netnography 127
  see also human services ethnography
everyday life, problematizing of 5–7
'everyday' practices 2, 4
evidence-based medicine (EBM) see
    EBM (evidence-based medicine)
evidence-based practice (EBP) see EBP
    (evidence-based practice)
'experience-nearness' in fieldwork 6

F

Facebook 127
facting, and concealed pregnancy 5, 10,
    133–135
  Baby Parker case 133–134, 135–150
'family insufficiency,' and dementia
    care 106
Fassin, D. 199–200, 202
feminist objectivity 22
Ferrell, J. 162
field notes
  and emotion 52
  and ethnographic distance 10–11
field-specific ethnography 2, 3, 7–8
fields 4–5, 153
  Dingwall, Eekelaar and Murray's
    research 155–156, 159, 161–
    162, 166
  as social constructs 154
fieldwork
  being 'experience-near' in 6
  nature of 5
'findings of fact' 133
Fine, Gary Alan 6, 70
Finland, fragmented human services in
    child protection 153–168
Floyd, George 204
following, as distinct from
    shadowing 119, 123
formula stories 40–41
Forsberg, H. 57

Foucault, Michel 4, 218
fragmented human services in child
protection 10, 153–154, 165–166
ethnographic challenge 154–158
field issues 164–165
multi-sitedness and gatekeepers 10,
156–161
time-in-place, and temporal
issues 161–164
Fraser, Nancy 86

G

Garfinkel, H. 84, 149n1
Garriott, William 123–124, 128
gender norms
and disability 77
in homelessness services 74
'global ethnography' 156
Goffman, Erving 68, 70, 71–72,
186, 211
grassroots activists 70–71
Grazian, David 7
grounded theory 173, 174
Gubrium, J.F. 87, 90
'guilt geography' 111–112

H

Hallet, Tim 70
Haraway, D. 22
Harper, R. 93
Hochschild, A.R. 60
Hollan, D. 129
homelessness, and agency and
authority 9, 67, 68, 73–77
Homo administratus 173, 183
Hubbard, G. 53
Huber, J. 72
human geography 157
human services ethnography
and dominant narrative
cultures 45–46
overview 1–4
problematizing everyday life 5–7
humility and ethnography 221
Hunt, J. 194

I

'impression management' 71
innovation, research as 219–220
'instant ethnography' 162
inter-agency consensus, in child
protection services 156
intervention, research as 219
intimate child protection 157–158
inventiveness, in home-based mental
health services 26–29, 29
investigation, research as 219
invisibility 32

hospital-based person-centred
care 19, 22, 29–32
and standardization 20–21

J

Jewkes, Yvonne 210
Jöhncke, Steffen 123

K

key incidents and key readings 171,
173–175, 178–179, 182–183
'key informants' 129

L

Leigh, Jadwiga 71
letter templates in child protection
services 163–164
Liebling, Alison 210
location for research 153, 154
see also fragmented human services in
child protection
'looking beyond' 5–6
Loseke, Donileen 40
Lundström, T. 173

M

Maynard, D.W. 140
media, and child protection 164
medical student culture 174–175
medication
in dementia care 104, 105–107, 108–
109, 110, 111, 112
see also addiction treatment, Norway
meetings, post-fieldwork ethnographic
discovery, Swedish youth care
project 11, 175–178, 181–182, 185
Meeuwisse, A. 186
Meyers, Todd 123, 130
migrants, and the Spanish police
service 191, 197–199
mobile ethnography 157
Mol, Annemarie 21, 101, 102
Moser, I. 21
Muir, W.K. 200
multi-sitedness, and fragmented human
services in child protection 10,
156–161
Murray, Topsy 7–8, 155–156, 159,
161–162, 166
Myanmar, prison ethnography 209,
215–218

N

Nader, L. 193
needs and needs-talk, disabled children
and families study 85–96
neoliberalism 153
netnography 127

Newburn, T. 193–194
Newman, Janet 10
Newman, Katherine 72
Nigeria, prison ethnography 209,
     211–213
non-accidental injuries to children 135,
     136–137, 138–139, 142, 148
Norway, addiction treatment 119–131
'nothing is happening' (seemingly)
     20–21, 32
noticing
  conceptual 37–38, 42, 44, 45
  empirical 37, 42, 44, 45
nursing homes 11
Nussbaum, M.C. 51

O

observational data, and analytical
     ethnography 69–70
oral communication 90
'othering', and disability 9, 67, 68,
     77–79

P

packaged goods 203
partiality 128–129
Peirano, M. 112
persistence, in home-based mental
     healthcare services 23–26
person-centred, multi-sited
     ethnography see addiction
     treatment, Norway
'Perspective Display Sequence' 140
police-as-control narrative in policing
     services 6, 11, 191–192, 204–205
  caring less 195–199
  caring more 199–200
  Danish police service 191–192,
     195–197
  difficulties in police
     ethnography 192–194
  duration of ethnographic study 201
  police culture 195, 199, 202
  police cynicism 200
  'police fetishism' 205
  police violence 194, 197, 200, 204
  recommendations 200–203
  Spanish police service 191, 197–199
'politics of what' 102
Pols, J. 101, 102, 107
post-fieldwork ethnographic discovery,
     Swedish youth care project 11,
     171, 187
  administrative struggles 179–181
  analytic implications 178–182
  context 171–172
  Eigendynamik 181–182, 185
  and ethnographic creativity 182–187

key incidents and key readings 171,
     173–175, 178–179, 182–183
  meetings 175–178, 181–182, 185
  research group 172–173
practice, as a concept 2
'praxis' 2
pregnancy see concealed pregnancy,
     and facting
Prior, L. 84
'prism of prison' 216
prisoners-of-life 11
prisons, non-Western 11, 209,
     221–223
  Myanmar 209, 215–218
  Nigeria 209, 211–213
  prison context and prison
     research 210–211
  status of knowledge produced by
     ethnography in 218–221
  Tunisia 209, 213–215
private sector agencies in child
     protection services 158–159
proportionality, in care
     proceedings 145, 147, 149n7

R

Rabinow, P. 203
racial issues, in homelessness services 74
Raikhel, Eugene 123–124, 128
rapport, in police
     ethnography 193–194
Reiner, R. 192, 193–194, 205
relationship-building, in home-based
     mental healthcare services 23–26
representation issues 53–54
'resource group assertive community
     treatment' 23
Riles, A. 84

S

Sacks, H. 84
Schatz, E. 211
schizophrenia, home-based mental
     healthcare service 19, 22, 23–29, 29
Schneider, L. 221
Schwartzman, Helen 181
sensitivity, in home-based mental health
     services 26–29, 29
sensitizing concepts 67, 68–69, 72–73
  disability and 'othering' 9, 67, 68,
     77–79
  homelessness 9, 67, 68, 73–77
shadowing 71–72
  of care workers 21–23, 32–33
  home-based mental healthcare
     service 19, 22, 23–29, 29
  hospital-based person-centred
     care 19, 22, 29–32

of children 164–165
as distinct from following 119, 123
see also facting, and
concealed pregnancy
Simmel, Georg 180, 182, 186
situatedness 22
Smith, Dorothy E. 5, 95
snapshots, of moments in
ethnography 162–164
social media 127
child welfare advocacy groups 158
social theory concepts 68–69
social work
strengths-based practice in 137
see also child protection
social worlds 42
society, sociological concept of 4
Spain, police service 191, 197–199
Spinoza, Baruch 71
standardization, and EBM/P 20–21
strengths-based practice in social
work 137
Streule, M. 154
Strong, Philip 70
Swedberg, R. 182
Sweden
young people in rural village 35–47
youth care project 171–187

T

tailored care, in hospital-based person-
centred care 19, 22, 29–32
talk-in-interaction 83
Thelen, T. 102
Timmermans, S. 20
torture prevention work 219–220
'total institutions' 186
trafficking, and the Spanish police
service 191, 197–199

trajectories 123–124
transport agencies, in child protection
services 159–161
Tsing, Anna 37
Tunisia, prison ethnography 209,
213–215

U

uniformity, resistance of in police
ethnography 202
'unique cases' 128
urban sociology 157

V

Vagli, Å. 57
Van Maanen, J. 193
violence, police 194, 197, 200, 204
visibility, and standardization 20–21

W

Wacquant, Loïc 72
Wales, facting, and concealed
pregnancy 5, 10, 133–150
Westmarland, L. 194, 196–197
Wetherell, Margaret 71
white supremacists 70, 71
Whyte, William Foote 6–7
work shadowing *see* shadowing

Y

young people
rural village setting, Sweden
human service agencies 35–37,
38–40, 44
problem-talk narrative 8, 35–42,
44–47
young peoples'
counternarratives 42–45, 46–47
youth care project, Sweden 171–187

www.ingramcontent.com/pod-product-compliance
Lightning Source LLC
Chambersburg PA
CBHW070922030426
42336CB00014BA/2493

* 9 7 8 1 4 4 7 3 5 5 7 9 3 *